Understa

Fifth Edition

ONE W   K

Understanding Equity & Trusts

Fifth Edition

Alastair Hudson

LLB, LLM, PhD (Lond.) FRSA, FHEA

Professor of Equity & Finance Law
University of Southampton
National Teaching Fellow
Fellow of the Royal Society of Arts
Fellow of the Higher Education Academy
Of Lincoln's Inn, Barrister

 Routledge
Taylor & Francis Group

LONDON AND NEW YORK

Fifth edition published 2015
by Routledge
2 Park Square, Milton Park, Abingdon, Oxon OX14 4RN

and by Routledge
711 Third Avenue, New York, NY 10017

Routledge is an imprint of the Taylor & Francis Group, an informa business

© 2015 Alastair Hudson

First edition published by Cavendish Publishing in 2001
Fourth edition published by Routledge in 2013

British Library Cataloguing in Publication Data
A catalogue record for this book is available from the British Library

Library of Congress Cataloging in Publication Data
Hudson, Alastair, author.
  Understanding equity and trusts / Alastair Hudson.—5th edition.
    pages cm
    ISBN 978-1-138-77468-1 (hbk)—ISBN 978-1-138-77467-4
  (pbk)—ISBN 978-1-315-77427-5 (ebk) 1. Equity—Great Britain.
  2. Trusts and trustees—Great Britain. I. Title.
  KD674.H833 2015
  346.42'004—dc23

                                                     2014007883

ISBN: 978-1-138-77468-1 (hbk)
ISBN: 978-1-138-77467-4 (pbk)
ISBN: 978-1-315-77427-5 (ebk)

Typeset in Times New Roman
by RefineCatch Limited, Bungay, Suffolk

Printed and bound in Great Britain by
TJ International Ltd, Padstow, Cornwall

Contents

Preface

This book offers a succinct analysis of the whole of a trusts law or equity course, whether for students or for those who want a concise explanation of the underpinnings of equitable doctrine and the practical use of trusts. While it cannot cover in detail all of the material contained in my full textbook *Equity & Trusts* (8th edition, 2014), which takes over 1,200 pages, this book nevertheless analyses the key components of any examination dealing with trusts law for the student who needs an introduction to their course, or a map through the thicket in the middle of that course, or help in that tense period revising for examinations. Podcasts, containing brief lectures recorded specially for my equity textbook readers, are available via the publisher's companion website. Other materials, including full lectures from recent years, together with vidcasts explaining some of the trickier areas, are also available at www.alastairhudson.com/trustslaw/trustslawindex. htm.

This book has been written so as to provide you with enough material to get through examinations successfully, while remaining both readable and concise. Free of the need to discuss every crevice of the case law, this book will give you an overview of the relevant law and focus on the most significant ideas without getting bogged down in unnecessary detail. What this book cannot do is replace the need to read the cases and study a full textbook, but it can shine a light on what might otherwise be in darkness. If you need help with trusts law, then this is the book for you. The main principles in the leading cases are set out and explained here, together with illustrations from other useful cases and some of the more interesting issues which flow from those cases. There are also many practical examples to illustrate how those principles operate. For the general reader, this book also presents a clear argument as to the importance and nature of equity which makes this complex subject more accessible.

Equity and trusts is a fascinating subject. The idea of equity can be traced back to Aristotle's *Ethics* as a means of achieving a fair result on the facts of a given case even if the common law or statute would appear to require something else. This approach is still observable in the law on constructive trusts, equitable estoppel and injunctions even today. The largest participants in most investment markets – such as pensions funds and unit trusts – operate on the basis of trusts law, as do the principles governing the operation of many wills. So, trusts law is a very important part of our life, from commercial activities right through to ordinary people's private affairs. The principles are a rich stew of strict rules and flexible doctrines which are gloriously malleable in practice. This is also an area of law which cultivates a large number of legal skills, particularly those concerned with organising matters so as to achieve the client's goals, like no other field. This subject also enables us to ask some searching questions about the way in which the legal system interacts with the needs and rights of the individual, and whether or not the idea of a 'conscience' is a feasible organising concept for an entire field of law like equity.

The image on the cover of this book represents a vintage racing car of the sort that Tony Vandervell – one of the key protagonists in a line of cases discussed in various places in this book – used to race. It puts a different perspective on our study of equity and trusts when we remember that there are real people behind the case law, and that some of them lead interesting lives. Vandervell was a wealthy philanthropist who gave money to the Royal College of Surgeons (there is still a lecture theatre in their building in Lincoln's Inn Fields in London which bears his name) and who raced cars in his spare time. Other characters in our cases were equally exotic: Nubar Gulbenkian travelled around London in a gold taxi, George Bernard Shaw is one of our most revered playwrights, and almost every litigant discussed in Chapter 9 seems drawn straight out of a soap opera.

Equity and trusts is potentially one of the most interesting components of any study of law. My task is to convince you of that. I defy you to read this book without encountering some parallel with your own life, or without being provoked by the problems it considers. Even if I only cause you to leap to your feet and hurl this book across the room with an oath, I will consider myself successful.

I would like to dedicate this book to the memory of Jeffrey Price, the man who started my learning in the law of trusts and who became a close friend in later life. I owe him a great debt of thanks for the time he took to help me (and everyone else) when I was an undergraduate. It was sitting in his office one dark November afternoon, as his colleagues swarmed in and out of the room in a cloud of badinage and bonhomie, that I first realised my vocation was to be an academic. (Something for which I may never forgive him.) It was from him that I learned the craft of explaining complex legal concepts to students, the importance of clarity, and the possibilities of infectious enthusiasm. It is no exaggeration to say that this book is the product of his kindness, his energy and his spirit. He is much missed.

Alastair Hudson
Haywards Heath
February 2014

Table of cases

Table of statutes

Table of International Legislation

Europe

France

Germany

Chapter 1

The principles of equity

Setting the scene

Equity is a means by which English law ensures fair outcomes in individual cases where the strict application of the common law or statute would otherwise generate injustice. Equity also presents a system of technical rules in itself (especially in relation to trusts) which operate in accordance with the doctrine of precedent and in accordance with clear rules in most circumstances. Therefore, equity is not simply about the creation of random, unprincipled exceptions to the common law. Equity has a third sense in which it contains a series of procedural devices which are significant in litigation. The study of equity and trusts law is a fascinating engagement with these different forms of legal principle.

Sometimes equity is criticised for being too unprincipled and too uncertain. In fact, what will emerge from this book is that equity and trusts law contains many clear rules, and their occasional exceptions to common law rules operate on a principled basis.

It has been said that certainty is the principal virtue of every legal system (Oakley, 1997). Whether or not that is true, chaos and complexity are the common characteristics of every problem that confronts a legal system. That is the tension at the centre of this book. While the law seeks to impose certainty, litigants bring only confusion. As Aristotle observed, the law can only create general rules such that there will always be circumstances in which those general rules will produce unfair results. A legal system therefore needs a mechanism to allow it to deal with those unexpected situations and to ensure fair outcomes. Equity is the way in which English private law does this.

Traditionally, equity and the law of trusts have been concerned with providing justice to balance out the rigour of the common law. Nevertheless, as we shall see, the modern law of trusts has developed principles of certainty and formal rules so as to achieve specific commercial, economic and sociological goals. This tension between a traditional flexibility and a modern desire for certainty underpins the many interesting developments in the law of trusts in the last twenty years. But before jumping into the complexity of the recent case law, we should begin at the beginning . . .

To begin at the beginning . . . what is equity?

There are two important senses in which equity should be understood. First, strictly speaking, the principles of equity are the rules which have been developed by the Courts of Chancery over the centuries. Understanding equity therefore requires a close consideration of those judicial decisions, together with the few statutes that have been introduced in this field. Second, philosophically, equity is a concept which is found in the works of the ancient Greek philosopher Aristotle and others. For Aristotle, equity suggests that a judge may ignore a legal rule if its literal application would cause an injustice which the legislator could not have intended. The purpose of equity in this sense is to prevent injustice being caused by the automatic application of legal rules.

I should explain that English courts have not expressly adopted the ideas of Aristotle nor of any other philosopher as part of equity, but it is suggested that the core principles of English equity are in sympathy with this philosophical tradition. The English concept of equity is built on the idea of *conscience* in that the courts consider the conscience of the individual defendant in any particular case. This idea of conscience and the main principles of equity will be considered in this chapter. The trust, as we shall see, developed in turn out of the principles of equity by preventing a defendant from using property in an unconscionable manner.

Let us begin by considering how the Courts of Chancery – which are the principal courts of equity – developed historically. The Chancery was originally a secretarial department of state and not a court at all. It was headed by the Lord Chancellor, who held the Great Seal of England and so could exercise the power of the Crown, making grants of land and so forth. Over time, the Chancery acquired the power to exercise a judicial function out of its role in administering the publication of common law writs. The Lord Chancellor was for centuries the monarch's principal minister before the evolution of the post of Prime Minister in Robert Walpole's time. The Lord Chancellor became a very powerful political actor by the 16th century in England – principally by means of the expanding range of writs which were served to bring nobles to account – a fact tacitly acknowledged by Henry VIII's determination to have so many Lord Chancellors executed. The Courts of Chancery evolved to hear petitions that would previously have been made directly to the Crown for clemency or justice. Much of the business of the early Courts of Chancery was procedural: issuing writs of subpoena, collecting fines and so forth.

Nevertheless, by the time of the *Earl of Oxford's Case* in 1615 it had become clear that the principles applied by the Lord Chancellor through the Courts of Chancery were very different from the ordinary common law which had been developed since the creation of the Courts of King's Bench by Henry II. Whereas the common law was concerned with the application of legal rules to individual sets of facts, equity as administered through the Courts of Chancery, was concerned to consider the conscience of the individual defendant. As Lord

Ellesmere put it in the *Earl of Oxford's Case* in 1615, the role of the Courts of Chancery was 'to correct men's consciences for frauds, breaches of trust, wrongs and oppressions of what nature soever they be'. So, the courts of equity would look at the conscience of the individual defendant and make an order which would avoid unconscionable outcomes. Furthermore, the role of equity was to correct any injustice which would result from the rigid application of the common law. As Lord Ellesmere said, the second goal of the Court of Chancery was 'to soften and to mollify the extremity of the law': which means that its second goal was to ensure justice where the common law would have produced unfairness or injustice.

Consequently, it is vital to understand from the outset one feature of English legal procedure. As the Courts of Chancery developed their own principles, there were clearly two completely separate streams of jurisprudence emerging in English law: the common law on one side and equity on the other. In practice it used to be a requirement that the litigant decide which of these systems of rules would be necessary to decide his case. The common law courts and the courts of equity were completely separate courts in completely separate places in London. Consequently, only courts of common law would hear cases to do with the common law (e.g. whether or not a contract had been created) and provide common law remedies (e.g. damages for breach of contract). Similarly, only the courts of equity would hear cases to do with equitable principles (e.g. the enforcement of a trust) or the award of equitable remedies (e.g. injunctions or specific performance).

If you were to read Charles Dickens's remarkable novel *Bleak House* you would read about the fictional case of *Jarndyce v Jarndyce*. At the start of the book, this case had droned on for such a long time that no one could remember what it was about and no lawyer could even explain it. Dickens himself had worked as a clerk in the now extinct court of Doctors' Commons (depicted in *David Copperfield*) and was therefore well acquainted with the painfully slow pace of English justice at that time. Part of the difficulty in the *Jarndyce* case was that the litigants had to move constantly between the courts of common law and the courts of equity as they tried to find out which court ought to decide on the case. The litigants could be sent back and forth for many years between the common law courts and the courts of equity simply to decide which court should hear the case, even before either court would resolve it.

Therefore, quite literally, common law and equity were physically as well as intellectually separate systems of law. Through the 19th century, as a result of the work of Dickens and others, the scandalous waste caused by the slowness of the courts led to reform. In 1873, the Judicature Act provided that the courts of common law and those of equity should be merged so that any single court could rule on any question, no matter whether it related to principles of equity or to rules of common law. However, that Act only removed the physical distinction between the courts – the intellectual distinction remains even today. The courts still make rigid distinctions between the award of common law remedies and equitable remedies. We will consider the difference between the various doctrines in the remainder of this chapter once we have thought a little more about the philosophical nature of equity in the next section.

The philosophical role of equity

Before proceeding to consider some of the core equitable principles I think it would be as well to attempt to convince you, albeit briefly, that equity does have a respectable intellectual pedigree. The final chapter of the book will try to map some of the ways in which equity is likely to become even more sociologically significant in the 21st century than it has been up until now.

Aristotle, in his *Ethics* (probably reduced to writing between 334 and 324 BC), spoke of equity as a more significant principle even than his theory of 'justice' because it enabled the courts in any particular case to come to the best possible result on those facts. Similarly, in Hegel's *Philosophy of Right* (1821) there is mention of equity as being that code of rules which permits the courts to use their discretion in individual cases not to apply statute or common law literally but rather to do what is 'right' between the parties, irrespective of the law. This notion perhaps has a parallel with the writing of Professor Dworkin, who writes of the role of the judge in *Law's Empire* (1986) as being to attempt to achieve the 'right' result and thus preserve the integrity of the law.

What these various thinkers have in mind is the following dilemma: although we might agree that the enforcement of a clear system of law is a necessary part of maintaining the fabric of our society, there may nevertheless be circumstances in which an overly strict application of the law would be unfair. Suppose the following example: a statute provides that any person wearing orange Doc Marten boots is entitled to receive a sum of money if they present themselves at the Town Hall on a particular date. Bertha has a splendid pair of orange Doc Marten boots that she wears to stride towards the Town Hall at the appointed time to receive her reward. Unfortunately, she is forced to walk through a muddy puddle in the car park which briefly obscures the orange colour of her boots in a dirty brown film of mud. A literal application of the statute would mean that Bertha would not be entitled to receive the reward because her boots were not orange at the time specified by the legal rule. Clearly, we would think such an application of that rule to be unfair because her boots were really orange and their colour was only temporarily obscured by the mud. In such situations, there is a need for judges to be able to reach a just conclusion, even if that is not the conclusion suggested by the literal application of the law. Equity, in its broadest sense, is exactly such a scheme of ideas which gives judges this scope for dispensing justice.

So is equity just an enlarged form of the 'mischief principle' in statutory interpretation, which allows judges to apply statutes in ways which achieve their underlying purposes? The answer is 'no'. Equity is much larger in scope and also much more technically sophisticated, having developed important legal devices such as the trust, injunctions, charges, rescission and so forth. The equity that will be considered in this book is an application of the philosophical ideas mentioned above to the core equitable principles considered below. Equity provides citizens with the possibility of liberty in the face of the legal system: the chance to have their individual stories heard by the court regardless of the strict letter of the law. Equity recognises the integrity of the individual as a being with identified rights in the broader context of achieving justice in our society. This is a difficult tension for political philosophers: how do we create the perfect system which applies equally to all without overlooking the needs of particular individuals? I will suggest in the final chapter of this book that a robust system of equity makes this goal possible.

The idea of conscience

As mentioned above, since at least 1615 with the decision in the *Earl of Oxford's Case*, it has been clear that equity operates on the basis of identifying and judging the conscience of the defendant. The idea of conscience which underpins equity strikes some people as being too vague to be useful. It appears to them to be an entirely subjective concept so that the law is based entirely on the beliefs of the individual defendant. But this is a misunderstanding of how a conscience works.

All of the great psychoanalysts – Freud and Jung are good examples – considered the conscience to be something that operated *outside* the conscious mind. If you think about the way in which a person experiences their conscience it is usually an uncontrolled force which comes unbidden to their mind and gnaws at them: Why did you do that? Why did you do it with them? Why did you have so few clothes on? It is said that the conscience is that still, small voice which speaks to us mainly of shame. There is no conscious control over the conscience. Instead, the conscience is the product of a lifetime of receiving messages from other people: from parents, from family, from schoolteachers, from society, from the law, through the media, and so on. Throughout life we receive messages about acceptable and unacceptable conduct. Even issues about which we feel strongly, for example our views on cruelty to animals or abortion, are only something we know about when the outside world confronts us with them. The conscience is therefore something which is formed in reaction to these outside forces, even though our individual consciences are experienced inside our own minds.

We might say that the conscience is objectively constituted (in that it is formed in reaction to external stimuli) even though it is subjectively situated (in that we experience it within our own minds). If the conscience is formed by these objective forces, then it is appropriate for the courts to judge what the conscience of the defendant *should* have prompted her to do. In essence, the court is assessing which messages the conscience should have absorbed and consequently which sorts of behaviour are suitable for judgment. So, when a court of equity acts on the conscience of the defendant, that is what it is doing. It is holding the defendant up to an objective standard of good conscience. And those standards of good conscience are contained in the principles of equity for the most part. This is the idea which we will pursue through this book.

The argument of this book

A book of this length on a subject as vast as equity and trusts is most useful if it presents an account of the main ideas while also developing a thesis about the way in which the principles of equity and trusts function. I come to this subject with a belief that the strength of equity is in its flexibility and that any attempt to over-formalise the principles of equity should be resisted. Over the centuries the possibilities which equity offered judges to examine the conscience of the defendant have given way to more formal, rule-based ways of thinking, principally in the development of the trust and its use to manage holdings of commercial as well as private property. There is clearly a paradox in equity being both so open and yet giving rise to formal rules in many contexts. That is the tension within equity and trusts law: between the flexibility offered by the general equitable principles and the frequent strictness of trusts law rules. In the case law one can see the ongoing pitching and yawing between the judges as they try to find the right balance between flexibility and certainty.

Nevertheless, there is still a great deal more flexibility in equitable doctrines such as constructive trusts and equitable estoppel than in the common law generally. That does not mean chaos; that does not mean that the courts are able to do whatever they want. Rather, it means that the courts have principles which govern the way in which they approach individual cases but which give them the scope to reach the 'right' result on the facts.

As considered earlier, equity was described in 1615 as being a collection of principles which allowed the courts to reach fair results in cases in which it appeared that the rigour of the common law would otherwise have led to injustice, and to enable the court to examine the conscience of the individual defendant, regardless of the detail of the common law. This use of equity was in tune with the ancient philosophical idea that every legal system must have this capacity to cut against the grain of rigid legal rules in some circumstances.

As society has become more complex over the centuries, so the rules of equity have become more formalised and slightly less flexible. For example, the trust became a more rigid institution in the 19th century as it was used by commercial people to develop the means of holding property and conducting trade during the social and industrial advances in Great Britain. The commercial use of trusts required great certainty in the creation and operation of trusts. In itself this demonstrates the flexibility of equity in allowing its doctrines to adapt to social change. It is my argument that the beginning of the 21st century is a time of unprecedented social complexity which requires another change in our understanding of equity: a change that requires us to celebrate the possibilities of achieving social justice in different social contexts through the use of equitable remedies and trusts. Equity is uniquely well constituted to cope with many of the challenges which are presented by the 21st century. Those ideas will emerge and re-emerge through this book.

The fundamental principles of equity

Equity has developed a range of very particular claims and remedies as part of its mission to dispense justice through the courts. One of the skills of the English lawyer is to understand which claims and remedies arise in equity and which arise under the common law. Therefore, it is necessary to continue to make a distinction between common law and equity.

The division between some of the more significant claims and remedies might be rendered diagrammatically in the following way. Note that there are many more equitable remedies than common law remedies.

Common law	Equity
Examples of claims:	
Breach of contract	Breach of trust
Negligence	Tracing property
Fraud	Claiming property on insolvency
Examples of remedies available:	
Damages	Compensation
Common law tracing	Equitable tracing
Money had and received	Specific performance
	Injunction
	Rescission
	Rectification
	Imposition of constructive trust
	Imposition of resulting trust
	Subrogation
	Account

Under the 'common law' column are some examples of common law claims that you are likely to have met already – there are plenty of others, of course. As an example, though, the law on contract contains the claim for breach of contract which frequently provides for common law damages. If the claimant wishes to force the defendant to a contract claim to perform their obligations under that contract, then it is the equitable remedy of specific performance which must be sought. Typically, the availability of equitable remedies is more dependent on the discretion of the court than common law remedies.

In general terms, it is only in equity that it is possible to receive discretionary remedies or declarations that are awarded in relation to specific factual circumstances – whether preventing unjust behaviour by means of injunction, forcing obedience of contractual provisions by specific performance, or providing that property be held on trust for the claimant by means of a range of techniques considered later in this book. However, the common law is organised principally around awards of money in relation to loss by means of damages, or exceptionally, by recovery of specific, identifiable property. The common law is concerned with the return of particular property or with making good loss, unlike the more complex claims and remedies which are available in equity.

Equity acts in personam

The most important equitable principle is that the jurisdiction of the court is to act *in personam*: that is, the court is concerned with the conscience of the individual defendant as much as with any strict rule. That equity acts *in personam* does not mean that it awards purely personal rights, such as damages at common law, as opposed to proprietary rights, because equity also awards proprietary rights in the form of rights under trust and so forth. This particular usage of the expression '*in personam*' refers back to Lord Ellesmere's description of equity in the *Earl of Oxford's Case* in 1615 as being concerned with the conscience of the defendant who appears before the court. In this sense, equity is concerned with that person's particular good behaviour, and thus with what their conscience should have told them.

A court of equity is therefore making an order, based on the facts of an individual case, to prevent that particular person from continuing to act unconscionably. This may relate to the manner in which a trustee is dealing with a beneficiary's property, or to a claimant's fear that the defendant will move their property out of the jurisdiction before judgment in a trial, or to a defendant's refusal to perform their obligations under a contract. Equity will intercede in all three of these circumstances by using principles of trusts, injunctions and specific performance, respectively. In each situation the underlying objective of the court is to make the defendant act in good conscience, by observing the trust, by refraining from taking property out of the jurisdiction, and so on.

One of the themes that we will observe in the modern application of equity is that the great flexibility which is identifiable in a court of equity's inherent jurisdiction to act *in personam* has been superseded in many circumstances by the introduction of more rigid rules to decide when these principles will and will not be deployed. This is true of some equitable doctrines, but not others. For example, the trust has become subject to more rigid principles – as considered in Chapters 3, 4 and 5 – whereas remedies such as injunctions – as considered in Chapter 13 – remain comparatively flexible.

The study of equity is concerned with the isolation of the principles upon which judges in particular cases seek to exercise their discretion. Therefore, it is an intricate task to find common threads between situations in which judges have necessarily been reaching decisions on the basis of particular facts. Bound up with the study of equity is the need to uncover common links or differences between judges. Clearly, if judges are able to reach decisions entirely according to their own discretion there are likely to be some disparities between the ways in which such principles are put into practice. Similarly, we might be concerned that this gives a great amount of power to individual judges to circumvent the wishes of Parliament when applying equitable principles to the interpretation of statute. In the era of human rights law in England – after the enactment of the Human Rights Act 1998 – we will also need to bear in mind the tension between traditional principles of equity and emerging principles of human rights law, in particular in relation to rights in the family home as considered in Chapter 9.

What is important about equity is that it never allows us to forget that people are individual human beings who have their own claims to be taken into account, whom we should not dismiss as just another case to be heard. Equity enables each individual citizen to have their claims for fair treatment heard in the private law context.

Equity never stands still. You will soon come to notice that, as soon as we think we have identified a clear rule, then a novel set of facts will materialise around the corner which call that rule into question, or we will encounter some cunning ruse used by a lawyer to avoid or manipulate that rule. The student of equity must therefore always be on guard. Having considered the principal tenet of equity – that it acts *in personam* – it will be useful to consider some of the other major equitable rules.

The core equitable principles

One thing to appreciate about the historical equitable principles is that they have a marvellously lyrical quality to them. All that has been said so far about the discretionary nature of these principles in the past is clear when you consider both how vague and how moral they are.

The core equitable propositions set out below are culled primarily from the many editions of *Snell's Equity* which have been published since 1868, with a few additions of my own which I think must now form part of the established canon. It might be useful if you thought of them as being a little like the Bible or the Koran: they are lyrical prescriptions for the way in which people should behave, which are open to interpretation, rather than strict rules in themselves. That is, equitable principles are the basis for the values that the courts should bear in mind when reaching their decisions. This is sometimes known as a 'high-level' principle which governs the application of more detailed rules to particular circumstances. You should not dismiss them because they seem too vague; they are still principles applied by the courts in line with established precedents about the application of those principles.

The core principles are set out in italics in the text of the following sections.

Ensuring the claimant will be provided for

It is worth briefly considering each of these principles in turn, to create a narrative of the way in which equity has operated historically. Perhaps the fundamental notion is that *Equity will not suffer a wrong to be without a remedy*, and thus equity establishes its core jurisdiction to ensure that a claimant will be entitled to acquire some redress for a wrong done to her or to protect some right in property. In this way, equity is also very creative in generating new doctrines or in extending existing doctrines into new contexts.

Preventing fraudulent or unconscionable behaviour

In deciding how equity and the common law interact it is usually said that *Equity follows the law*, which means that equity is generally required to follow statutes and common law rules in all circumstances. This is clearly constitutional. However, there are doctrines such as the secret trust (discussed in Chapter 4), which exist solely to circumvent the Wills Act 1837 by requiring that property willed to a legatee can be subject to a trust where that legatee had promised the deceased that she would hold the property on trust for another person. The secret trust enforces that informal arrangement even though it is in flat contravention of the Wills Act. The doctrine of secret trust is perhaps illustrative of a more important equitable principle to the effect that *Equity will not permit statute or common law to be used as an engine of fraud*. So it is that a legatee, Sidney, who has promised to hold property ostensibly left to him by Tony's will on trust for Bill, will be precluded from claiming to be a legatee under Tony's will, entitled to take that property entirely free of any obligation to Bill, because that would mean that Tony would have been defrauded when Sidney promised to hold the property on trust for Bill rather than keeping it for himself.

The common law will be applied only where it is impossible to choose between the parties to the litigation, in accordance with the principle that *Where there is equal equity, the law shall prevail*. So in a situation in which there is no clear distinction to be drawn between parties as to which of them has the better claim in equity, the common law principle that best fits the case is applied. In circumstances where two people have both purported to purchase goods from a fraudulent vendor of those goods for the same price, neither of them would have a better claim to the goods in equity. Therefore, the ordinary common law rules of commercial law would be applied in that context.

A trace of commerce

There is a sense in which even equity in the English courts is driven by commercial considerations as to the need for contracts to be completed on time, for there to be an adequate level of certainty, and for the courts to enforce only valid bargains. Those themes emerge from the following principles.

It may be that the common law has nothing to say about the dispute at issue. In that case the following principle would be applied: *Where the equities are equal, the first in time shall prevail*. Suppose that two people have equally valid claims in equity to land that was purportedly transferred to each of them separately by a fraudster. In that situation the merits of the parties' claims would be equal – where both had been defrauded in the same way – and therefore the court would simply prefer the claim of the person whose rights were created first. Time is important to equity, reflecting, perhaps, its commercial element. The only reason for defeating the claim of the person whose rights came into existence first would be if that claimant had delayed for a sufficiently long time before bringing his or her claim: *Delay defeats equities*. So if Anna had acquired rights from the fraudster but had delayed for ten years before doing anything to protect them, such that the fraudster was able to claim to sell that same land to Bertha ten years later, then Anna's claim may be relegated behind Bertha's claim unless Anna had a good reason for that delay.

The most significant equitable principle in this context is that *Equity will not assist a volunteer*. What that principle means is that a person will have no enforceable rights unless there is a valid contract, a valid trust, or some statutory provision to help them. Only a person who provides consideration is entitled to rely on the law of contract; providing consideration means that you are not a volunteer. Someone who is merely promised that they will be given a present of a bouquet of flowers, for example, acquires no rights in those flowers unless they have given consideration as part of a valid contract or unless a valid trust has been created over those flowers. This concept is considered in detail in Chapter 3.

Requirements of conscionable behaviour in litigation

Equity is also keen to ensure that a claimant is not seeking to establish a claim in circumstances in which she has not acted conscionably herself. Therefore, it is said that *He who seeks equity must do equity*. Suppose that Charles and Dipali had entered into a contract and that both were refusing to perform their obligations under that contract. Charles would be restricted from seeking specific performance of Dipali's obligations because Charles was also refusing to perform his duties: if Charles seeks equity, he must also do equity by performing his part of the contract.

Similarly, it is possible that a fraudster will seek to come to a court of equity and ask the court for an equitable remedy. Equity provides that *He who comes to equity must come with clean hands*. What this principle requires is that a claimant has acted in good faith. Therefore, in Chapter 7, we will consider the case of a company director who had committed criminal offences in the course of his duties as a director which required him to hold profits from those crimes on trust for the company (*Guinness v Saunders* (1990)). The director asked the court for some money from the company in recognition of the work which he had done for the company. The court refused to make an award of equitable accounting in his favour because he had acted illegally and therefore had not acted with 'clean hands'.

Equity and common sense

In many situations it will be difficult to differentiate between the relevant merits of two claimants' arguments. One example considered in detail in Chapter 9 in relation to trusts of homes is the difficulty of deciding which of an unmarried couple should have what equitable interest in the home at the time of separation, how the rights of the children are to be taken into account, and the comparative rights of mortgagees, and so forth. In situations where there is no clear answer as to which party ought to be entitled to a larger share, the courts may retreat to the principle that *Equality is equity* (see *Midland Bank v Cooke* (1995)). In other words, claimants should be treated equally as a last resort if no other clear answer presents itself. This is a principle that is resonant of the more common synonym for 'equity' in the other social sciences as meaning 'equality': in the economist's lexicon to act 'equitably' is to 'treat everyone the same'.

Another example of equity employing common sense is when *Equity looks to the intent rather than to the form*. Therefore, when Anna attempts to describe Bertha's rights as being 'not a trust' because she had written those words across the bottom of their agreement in felt-tip pen, a court of equity will nevertheless treat Bertha's rights as being those of a beneficiary under a trust if the true substance of their arrangement was to create a trust in her favour. In that sense, equity will seek to identify the trust intention of the parties' actions, rather than looking only at the form suggested by Anna's felt-tip comments on the bottom of the document. A court of equity will always try to cut to the heart of the parties' intentions and not just be satisfied with the performance of some trifling formality. As we shall see in Chapter 3, even where the parties do not use the expression 'trust' the courts will give effect to something which is in substance a trust as a trust (see *Paul v Constance* (1977)).

A third example of this common-sense attitude used to achieve fairness is demonstrated by the principle that *Equity looks upon as done that which ought to have been done*. One of the oldest examples of this principle is the case of *Walsh v Lonsdale* (1882), in which a binding contract to grant a lease was deemed to create an equitable lease, even though the formal requirements to create a valid common law lease had not been observed. The rationale behind equity finding there was a valid lease was the principle that the landlord was bound under contract law by the equitable doctrine of specific performance to carry out his contractual obligations and to grant a formally valid lease to the tenant. Therefore, the landlord ought to have granted such a lease. In the eyes of equity then, the grant of the lease was something that ought to have been done and which could therefore be deemed (in equity) to have been done such that the tenant acquired a lease in equity.

Furthermore, it is said that *Equity imputes an intention to fulfil an obligation*. This doctrine assumes an intention in a person bound by an obligation to carry out that obligation, such that acts not strictly required by the obligation may be deemed to be performance of the obligation. For example, if a deceased woman had owed a money debt to a man before her death, and left money to that man in her will, equity would presume that the money left in the will was left in satisfaction of the debt owed to that man. This presumption could be rebutted by some cogent evidence to the contrary; for example, that the money legacy had been promised long before the debt arose.

It is also observable that *Equity abhors a vacuum*, which is an idea resonant in Chapter 6 on resulting trusts, where a failure to make a gift of property to someone (e.g. by failing to comply with some formality required by the law of property) leads to the rights in that property returning automatically to their previous owner on 'resulting trust'. This device exists to prevent there being some property in the world which does not have an owner: that is, to prevent there being some vacuum in the title over that property. For example, if I could simply abandon my property rights in my horse, that would mean that I would no longer be obliged to feed and care for it, and that I would not be liable to compensate a farmer whose crops my horse ate, and so on. Importantly, if my rights were simply abandoned there would be nobody who could be obliged to do these things. Therefore, rather than say 'this property belongs to no one', the courts say 'this property should be deemed still to belong to its previous owner', so that there is someone responsible for the obligations attached to that property as well as being entitled to its benefits.

The trust

However, the most significant of the equitable constructs is the *trust*, under which a beneficiary is able to assert equitable rights to particular property held by a trustee and thus control the way in which the trustee of that property is entitled to deal with it. The detailed rules surrounding the trust form the bulk of this book; the introductory concepts are considered in the next chapter.

Chapter 2

The nature of the trust

The roots of the trust

The trust is peculiar to systems of law that are based on English law; therefore, the trust is found in the USA, Australia, New Zealand, Canada, India and other Commonwealth countries, but it is not indigenous to the civil code jurisdictions of Europe and elsewhere based, for example, on the Napoleonic *Code Civil* or the German civil code. The modern form of trust considered in this book is unique to Anglo-centric legal systems because it is a product of English history. We should be careful with this idea, however, because there is reason to suppose that the idea of the trust was first developed in the Middle East to provide for quasi-charitable purposes within families in the form of the *'waqf'* (Lim, 2001) or in monastic orders where the monks were required to live in poverty. Therefore, the trust idea may not have been English originally.

What is clear is that it was in England and Wales that the trust idea was incubated and raised into its current form. The trust idea is so important and so useful in commercial and non-commercial contexts alike that latterly other jurisdictions have enacted statutes to import the trust concept into their jurisdictions. The trust established the simple idea that one person could act as the steward of property ultimately for the benefit of someone else. As is explained below, this separation in the ownership of the property and the flexibility inherent in this structure are key to its success over the centuries. Today, trusts are the means through which many wills are effected, through which commercial people take security in their transactions, through which the most significant investment activity is conducted in this jurisdiction, and through which issues as to the ownership of many millions of homes are resolved.

There are two important roots of the English trust – one historical and the other intellectual. We shall deal with the historical development of the trust before coming to its intellectual roots a little later in this chapter.

The historical root of the trust can be explained most dramatically by reference to the so-called 'crusades' (from the late 11th century onwards) in which English noblemen fought and which meant that they were away from England for years at a time. These nobles were also the most significant landowners in England under the old feudal land system. The problem therefore arose as to who would be able to direct how the land should be used if the nobleman was out of the country. In consequence, equity recognised that land could be left by the nobleman 'to the use' of another while the nobleman was unable to exercise his legal rights in person. Importantly, equity recognised that in such an arrangement the nobleman should be treated as retaining some property rights. The nobleman was therefore recognised as being the person who had the ultimate beneficial right to the land and for whose benefit the arrangement was created: that person was known as the 'beneficiary'. The steward who took charge of the land in the nobleman's absence of several years would need to have all the common law ('legal') rights to raise taxes on the land and so forth. Consequently, equity came to recognise an arrangement by which the nobleman would pass the legal rights in the land to a trusted person (or 'trustee') so that the trustee could control the use of the land, but on the understanding that the ultimate beneficial rights to the property remained with the nobleman as the 'beneficiary' of this arrangement. It was equity which would recognise and protect the rights of the beneficiary, and therefore the beneficiary is said to have an 'equitable interest' in the property.

Therefore, the trust device was created originally to deal with a situation in which a number of people had claims to land which arose simultaneously. What is clear about dealings with land is that the land is immovable: there will be no question of the land being mixed up with other land in the way that water in one glass can be mixed with water from another glass so that the two pools of water become impossible to separate out.

By the 21st century trusts take effect in relation to all forms of property: from land through tangible chattels and into all forms of intangible property. Anything which is considered to be property under English law can be held on trust. With the advent of trusts over these new and complex forms of property, the rules which were developed originally in relation to land did not always work properly, and so trusts law has had to develop in reaction to circumstances ever since. You should remember that when two trusts cases conflict, or when the principles are difficult to apply to a novel situation, that it may well have something to do with the fact that trusts law has been made up on a case-by-case basis since the 11th century and therefore its logic is bound to creak occasionally. Our task will be to question the suitability of those old principles of trusts law in their modern context and to map some of the judicial sleights of hand that have been necessary to make them appear to fit the modern context.

The modern trust

Some important vocabulary in the creation of an express trust

A trust exists in relation to identified property (known as the 'trust property' or the 'trust fund' or the 'subject matter of the trust'). The absolute owner of the trust fund (the 'settlor') creates the trust by appointing a trustee or trustees to hold the trust fund on trust for the identified beneficiary or beneficiaries. When a trust is created it is said to have been 'declared'. In Chapter 3 we will consider the formalities that may be necessary to create such a trust in some circumstances, although in most cases there is no formality; for present purposes it is enough that the settlor merely demonstrates an intention to create such a trust, without needing to do anything more.

When the settlor creates a trust, the settlor is said to 'settle that property on trust' or to make a 'declaration of trust'. Both expressions mean the same thing. (This use of the two synonymous expressions demonstrates the tendency of English lawyers to have more than one name for the same concept – arguably because it helps to maintain the mystique of the law and to ensure that clients are sufficiently impressed by their counsel's knowledge of so much complicated terminology.) The trustee holds the trust fund on trust for the benefit of the beneficiary. There can be any number of trustees and beneficiaries in theory in relation to most types of property. More simply, it could be said that the trustee holds the property on trust for the beneficiary.

In the sorts of cases which arose in Jane Austen novels in which the property of wealthy English families was passed down within those families (including their home, their chattels and so forth), it was usual to create a formal trust known as a 'settlement' in which the rights of the various members of the family (present and future) were set out. The term 'settlement' can be treated as a synonym for 'trust' in this context. It was common to say that property was 'settled on trust' when a trust was declared over it in the older cases. The term 'settlor' comes from the concept of a 'settlement' and refers to the person who created the trust originally.

The mechanics of creating express trusts

To be able to declare a trust over property, the settlor must have had all of the rights in the property which is to be settled on trust, or 'absolute title', before the declaration of the trust. Clearly, one cannot deal with property in which one has no rights: therefore, the settlor must hold all of the rights to be settled on trust before that trust can be declared. Before the trust is created, there is simply absolute title in that property vested in the settlor; we do not think of there being legal title and an equitable interest lurking latent within an item of property such as the albumen and the yolk lying hidden inside an egg. Rather, the legal title and the equitable interest are brought into existence when the trust is declared. At the moment that the trust is created, the trustee acquires 'legal title' in the trust fund and the beneficiaries acquire the 'equitable interest' (or, as it is sometimes known, the 'beneficial interest') in the trust fund in accordance with the terms of the trust. One does not talk, however, of there being legal title and equitable title latent in property before the creation of the trust; rather, the settlor simply has absolute title before the declaration of the trust (*Westdeutsche Landesbank v Islington* (1996)).

The rights of the various parties are represented in the following diagram.

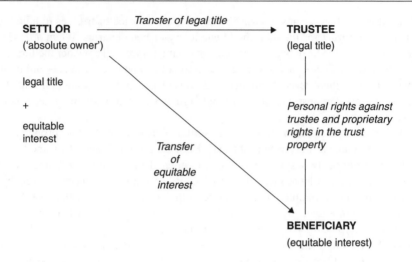

What emerges from this diagram is the following. The settlor declares a trust. At that point in time there is a division in the title in the property, which is to be held on trust. The legal title is transferred to the trustee. The trustee thus acquires all of the common law rights in the property. If the property were land then the legal title at the Land Registry would be in the name of the trustee; if the property were a bank account, the name on the account and on the chequebook would be in the name of the trustee; if the property were shares in a company then the share register would record the trustee as being the owner of the shares, and so on. Therefore, from the perspective of the outside world, the trustee appears to be the owner of the property; although the truth is that the beneficiary has the beneficial interest in the trust property. The advantage of this arrangement is that the trustee does all of the work of managing the trust property, while the beneficiary takes all of the benefit. As will emerge through this book, to be a trustee is a weighty responsibility with many duties and obligations. Those rights and obligations of the trustee are considered in detail in Chapter 5, and the potential liabilities for breach of trust are considered in Chapter 10.

Meanwhile, on the declaration of the trust the equitable interest in the trust fund is vested in the beneficiary. From the perspective of the law of trusts this equitable interest is the ultimate interest in the trust fund. What this means for the beneficiary is that she acquires equitable proprietary rights in the trust fund and also a set of personal claims against the trustee to ensure that the trustee carries out the terms of the trust. Among the proprietary rights is a recognition that the beneficiary holds the property rights in any property held on trust. Among the personal rights of the beneficiary, the trustee is required to protect the interests of the beneficiary, to observe faithfully the terms of the trust as set out by the settlor, and to protect the trust property. The trustee is subject to a potential personal liability for any loss suffered by the beneficiary as a result of any breach of trust. The rights of the beneficiary are considered in more detail in Chapter 4.

It may be that there is only one beneficiary, which is known as a 'bare trust'. However, it is more often the case that there are a number of beneficiaries, and it is common to provide that different beneficiaries (or different groups of beneficiaries) will have different rights. The difficult question is therefore how should the trustee conduct herself so as to act fairly between this range of beneficiaries? These issues are considered in detail in Chapter 5. Typically, all such questions would depend on the terms of the trust as set out by the settlor. As will emerge in the next chapter, trusts can be created orally in most circumstances and therefore there may not be any detailed terms created to govern the trustees' obligations. A well-organised trust, however, would have a trust instrument which records the trustees' obligations, the beneficiaries' various rights and so forth in a written document drafted by a lawyer. Trusts can be quite simple or they can be very complicated. Pension funds with thousands of members are organised as trusts and are subject to very detailed provisions as well as detailed statutory and regulatory codes. Similarly, as considered in Chapter 3, it may be that a bank account holding money contributed by only two people will also form a trust, but without either of the parties realising they had created a trust or specifying any terms of their trust. That sort of trust will be very simple indeed, with the general law of trusts supplying the trustees' obligations. As such the law of trusts is required to deal with a very broad range of factual circumstances.

Capacities, not people

The settlor drops out of the picture *in her capacity as settlor* at the moment when the trust is created. It is important to understand that trusts law is not concerned with people as people; rather, trusts law is concerned with *the legal capacities* in which people are acting on each occasion. To make that point clearer: it is possible for Adam to decide that he wants to create a trust over the family home over which he is absolute owner so that, after his death, his children will have title in it. It might be that Adam wants to avoid tax and so wishes to create a particular kind of trust over his home. It would be possible for Adam, as absolute owner of the property, to be settlor and thus to declare that he will act as trustee himself and hold the home from the date of the declaration on trust for himself for life and, after his death, for his children absolutely. (Strictly, after Adam's death, it would be Adam's personal representatives who would act as trustees on his behalf.) In this situation Adam will be settlor, trustee and also one of the beneficiaries. This is perfectly normal: one person can act in those different capacities. Importantly, when Adam is acting as trustee he will be treated by trusts law as though he was a different person from Adam acting as beneficiary: when acting as trustee, Adam would be prevented by trusts law from giving advantages to himself as opposed to acting impartially for all of the beneficiaries. It is in this way that trusts law is concerned with *capacities* and not simply with *people*.

The only structure that would be logically impossible would be for Adam to declare that he holds the property as the sole trustee on trust for himself as the sole beneficiary because, in that example, he would retain all of the available rights in the property. In that situation we would say that no trust had been created and that Adam simply remained absolute owner of the property. What would be possible would be for Adam to appoint someone, Bernice, to hold property on trust as the only trustee for Adam as the only beneficiary. In that situation, Adam would not be trustee.

Because Adam would be the only beneficiary in this example, we would refer to the trust as a 'bare trust' and we would refer to Bernice as being a 'bare trustee' or, more usually, as a 'nominee'. (You may be becoming bemused by all of these synonyms for the same concept. Do not be downhearted for there are clear benefits in it. In practice, your clients will soon come to understand the jargon terms you are using and as a result your allure will fade in their eyes. So think how useful it is to be able to use a synonym for that concept which your client will not understand, with the result that their admiration for your learning will be instantly rekindled and that they will consider themselves very lucky indeed to be paying only a fraction of the fee which a person of your staggering intellect so clearly deserves.)

The rights of beneficiaries

In ordinary circumstances, the settlor transfers the legal rights in the trust property to a trustee so that the trustee will use the trust property in accordance with the settlor's instructions. No rights are owed by the trustee to the settlor (in her capacity as settlor) from that moment. Instead, the courts of equity recognise that the trustee holds the trust fund on trust for the beneficiary. Therefore, all of the beneficial interest resides with the beneficiary.

Division of title

It is a neat trick that the trust performs – two or more people are able to hold rights simultaneously in the same item of property. The trustee is recognised by the common law as being the owner of the property – therefore the trustee is said to have the common law, or 'legal', rights in the property; whereas the beneficiary is recognised by equity as having rights in the property – therefore the beneficiary is said to have the 'equitable interest' in the property. The nature of these equitable rights is considered in more detail in Chapters 5 and 10. In short, the beneficiaries have both proprietary rights in the trust property and also the right to ensure that the trustees observe the terms of their trusteeship.

Multiple beneficiaries

Where there is more than one beneficiary, the proportionate rights of the beneficiaries in the trust fund are dependent on the terms of the trust. It may be that the settlor intends one person to be entitled to enjoy the rights of beneficiary during that person's life and for the equitable interest to pass to another beneficiary on the death of the first. To achieve that structure the settlor would provide that the trustee 'shall hold the property on trust for A for life, remainder to B absolutely'. That provision means that A is entitled to the income from the trust fund and the use of the fund during her life but without any power to dispose of the trust fund before her death. B has the rights to the capital of the fund after A's death. The interests of these two beneficiaries are clearly at odds with one another: A will want the trustee to generate as much income in the short term as possible, even if that means risking the capital; whereas B would prefer a cautious treatment of the capital so as to preserve as much of it as possible. A is known as the 'life tenant'. B is known as a 'remainderman' (or 'remainder beneficiary') who has sufficient rights to prevent A and the trustee disposing of all of the value in the trust fund before A's death and is then a beneficiary under a bare trust after A's death.

It might be that the beneficiaries are all entitled to income from the trust or to the use of the trust property during their lifetimes. Alternatively, it may be that the income from the trust fund is to be held on trust for the beneficiaries equally – which would mean that the trustee would make a periodical, outright transfer of the income in equal shares between the beneficiaries. This will depend on the terms of the trust.

Discretionary trusts and mere powers of appointment

The trust may be a 'discretionary trust' under which the trustees have the power to make apportionments of the trust property to one or more of the members of the class of beneficiaries in accordance with the terms of the powers given to the trustees by the settlor. An example of such a discretionary trust would be a term in a trust which provided: '*My trustees shall pay £10,000 out of the trust fund to whichever of the beneficiaries achieves the most impressive examination results at university.*' In this example, the trustees are obliged to make an apportionment of property but the decision as to which beneficiaries are to be the recipients will be in the trustees' power alone, provided that they apply it in accordance with the terms of the trust. The trustees therefore have a discretion as to *how* they exercise their power, but they have an obligation to exercise that discretion in favour of one of the objects of that trust.

There is a further structural alternative. The trustees may have a power to transfer (or 'appoint' or 'advance') given amounts of the trust income or capital to an identified class of beneficiaries – this is known as a 'power of appointment' or a 'power of advancement'. An example would be: '*The trustees may appoint £1,000 out of the trust fund to any of the beneficiaries whose bank account is overdrawn.*' In such a situation, the trustees are not obliged to transfer money to any of the beneficiaries; rather, they would have an ability to do so in defined circumstances if they considered it to be appropriate. The trustees also have a discretion as to the recipient of the appointment. It might be that the settlor wanted to give the trustees the flexibility to pay money to one or other of the beneficiaries if they should encounter financial difficulties. When creating a trust, the settlor and her advisors have to build enough flexibility into the trust from the outset to meet all future contingencies. At the same time the professional advisors must take care to consider the tax law treatment of the various forms of trust which they may create.

The way in which you can distinguish between a discretionary trust and a power of appointment is by examining the precise terms of the trust and determining whether or not the trustees are compelled to act or merely enabled to act. Therefore, the word 'shall' in a trust deed usually indicates that the trustee 'must' exercise her discretion: it is that compulsion which distinguishes a discretionary trust from a power of appointment. Further, the word 'may' usually indicates that the trustee is not obliged to exercise a discretion but rather has merely a power to do so if she considers it appropriate.

The rule in Saunders v Vautier

Exceptionally, the case of *Saunders v Vautier* (1841) gives the beneficiaries the right to instruct the trustees to transfer the property to them absolutely. They can exercise this power only if they hold between them the entirety of the equitable interest and if they are all legally competent to act. The rule in *Saunders v Vautier* demonstrates one particular important facet of the rights of a beneficiary: the beneficiaries under a trust have proprietary rights in the trust fund and not merely personal rights against the trustees. This rule is considered in greater detail in Chapter 4.

The intellectual roots of the trust

It is the central contention of this book that the trust is best understood as being a creation of equity under which the actions of the legal owner of property are controlled to prevent unconscionable conduct. This is so even though the modern trust is in fact far more formalistic than this root in 'good conscience' would seem to suggest – a dichotomy that is considered further in Chapter 14. Nevertheless, the speech of Lord Browne-Wilkinson in *Westdeutsche Landesbank v Islington* (1996) re-emphasised the importance of the concept of 'conscience' in relation to the trust:

> Equity operates on the conscience of the owner of the legal interest. In the case of a trust, the conscience of the legal owner requires him to carry out the purposes for which the property was vested in him (express or implied trust) or which the law imposes on him by reason of his unconscionable conduct (constructive trust).

Thus, the trust is imposed in any circumstance in which the owner of property is bound by good conscience to recognise that someone else ought to have rights in that property too. This may be because the settlor has consciously created an express trust or because the court interprets the parties' behaviour to disclose sufficient intention to create something that the law would recognise as being a trust.

The various types of trust

There are three forms of trust. The simplest is the 'express trust', which is a trust created intentionally by the settlor. The rules of formality in the creation of an express trust and the factors necessary to constitute such a trust are considered in Chapters 3 to 5 below. There are also two other forms of trust that are imposed by the courts: the 'resulting trust' and the 'constructive trust'. These trusts are discussed at length in Chapters 6 and 7 respectively. A short outline of each is given below.

Resulting trusts

The resulting trust is a means by which equity supplements the ordinary law of property in two circumstances (*Westdeutsche Landesbank v Islington* (1996)). What is common to both circumstances is that it is the court that imposes the trust: by definition the parties have not declared an express trust.

The first circumstance is the automatic resulting trust. If a settlor has purported to create a trust by transferring legal title to trustees but has not made clear who the beneficiaries will be, that trust will fail for uncertainty (as considered in Chapter 3). The problem is then: what happens to the equitable interest in the trust property? The resulting trust provides that the equitable interest passes back to the settlor such that the trustee holds the property on resulting trust for the settlor.

The second circumstance concerns purchase price resulting trusts. In a situation in which two people contribute to the acquisition price of property, equity provides that each of them will acquire an equitable interest in the property in proportion to the size of their respective contributions to the purchase price. The legal owner of that property will hold the property on resulting trust for the two purchasers according to those proportionate shares.

Constructive trusts

Constructive trusts arise in a broad range of circumstances by operation of law. That means that it is the court that imposes the trust on the parties instead of it being an express trust declared by the parties. In general terms, a constructive trust arises in circumstances in which the defendant deals with property knowing of something that should affect her conscience. The term 'constructive trust' refers to the fact that the defendant is 'construed' to be a trustee of that property. In such a circumstance, the defendant would become constructive trustee of that property. An example would arise in a shop if a customer gives the shopkeeper a £10 note and receives change from the shopkeeper who mistakenly believes that she had been given a £20 note. If the customer noticed that she had been given too much change, then she would be a constructive trustee of that excess change because she knew of the mistake and so it would be unconscionable to keep the excess change.

There are many constructive trusts considered in Chapter 7. Examples are where a trustee makes unauthorised profits from the trust, where a trustee receives a bribe, where a person acquires property through fraud, where a person enters into a contract promising to transfer property to someone else, or where two cohabitees create a common intention as to their respective rights in their home. In each of these situations the particular property dealt with will be held on constructive trust.

There is another species of so-called constructive trust in which the defendant either knowingly receives property in breach of trust or dishonestly assists in a breach of trust. In these situations it is a person who is neither a trustee nor a beneficiary who becomes personally liable for any loss suffered by the beneficiaries for their role in the misapplication of trust property. These doctrines are considered in Chapter 10 in relation to breach of trust.

Proprietary estoppel

One further equitable doctrine which is worthy of mention at this juncture is that of proprietary estoppel. Given that the significance of the trust is that it grants the beneficiary rights in property, proprietary estoppel may also grant rights in property. The doctrine of proprietary estoppel operates so that where Eve gives an assurance to Adam that Adam will acquire rights in property, if Adam acts to his detriment in reliance on that assurance then Eve will be estopped from denying Adam any rights in connection with that property. Estoppel gives the court a wide discretion to identify the remedy that best avoids Adam from suffering detriment. The court may grant Adam an absolute right in the property or merely order that he be entitled to receive some financial compensation to alleviate his detriment. This doctrine is considered in Chapter 8. In relation to express trusts it is occasionally the case that estoppel will grant proprietary rights to an applicant even if the formalities necessary to create a trust have not been complied with. The doctrine is also important in relation to trusts of homes, as considered in Chapter 9.

Distinguishing between other kinds of trust

I have a further series of divisions to make in the law of trusts beyond the long-established divisions considered above, based mainly on the contexts in which those trusts are created.

The historical roots of the trust

The roots of the trust, as considered above, are in equity's control of the conscience of the trustee. These principles were developed in relation to trusts over land and, primarily, over family homes. In time, trusts were also used to allocate rights to other property, such as money, family businesses and so forth. As such the judiciary took the view that it ought to protect the beneficiaries above all else because the beneficiaries' entire livelihood was usually what was at issue. However, the trust device is deployed in a broader range of circumstances than in relation to these early family trusts.

In the novels of Jane Austen and Charles Dickens much of the drama turned on the rights of wealthy, landed families under complicated family settlements. So in *Sense and Sensibility* and *Bleak House* the protagonists are in desperate financial straits because their ancestors had created trusts that provided that only identified members of the family would be entitled to inherit property, thus leaving other relatives destitute. It was common, especially in the circumstances of Jane Austen novels like *Pride and Prejudice*, for the family home to pass to male heirs, with the result that female family members were required to find rich husbands so as to avoid having to scrape by on small incomes from the family settlement. The family settlement and a trust set out in a will were the most common forms of trust before the mid-19th century. Therefore, the management and conduct of these trusts were of vital importance to the beneficiaries because their entire livelihood was bound up in them. An entire, genteel social class was dependent upon these sorts of trust. In consequence, the law of trusts developed strict principles to ensure that the beneficiaries would not be prey to unscrupulous trustees bent on defrauding them – as considered in Chapter 5.

Commercial and non-commercial trusts

In the 19th century there was an economic boom in the British Empire which created a hunger for investment capital. As a result, the trust device was used to raise capital from the public at a time when companies were still unlawful associations after the cataclysmic collapse of the South Sea Company in 1720. Trusts were used either in the form of joint stock arrangements whereby members (or, to use modern jargon, 'shareholders') became partners in the pursuit of commercial profit, or alternatively in the form of unit trusts (considered briefly in Chapter 11) as a mutual fund in which investors pooled their money in expectation of a financial return.

However, there is at least one more commercial use for the trust: as a receptacle for property used in commercial transactions. Suppose that Ernest wants to have an expensive suit made to measure for him by a tailor whom he has never met before. Ernest will not want to pay for the suit until he is content that it is suitable for his purposes. The tailor will not want to spend a lot of his time and use expensive cloth to make a suit for Ernest in case Ernest does not pay. Therefore, they might use a trust to secure their positions. Ernest could pay the price of the suit to a trustee on the following terms: if the suit proves satisfactory then title in the money would be transferred to the tailor, whereas if the suit proves unsatisfactory title in the money would remain with Ernest. The trustee would therefore hold the money on trust for both Ernest and the tailor until the suit was completed. In this way, trusts are used very frequently by commercial people to facilitate their transactions and to absorb the risks of the other party to the contract not performing their obligations.

Significantly, where a person has the rights of a beneficiary under a valid trust, that beneficiary is entitled to retain its rights in the property even if the trustee or her fellow beneficiaries go into insolvency. The beneficiary is considered to be a secured beneficiary protected against insolvency. Ordinarily, if a person did not have rights in property held by the insolvent person, that person would be only an unsecured creditor of the insolvent person (entitled only to a personal claim) and therefore unlikely to receive anything more than a small percentage of the money owed to it under insolvency law. Therefore, the trust provides protection against insolvency by granting the beneficiary a proprietary right in the property held by the insolvent person as trustee.

Even though commercial trusts are very common, there is an uneasy assimilation in the law of trusts between the roots of the law in the allocation of rights in family property and the increasing volume of litigation attempting to apply those same principles to complex commercial contracts. The House of Lords raised the question in recent cases as to whether the existing principles of equity and trusts are suitable to cope with the broad variety of cases in the modern world. These sentiments are best expressed by Lord Browne-Wilkinson in *Target Holdings v Redferns* (1995), p 475:

> In the modern world the trust has become a valuable device in commercial and financial dealings. The fundamental principles of equity apply as much to such trusts as they do to the traditional trusts in relation to which those principles were originally formulated. But in my judgment it is important, if the trust is not to be rendered commercially useless, to distinguish between the basic principles of trust law and those specialist rules developed in relation to traditional trusts which are applicable only to such trusts and the rationale of which has no application to trusts of quite a different kind.

Therefore, one theme that we will observe at various points throughout this book is the difficulty in taking those rules of the law of trusts which were developed in relation to land and to family settlements and applying them to commercial situations (especially complex financial transactions in recent cases).

It is important to understand that the broad application of trusts in commercial and financial transactions operates across national borders. As the world has become more globalised, so the techniques that commercial people use have similarly become more globalised. The trust has been seized upon by the commercial and financial communities as a particularly useful means of securing their positions. The trust therefore faces the challenge of breaking loose from its moorings in English social history and adapting to this new world. However, we should never lose sight of the very significant role which the trust continues to play in

England and Wales in relation to the way in which people acquire rights in their homes. Therefore, as we develop trusts law principles to meet commercial practice we run the risk of ignoring the social impact of trusts law, and vice versa. These issues are pursued in Chapter 14.

Distinguishing between personal and proprietary rights

Beneficiaries under a trust have equitable *proprietary* rights in the trust property, as is explained in detail in Chapter 4. This means that the beneficiaries have rights of ownership in whatever property is held on trust, whether that property increases or falls in value over time. As considered in the next section, this has the advantage in relation to insolvency that beneficiaries receive special protection. By contrast, having merely a *personal* right means that the claimant has no right to any specified property, and therefore if the defendant were to go into insolvency or were to leave the jurisdiction then the claimant would have no property against which she could enforce her rights and would instead have only a worthless right (in practice) to compensation in money. For the purposes of this book, having a proprietary right will be seen as being advantageous because the claimant has rights in some identified property if she has proprietary rights, as opposed to having merely personal rights to compensation. It is important to bear this distinction between proprietary and personal rights clearly in mind because some rights will be proprietary and other rights will be merely personal – the analytical difference between the two is often vital.

Trusts and insolvency

The significance of trusts in cases of insolvency is this. If a trustee goes into insolvency, the beneficiaries under that trust continue to hold a proprietary right in the trust property and therefore any property held on trust does not fall to be distributed generally among the trustee's creditors, but rather is held solely for the beneficiary. Consequently, a beneficiary is described by insolvency practitioners as being a 'secured creditor'. In insolvency proceedings it is therefore advantageous for the insolvent person's creditors to seek to argue that some sort of trust should be understood as having come into existence in their favour so as to elevate them from being unsecured creditors into being secured creditors who therefore have rights in identified property. Many of the cases we shall consider in this book have insolvency as their background as a result.

The way ahead

The next three chapters will consider the detailed rules as to the creation and management of trusts from the perspectives of the settlor, the beneficiary and the trustee, respectively. The aim is to consider how an express trust comes into existence and the nature of the rights and obligations that are created. After that,

Chapters 6 and 7 will consider those trusts that are implied by law as opposed to being expressly declared by a settlor. Chapter 9 will consider how those trusts that are implied by law apply to the family home. Chapter 10 will consider the various claims and remedies available when any trust, express or implied, is breached. Chapters 11 and 12 will then consider how those trusts principles are applied in commercial and welfare contexts, respectively.

First, it is important to know how the principle of conscience identified above is put to work in the creation of express trusts in Chapter 3.

The settlor: certainties and formalities

Introduction: creating a trust

There are at least as many reasons for creating a trust as there are people in the world. This chapter will consider how equity treats the creation of trusts and it will explore some of the main reasons why trusts are used at all by settlors. Our principal focus will be on the formalities and the certainties with which the settlor must comply before a valid trust can be created. Once the trust is created we will see that the settlor's role ceases to exist: a little like the chrysalis once the butterfly has emerged from it.

In short, it should be said that it is open to the settlor to do almost anything she wishes when creating a trust: the terms of the trust are the rulebook that the settlor creates to govern the way in which the trustee is to behave and to set out the entitlements of various classes of beneficiary. So, the common answer to the question 'What must the trustees do?' is quite simply 'Read what the terms of the trust say', if there is a trust instrument. In some situations, however, it is necessary to look at some of the mandatory rules of the law relating to trusts: that is, those rules that prohibit or require certain kinds of activity before a trust will be enforced. Where the trust is created entirely orally, then there will not be a trust instrument and so the terms of the trust will be contained in the settlor's words and supplemented by the general law of trusts. (As considered in the previous chapter, trusts can be created orally (unless, like land, there is a statutory rule requiring that the trust be in writing) although a well-drafted trust would normally be contained in a trust instrument.)

It will be useful to bear in mind that settlors' intentions are important only in relation to express trusts. Therefore, the discussion in Chapters 3 to 5 will focus on express trusts and the interaction of settlor, beneficiary and trustee. In later chapters it will be seen that implied trusts are imposed by the courts without the need for a settlor to have sought to create a valid trust.

Contract, or simple giving

There are two principal kinds of express trust: trusts created out of a simple intention to transfer property to someone and trusts created as part of a larger transaction. Trusts created in a contract, as considered below, might arise in a number of circumstances. Commercial parties may use a trust to provide for protection of their title in property that is being used for the purposes of their contract as considered in the previous chapter (see p 25). Alternatively, the contract might be for investment purposes (as with pension funds, for example) in which the investor will form a contract with the investment manager to the effect that the investment manager holds funds on trust with an obligation to invest them on behalf of the investor–beneficiary: the contract will provide for the trustee to be paid its fee and for any limitations on the investment manager's liability for losses suffered. In such situations it is the contract which creates the underlying rationale for the existence of the trust; the contract will therefore also contain the terms of the trust in many circumstances.

Trusts are, more traditionally, a means of giving property 'over the plane of time', to borrow Moffat's expression (1999). In other words, rather than simply make an outright gift of property at one time and transfer all of the rights in property absolutely to a donee, a person may prefer to ensure that the gift will continue over a long period of time. So, a grandparent in a will may decide to divide up an estate so that each of their children and grandchildren become beneficiaries under a trust that provides for some to live in the family home and for others to receive a regular cash income during their lifetimes. Thus, a trust is a means of creating more complex relationships than a simple gift.

Bearing some of these different objectives in mind, this chapter will consider the requirements placed on the settlor when seeking to create a trust.

Irrevocability of a trust

One of the key rules in relation to the settlor's interaction with a trust is that once a trust is created the settlor cannot undo that trust. So, in the case of *Paul v Paul* (1882), a husband and wife had entered into a marriage settlement before their marriage. A marriage settlement, as considered in Chapter 2, is a trust created before marriage whereby the parties to the marriage and their families set out which property passes to the married couple and which of their future children and other members of their extended families are entitled to acquire rights in that property in the future. In *Paul v Paul* the marriage settlement created rights for the couple and for others as beneficiaries. The marriage was unsuccessful and the couple therefore sought to undo the trust and recover title in the property for themselves. The court held that the trust could not be undone by the settlors or anyone else after it had been constituted. Therefore, the trust continued in existence.

This is a salutary lesson for the settlor: be sure of your intentions before creating your trust. Or, at least ensure that you have a power built into the trust instrument to undo the trust if your expectations are not borne out.

The only exception to the general rule in *Paul v Paul* would be if the settlor created some express right in the terms of the trust that she could recover title in the property. No such right was contained in the trust in *Paul*. So, how would such a mechanism operate?

Suppose, for example, that two commercial parties form a contract whereby Industrial Ltd agrees to buy a very large consignment of components from Supplier Ltd over a period of five years. That contract will contain provisions that Industrial Ltd is to pay Supplier Ltd amounts for the components at various stages over the five-year period. However, Industrial Ltd would be nervous of paying for parts in advance of delivery. A trust could therefore be contained in the contract which provided that Industrial Ltd would make payment to Bank so that Bank held those payments as trustee. The terms of the trust would be that Bank would hold the money on trust until Industrial certified that the components were of sufficient quality – from that point in time Bank would hold the payment on trust solely for Supplier. If a term were inserted into the trust to the effect that Industrial was entitled to recover the money from the trust absolutely and terminate that trust, then it would be possible for it to guard against the risk of Supplier going into insolvency or failing to deliver suitable parts.

There are two ways in which Industrial could recover its money. First, the term contained in the trust could be to the effect that Industrial as one of a number of beneficiaries would be entitled to recover property from the trust. Alternatively, Industrial could be expressed to become entitled to the money absolutely as the sole beneficiary under a bare trust: that is, as though Supplier's equitable interest was terminated if it failed to deliver suitable components.

Suppose then that a parent wanted to create a trust for a child but was concerned that the child might use the money in an inappropriate way. The parent acting as settlor might express the child's equitable interest as being subject to a power held by the settlor to terminate the trust in the event that the child performed one of a specified type of action. Alternatively, it might be that the settlor created a trust with the provision 'so that my child shall acquire no rights as a beneficiary unless and until' certain actions were performed: a kind of condition precedent. As we shall see in Chapter 4, it is not always easy for the settlor to prevent the beneficiaries from attempting to rewrite the trust after it has been created. In some (non-commercial) situations, there may be tax disadvantages if the settlor retains an interest under a trust fund.

The trust as an institution

As was considered in Chapter 2, the express trust is something that is becoming ever more important in modern commercial life, despite its heritage as a means for families to organise the way in which their property will be made available to future generations. This chapter considers some of the detailed rules concerning the creation of express trusts with the intention both of summarising those rules and also of providing a map of the legal treatment of express trusts at this stage. This chapter divides then between the rules relating to certainties, the rules relating to perpetuities and the rules relating to formalities.

There is a more general point to be made at the outset. Whereas the trust was born to act as a means by which equity was able to control the conscience of the common law owner of property, the development of the rules considered in this chapter has had the effect of changing fundamentally the nature of the express trust. In short, the trust has become 'institutionalised'. If you recall the discussion in Chapter 1, the claims and remedies identified with equity were remarkable for their flexibility. The principles on which equity operated were considered to be more lyrical than legal. However, introducing the sort of rigid prerequisites to the creation of trusts which are considered in Chapters 3 to 5 has meant that the express trust has become similar to the contract in one particular sense: that is, a range of formalities has to be performed, and if they are performed the courts will recognise that you have created a trust.

Constituting the trust

The settlor must constitute the trust, which means that legal title in the trust property must be vested in the trustee(s) by the settlor. Recalling the discussion in Chapter 2 that the settlor must have absolute title in the property rights that are to be settled on trust, for a trust to come into existence legal title in those property rights must be transferred to (or, must *vest* in) the trustee. In most trust situations this is a simple process of the settlor passing title to the trustee. It may be that the settlor is proposing to act as trustee herself, in which case all that is required is a valid declaration of trust that the legal title in that property is now held by the settlor as a trustee. If the trust property is land, the settlor would be required to manifest or prove the declaration of trust by signed writing (Law of Property Act 1925, s 53(1)(b)); otherwise it is required that the settlor evidence sufficient intention to declare such a trust, as considered below.

What is more complex is the situation in which a person will argue that they ought to be considered to be a beneficiary where it is not clear whether or not a trust has been created. For example, suppose that Sam intended to make a gift of shares in a company to Benny but Sam failed to comply with the company law formality of re-registering the title in the shares in favour of Benny as their new absolute owner. In such a situation there would be no valid transfer of any title in the shares to Benny. A gift requires the transfer of absolute title, unlike a trust. A gift and a trust are different things. Benny may seek to argue that he should be considered to be the beneficiary under a trust of those shares on the basis that Sam *intended* to transfer them to Benny but failed to complete a formality. This type of argument is used regularly by people who want property to be vested in them and who therefore attempt to suggest that the transferor should be bound by good conscience to transfer title.

The Court of Appeal's decision in *Milroy v Lord* (1862) is very clear on this point: you cannot try to give effect to a failed gift by calling it a trust instead. Therefore, Benny would not be entitled to interpret Sam's clear intention to make a gift as being really an intention to make a trust just so that Benny can take good title in the property. The trust device is not to be used as a means of perfecting imperfect gifts. (The term 'perfect' here comes from the Latin *perfacere* meaning 'to complete'.)

In the case of *Milroy v Lord* itself a deed had been created that purported to transfer 50 shares in a Louisiana railway company to Samuel Lord for him to hold on trust for Milroy's benefit. The transfer was to have been carried out through an agent. It was a requirement of the applicable company law that there could not be a transfer of those shares unless the transfer was registered in the company's register. There had not been a re-registration of any transfer and therefore Milroy had no rights in the shares. Instead, Milroy tried to argue that the intention to transfer the shares to Lord ought to mean that the current owner ought to be considered to be a trustee of them. It was held that an ineffective gift does not constitute a declaration of trust without there being a clear intention to create a trust in that way.

That much would appear to be perfectly clear if it were not for the case of *Re Rose* (1952). The problem that arises after *Milroy v Lord* is this: what if the transferor has done everything necessary to transfer the shares? In that situation, should the transferor be considered to have transferred an equitable interest to the claimant (and thus to have created a trust)? For example, suppose that Derek is shipping shoes to Clive and that Derek has filled in all the forms necessary to transfer title in the shoes to Clive and that the final legal formality that remains is for the shoes to be delivered by ship to Clive in India; should we consider that Derek has given up all of his rights (in equity at least) to Clive as soon as the ship sets sail and there is nothing Derek can do to recover the shoes? The approach that trusts law takes is to accept that once the transferor has done everything necessary to effect the transfer, then the equitable interest should be treated as passing to the transferee by way of constructive trust. This is so, even if the transferor intended only a gift of the property originally – thus making the trust appear to be a constructive trust (as considered in Chapter 7).

The reader may now be thinking: but surely the decision in *Re Rose* completely contradicts what was said in *Milroy v Lord*? This is a key point in the technique of trusts law: it is important to understand the subtle distinctions on which the cases turn because it is precisely these subtle distinctions in structure which are exploited by trusts lawyers in advising their clients. In *Milroy v Lord* it was said that one cannot intend to make a gift, fail to make that gift properly, and then simply call it a trust so as to give effect to it. However, in *Re Rose* the court found, in effect, that in the situation where the transferor had done everything necessary *for her to do* to effect a valid transfer, it would be unconscionable to allow her to renege on her promise to transfer. Therefore, the *Rose* trust comes into existence to stop that individual transferor acting unconscionably.

To give one more illustration by comparing two cases, in *Re Fry* (1946) an American had filled in a transfer form with the intention of transferring shares in a private company but had not received the required consent of Her Majesty's Treasury to effect a valid transfer of those shares. In consequence, it was held that he had not done everything necessary *for him to do* to transfer the shares because he did not have the Treasury's consent. In *Re Rose* a husband intended to transfer shares to his wife and at the material time all that remained to be done was for the board of directors to agree to the transfer; importantly, Mr Rose had done everything that was required of *him* to effect a valid transfer. As a result, the Court of Appeal in *Re Rose* held that equitable title ought to be deemed to transfer to Mrs Rose as soon as Mr Rose had finished the formalities.

Now, the reader may be thinking: what is the difference between Fry needing to get the Treasury's consent and Rose still awaiting the consent of the directors? The answer is probably revealed by the context. In *Rose* the board of directors did eventually give consent to the transfer; the only reason for the case to come to court was because, under tax law at that time, if Mr Rose could be shown to have transferred his equitable interest in the shares to his wife as soon as he completed the forms there would have been no inheritance tax to pay on the shares after his death, whereas there would have been tax to pay if the court had held there was no transfer until the date of the directors' agreement. Therefore, the court was looking at the surrounding factors in the case of *Rose*. This is something the student of trusts law should never forget: courts of equity will always be sensitive to context and therefore it may be difficult, occasionally, to reconcile the logic of one decision with the logic of another decision entirely in the abstract: only a close reading of the cases will make sense of these points.

The Privy Council has subsequently accepted that when a man lying on his deathbed sought to declare a trust over his own property with himself as one of nine trustees, a valid trust was created over that property even though the dying man did not transfer the legal title in the trust property to the other eight people who were to have acted as trustees (*T Choithram International SA v Pagarani* (2001)). There would have been no issue of formality had the deceased simply declared himself to be sole trustee of that property because transfer of title would have been necessary to constitute the trust. However, in that instance, he had purported to create nine people as trustees. Subsequently, the Court of Appeal has applied this principle so as to perfect a gift of shares in circumstances in which the donor had neither effected a declaration of trust over the shares nor done everything that was necessary for him or her to do to effect a transfer of the shares (*Pennington v Waine* (2002)). This decision extended the *Re Rose* principle beyond its former boundaries where it could be demonstrated that the donor had indeed done everything necessary for her to finalise the transfer. In that case, Clarke LJ accepted that the principle operated in general terms and that the equity identified by the Court of Appeal in *Re Rose* was capable of such general application.

In *Curtis v Pulbrook* (2011) Briggs J held that where a man had not completed the formalities for transferring shares to his wife and daughter then the *Re Rose* principle could not be relied upon because he had intended to make a gift and yet had not done everything necessary for him to do. His Lordship also expressed concern at the lack of apparent principle in the decisions in *Pennington* and in *Choithram*. Similarly, in *Kaye v Zeital* (2010) the Court of Appeal refused to accept that *Re Rose* had been satisfied where the transferor had failed to do everything necessary for him to do to transfer property.

Certainty in express trusts

Whereas the trust began life as a means of achieving justice in relation to the treatment of property held by one person ultimately for the benefit of others, it is now an institution that has lost much of its flexibility. Part of that loss of flexibility was due to the development of the principles of certainty and the rules of formality in the creation of trusts.

As long ago as *Knight v Knight* (1855), it was held that there must be three forms of certainty in the creation of an express trust: certainty of intention; certainty of subject matter (or, the trust property); and certainty of objects (or, beneficiaries). Each of these three is considered in turn in the three sections that follow.

Certainty of intention

No formality, but evidence of sufficient intention

Certainty of intention requires that the settlor intended to create a trust rather than to achieve some other end. There is no particular formula that has to be used in the creation of an express trust – that is, there is no form of abracadabra that will bring a trust into existence. The clearest means of creating a trust would be for a settlor to visit a solicitor and prepare a deed of trust that began with the words: 'I hereby declare that the following property shall be held on trust by the following trustees on the terms of this trust . . .' However, that level of formality is not required by the law of trusts, even though it may be desirable to make your intention as clear as possible. The courts will be prepared to infer an intention to create a trust from the circumstances in which the settlor deals with the property.

In many situations it will be difficult to know quite what the settlor intends. For example, in relation to wills, aside from straightforwardly making ordinary gifts of property to legatees, it is common for people to leave property subject to some obligation as to how the property is to be used: for example, 'this money is to be left to my wife in the hope that she will use it to take care of the children'. In such a situation it may not be clear whether the testator intends that the legatee should hold that property as a trustee for someone else or whether the legatee is merely under a moral obligation to use the property in a particular way. In this context, to be under a merely moral obligation means that there is no trusteeship imposed by the court – the obligation is therefore not a legally enforceable one.

In the interesting case of *Paul v Constance* (1977), a claim was brought by Mr Constance's widow arguing that money left in a bank account after Constance's death ought to pass to her as next of kin. Constance had previously left his wife to live with Mrs Paul. The bank account had been intended by Constance and Paul to be a joint bank account but, after persuasion by their bank manager, legal title in the bank account was placed in Constance's sole name. Constance assured Paul that 'this money is as much yours as mine'. The account contained money Constance had been given as compensation for an accident and some joint bingo winnings acquired by the couple together. The court held that it was Constance's intention to hold that bank account on trust for himself and Paul as beneficiaries. Consequently, Constance's widow could not assert any right in the property because it was found to have been held on trust for Paul. Here, significantly, the court inferred an intention to create a trust from the circumstances despite the fact that Constance and Paul did not know that that was what they were creating.

Examples of intentions to create express trusts abound. Importantly, the same principles apply to small-scale, non-commercial situations and to large-scale commercial situations. So in *Annabel's (Berkeley Square) Ltd v Revenue and Customs Commissioners* (2009) it was held that when tips were paid at a night-club and held by a 'troncmaster' as part of a tronc system, such that the tips would be divided equally by the troncmaster periodically among the nightclub staff, it was found that the tronc constituted a trust over which the troncmaster was trustee and the staff were the beneficiaries with shares in accordance with the rules of the tronc system. What was significant was that one person was deputed to hold the money for the benefit of other people in accordance with the terms of their arrangement: this suggested a split in the ownership of the money between the legal title of the trustee and the beneficial interests of the beneficiaries.

Express trust and commercial insolvency

A trust is particularly useful in commercial situations to guard against the insol-vency of the other party to a contract. If a person holds property as trustee then that trust property does not form part of their personal estate in the event that they go into insolvency; but rather it continues to be held on trust for the beneficiaries. That the same principles apply in commercial situations as in domestic situations is illustrated by the important case of *Re Kayford* (1975). In *Kayford* a mail order company was known to be on the brink of insolvency by its accountants and management. The company received pre-payments from its customers prior to sending them the goods which they had ordered. The risk which those customers bore was that the company would go into insolvency before sending off their goods but after their cheques had been banked. Consequently, the company decided to set up a separate bank account into which it paid its customers' money until such time as each customer's order had been completed. When the company did indeed go into insolvency the question arose as to who owned the money in that bank account. Megarry J held that because the money had been segregated from other money for the purpose of protecting the position of those customers, the only inference was that there had been an intention to create a trust over that money in favour of the customers whose orders had not been fulfilled. Therefore, an intention to create a trust was found. Interestingly, even though it was a commercial situation, there was no formality which was required to be fulfilled to effect a trust. Instead, the case was approached on the basis of the same principles as in *Paul v Constance*, a non-commercial situation.

These questions can arise in the most complex situations. Let us have just a taste of some of the complex banking law cases which have arisen in recent years since the global financial crisis which became a full-blown catastrophe on 15 September 2008 with the failure of US investment bank Lehman Brothers. In *Brazzill v Willoughby* (2009) the City of London financial institution KSF was in financial difficulties when its parent company, the Icelandic bank Kaupthing, went into insolvency in October 2008. Consequently, the UK regulator, the Financial Services Authority, issued an order that KSF must set up an account into which it would pay amounts equal to deposits from its customers in case it should go into insolvency itself. Relying, *inter alia*, on *Re Kayford*, Smith J held that the establishment of this account should be interpreted as being a trust in favour of those customers. This conclusion was bolstered by the use of the term 'trust' in the regulator's order, although the terms of the arrangement were otherwise unclear.

Similarly, in *Mills v Sportsdirect.com Retail Ltd* (2010) a corporate customer had entered into a financial transaction with KSF, the same entity as before. Unusually for a 'repo' transaction of that type, because the customer was concerned about KSF's financial position, the securities which were a part of that deal were passed to a specific subsidiary of KSF as nominee to be held for the purposes of that deal. The parties were vague about the precise legal nature of this aspect of the transaction although their representatives did use language to the effect that the (intangible) securities would be 'ringfenced', that they were in the customer's 'box', and that they were owned by the customer. Lewison J held that this was sufficient to demonstrate an intention to create a trust. Again, in spite of the fact that the parties were acting commercially and that a very large amount of money was involved, the case was decided on ordinary trusts principles by inferring an intention to create an express trust from the circumstances of the case.

Types of express trust

What emerges from the foregoing discussion is that there are, in truth, a range of types of express trusts. This issue was raised in Chapter 2. When the court infers an intention as in *Paul v Constance* this raises a number of questions about the more complex rights of the parties. Suppose that Mr Constance had held the property for two years before the matter came to trial and suppose that Mr Constance had attempted to use the money for an investment that Mrs Paul objected to. Ought Constance to be deemed subject to the same principles relating to investment of trust funds as ordinary trustees? There seems no reason to absolve Mr Constance from such liability – but it might seem unfair to subject him to those obligations at a time when he was ignorant not only of his status as a trustee but also of the very existence of such a legal office.

It seems reasonable to suggest that a different treatment ought to apply to trustees who accept their office as trustees in full knowledge of their obligations to invest the trust fund, unlike Constance, who would not have known that he was a trustee at all. Indeed, in this circumstance those trustees will frequently be professional investment managers whose liabilities under the law of trusts will typically be limited by their contractual obligations, as considered in Chapter 5. This will often mean that the professional investment manager will have restricted her liabilities for any failure connected to the investment under the terms of a contract with the settlor. Ironically, the professional trustee will usually bear a lesser standard of care than an amateur trustee without investment experience as a result of this exclusion of liability provision (*Armitage v Nurse* (1998)). For a more detailed discussion of the various possible forms of express trusts, see my *Equity & Trusts*, Chapter 2 (Hudson, 2014).

Certainty of subject matter

The importance of certainty

One of the key tenets of the law of trusts is that the trust fund itself must be certain (*Re London Wine Co* (1986)). There is logic in this classic approach: a trust is a relationship between trustee and beneficiary, which requires both to observe the terms created by the settlor in relation to the property that is held on trust. Without the property, there could not be a trust. In truth, the trust is a mixture of property law concepts and concepts of equitable obligations between trustee and beneficiary. Without the property, there could be no other obligations.

In most circumstances it will be clear which property is intended by the settlor to be held on trust. The difficulty arises when the settlor seeks, for example, to create more than one trust and does not explain which property is intended to be held for which trust. Alternatively, it may be that a number of people are claiming entitlement to property held by a company that goes into insolvency: to establish those property rights the claimants would have to demonstrate that they were beneficiaries under a trust. However, to demonstrate rights under trust, the claimants would have to be able to prove that identified property was held on trust for them.

An example will make the point. In *Re London Wine Co* a wine shipper bought and held wine for clients to their order. The wine was stored in a cellar. Importantly, all of the wine shipper's stock of wine was held together without distinguishing which particular bottles were held for which client. The wine shipping company went into liquidation and the customers attempted to demonstrate that they were secured creditors: that is, people entitled to specific property in the insolvency. The plaintiffs argued that the wine they had ordered from the shipper was held on trust for them under the terms of their contracts. It was held that there could not be a valid trust because the plaintiffs could not identify which wine was held for them out of the general store. It would have been necessary for the plaintiffs' wine to be segregated: that is, to be separately identifiable from the general stock of wine.

Similarly, the Privy Council decision in *Re Goldcorp* (1995) concerned a bullion exchange that had gone into insolvency. In that case, the customers of the exchange entered into standard contracts that required the exchange to acquire bullion for their customers and to hold the total amount of their customers' orders in their vaults. According to the terms of their contracts the customers should have been very happy with the arrangements: because the exchange was required to buy and to hold the total amount of their customers' orders, it would (in theory) have been possible for the customers to know that the whole of their order and the whole of every other customer's orders were held physically by the exchange in its vaults so that there could have been no question of the exchange failing to satisfy an order. Those contracts purported to create proprietary rights in favour of the customers over the bullion that the exchange was required to acquire on their behalf. Unfortunately, the exchange broke its contracts. It only acquired enough bullion to meet the usual requirements of its customers on any working day and did not hold the entirety of the customers' orders. In consequence, when the exchange went into insolvency it could not meet its customers' orders.

It was held that only those customers who could prove that their order of bullion was in fact held separately from the general store of bullion would be entitled to enforce a trust against the exchange and consequently be able to take their bullion away as secured creditors. Those customers who could not demonstrate that their orders had been segregated from the general store of bullion could not demonstrate that they were beneficiaries under a trust because the subject matter of that trust was uncertain.

To make this point more explicit, let us dramatise the proceedings slightly. If you have seen films such as Steve McQueen's *The Thomas Crown Affair* or even James Stewart in *It's a Wonderful Life* that may help you to visualise what is happening. Imagine the scene: hearing of the exchange's insolvency, the customers race down to the exchange's vaults to recover their bullion. A huge crowd of nervous, shouting customers breaks through security and rushes down to the basement. On opening the doors of the vaults the customers tear into the steel-lined room. Imagine that the steel walls of the vaults are made up of metal cages or deposit boxes and that in the middle of the floor is a suspiciously small pile of gold bars: there should by rights be a whole lot more. On the doors to some of the deposit boxes are neatly written labels identifying the owner of the contents of that box. Anyone with their bullion in a box with their name on the door would be able to demonstrate that their bullion had been sufficiently segregated from the rest: therefore, they would be able to show that the subject matter of their trust was sufficiently certain and consequently valid. Happy, these fortunate few people begin to drag their bullion out of the vaults.

Those other customers who could not find their names on any of the boxes would then realise that the only bullion they could claim was in the small pile in the middle of the floor. After a while a large crowd of customers is gathered round the remaining bullion waving their order contracts angrily, all of them convinced that they are entitled to the amount of bullion specified in the contract. Undoubtedly, those customers were entitled to the bullion under the law of contract – but the contracts had been breached and the insolvent exchange had no money to pay damages. At length, an awful silence dawns as the customers realise that there are many more people shaking order contracts than there is bullion to go around. Lord Mustill in *Goldcorp* held that those customers were not able to rely on the terms in the contract which purported to create trusts because they could not identify which bullion out of the general store of bullion had been held on trust for them.

In the House of Lords in *Westdeutsche Landesbank v Islington* (1996), the approach taken by the Privy Council in *Goldcorp* was accepted as being the right one. It was said that there could be no valid trust without certainty of subject matter.

An exception for intangible property?

As you are doubtless becoming aware, when considering English law one no sooner identifies a general rule before becoming suspicious that there is bound to be an exception to it lurking round the corner. After all, that is the purpose of equity – to balance rigidity with fairness.

So, in the Court of Appeal in *Hunter v Moss* (1994) it was apparently accepted that there is no need for certainty of subject matter in circumstances in which the property in question is intangible. This was the argument that was accepted in *Re Harvard Securities* (1997), that there should be a distinction between tangible and intangible property, following *Hunter*. In the *Re Harvard* case a securities dealer acquired financial securities (intangible property) for his clients and held them as a general fund. When the dealer's business went into liquidation, the question arose as to whether or not those securities were held on trust according to the clients' contracts, or whether they were insufficiently identified because they were held as part of a general fund. It was held that there was no need to segregate the property because the securities were identical and therefore it would make no difference which securities were held on trust for which client.

In *Hunter v Moss* an employer had agreed that an employee was entitled to 50 shares out of 950 shares held by the employer, as part of the employee's remuneration package. Relations between employer and employee broke down and the contract of employment was terminated. The employee argued that the employer was required to hold 50 shares on trust for the employee. The employer argued that no 50 shares had ever been segregated from the general fund of 950 shares and therefore that there could be no valid trust in favour of the employee. The Court of Appeal held that cases like *Re London Wine* could be distinguished because they were concerned with title in chattels whereas *Hunter v Moss* itself was concerned with whether or not there had been a declaration of trust over intangible property in the form of identical ordinary shares in a company. On the basis of this unconvincing distinction, Dillon LJ was prepared to hold that a valid trust had been created.

A decision of the Supreme Court of New South Wales in *White v Shortall* (2006) explicitly rejected the approach taken by Dillon LJ in *Hunter v Moss* in a carefully argued judgment, primarily on the basis that the purported distinction between chattels and other forms of property was so unconvincing. In *White v Shortall* the defendant was contractually obliged to declare a trust over 1,500,000 shares so that the claimant would acquire an equitable interest in 222,000 of those shares. However, no segregation of the 222,000 shares took place. The court inferred from the facts that the intention was that a single trust would be declared over the 1,500,000 shares in favour of the claimant and the defendant, with the claimant's share in that trust being equal to 222,000 shares. Therefore, there was a single, large trust with two beneficiaries rather than the separate trust over 950 shares which was purportedly found in *Hunter v Moss*. Importantly, it is suggested, to use this analysis in other cases it would be important to be able to find such an intention on the part of the parties.

So, where does that leave us?

It is suggested that the decisions in *Re Goldcorp* and in *Hunter v Moss* are very different from the standard principles of trusts law, but possibly reach back into an earlier tradition of equity. It is not possible to say that there has always been such a distinction between tangible and intangible property in this context. Let us consider the traditional approach in the law of trusts as exemplified by the Court of Appeal in *MacJordan Construction v Brookmount* (1992). In that case it was held that, in relation to money held in a bank account, there could not be a valid trust created over part of the money held in the account because that part of the money was not segregated from the other moneys held in the account. However, what was at stake in *Hunter v Moss* was whether or not a party to a contract of employment ought to have been able to renege on his contractual obligations so as to deny an employee part of the salary owed to him. In that sense we could understand that, perhaps, Dillon LJ was reaching back into the grander traditions of equity which assert that the courts of equity act *in personam* against the good conscience of the defendant; in that case to prevent him from deliberately breaching his contractual obligations to pay an agreed wage.

The reason why the *Goldcorp* approach is preferred by property lawyers is that its certainty avoids many problems. The principal question was that exemplified by *Goldcorp* itself: what should the law do when there are more claims than there is property to satisfy them? Answer: only allow claimants to have proprietary rights if they can demonstrate with sufficient certainty which property was being held separately for them. Otherwise, it is said, this would be to break one of the core principles of insolvency law: that no unsecured creditor is to be permitted to gain an advantage over any other unsecured creditor. If such an unsecured creditor were to be granted rights to property, that would be just such an advantage. It is the lot of unsecured creditors to wait nervously for the liquidators to finish winding up the company in the hope that there will be some money left to pay off part of the debts owing to those creditors. In cases like *Hunter v Moss* there was a luxury available to the courts: in that case there was the same amount of property as there were claims to the property and everyone was solvent. The question was not 'Is there enough property to go round?' but rather 'Should the defendant have to transfer the property he has got?' Therefore, the issue of whether or not the property was segregated was not of the same critical importance as in *Goldcorp*. This indicates the pragmatism at the heart of the law in this area.

Certainty of subject matter in the wake of the global financial crisis

The financial crisis demonstrated that a number of investment banks had been breaching their financial regulatory obligations under the 'CASS' rulebook created by the Financial Services Authority in the UK. The CASS regulations obliged investment banks to segregate their clients' assets into separate accounts so as to protect those clients against the insolvency of the banks. The regulations were clear that there would be a statutory trust. What was not clear were the terms on which that trust was supposed to operate. Many of the banks (particularly Lehman Brothers) had breached their regulatory obligations and had not segregated client money. Instead, all of the assets which should have been held for customers were simply held in a large pool with Lehman Brothers' own assets. Similar to the facts in *Re Goldcorp*, the issue was whether or not there had been sufficient certainty of subject matter to create trusts in favour of those customers.

There were many cases flowing from the Lehman Brothers insolvency. Perhaps the most significant case was *Re Lehman Bros International (Europe) (No 2)* (2009), in which Briggs J considered Lehman Brothers' practice of holding client assets in a central pool for long periods of time rather than in segregated accounts. His Lordship held that this lack of segregation meant that each client of the bank with assets in that pool could not have a trust in their favour precisely because their moneys were merely held in a central, mixed pool.

However, this decision was appealed successfully to the Court of Appeal under the name *Re Lehman Brothers International (Europe) (in administration) v CRC Credit Fund Ltd* (2010), in which it was held that there was one, large trust fund constituting the entire pool in favour of all of the clients as beneficiaries, with each client having a share in accordance with their rights against the bank (until amounts were segregated to the accounts of specific clients). In practice, this meant that the clients had valid trust rights in the Lehman Brothers insolvency. The Court of Appeal was able to take this view because the regulations were so ambiguously drafted as to the precise nature of the regulatory trust and because the Court of Appeal made very little reference to any case law. In essence it was held that a single '*White v Shortall* trust' took effect over all the client assets.

On appeal, the Supreme Court in *Re Lehman Brothers International (Europe) (in administration) v CRC Credit Fund Ltd* (2011) held, by a three-to-two majority, that the CASS rules should be interpreted so that it would be permissible for a single trust to take effect over all of the assets held by Lehman Brothers for the benefit of all of the customers with some assets in that pool of assets. Consequently, it was not found to be necessary for there to have been segregated assets to their account. The majority, primarily through the judgment of Lord Dyson, chose to adopt an interpretation which offered the largest amount of protection to the largest possible number of clients of the bank. This was achieved by interpreting the wording of the CASS regulations, and the EU Markets in Financial Instruments Directive from which they were derived, benignly.

For the minority, Lord Walker doubted the efficacy of the large 'single trust' trust approach which had been taken in the Court of Appeal. Lord Walker was convinced of the dangers to trusts law, and to the orderly administration of insolvencies, if this approach was maintained instead of the rigour of requiring that trusts must be predicated on a clear segregation of the trust property. At one point Lord Walker held that 'a trust without segregation is a very precarious form of protection'.

The fault here lay entirely with the reprehensible business practices of Lehman Brothers. We could be forgiven for assuming, in accordance with the old adage, that hard cases (such as the litigation following the collapse of Lehman Brothers) make bad law. It remains to be seen whether this case will be taken to have changed trusts law or simply to have interpreted the CASS regulations.

Certainty of objects

The third certainty required is that there be certainty as to the identity of the beneficiary. If the beneficiaries are uncertain the trust will be void. In Chapter 2 we considered different forms of express trust: bare trust, fixed trust, discretionary trust, mere fiduciary power and personal power. That division between forms of trust is important because different principles apply to different forms of trust power.

The rules for certainty of objects

The first category is the bare trust. That is a trust in which the trustee holds on trust for one beneficiary absolutely. In relation to such a trust, the identity of that beneficiary must be capable of being established.

The second category is the fixed trust. This is a form of trust in which the trust fund is to be held on trust for a fixed group of beneficiaries. For example, '£10,000 to be held on trust for my two children now living.' No other beneficiaries acquire a right in that trust, therefore it is a fixed trust.

Similarly, '£10,000 to be held on trust for everyone who bought the book *Understanding Equity & Trusts* on 1 December.' That would be a fixed trust because only those people who bought that book on that date are entitled to benefit. For such a trust to be sufficiently certain it must comply with the 'complete list' test which requires that a complete list of all the beneficiaries be capable of being drawn up. If a complete list cannot be drawn up, the trust fails: *IRC v Broadway Cottages* (1955).

The third category is the discretionary trust. That is a trust in which the trustees are obliged to make a distribution of property to any persons drawn from a general class of beneficiaries. For example, 'My trustees shall pay £1,000 annually to any of my good friends.' The trust is 'discretionary' in that the trustees have the ability to use their discretion to decide which of the class of beneficiaries is to benefit. It is a discretionary trust, rather than a mere power (considered below) because the trustees 'shall' (or, are obliged to) pay the money out. The problem of certainty in this example is that it is not possible to know what is meant by the concept of 'good friends'. The test set down by the House of Lords is the 'is or is not' test (or, 'any given postulant' test) (*McPhail v Doulton* (1970)). That test requires that, for a discretionary trust to be valid, it must be possible to say of any given claimant to the trust that that person either is or is not within the class of beneficiaries. (What the judges differ on is whether that means any claimant who actually turns up to ask the trustee to consider her, or whether that means any hypothetical claimant who might turn up.) In the event that any one person cannot be categorised as falling either within or without the class of beneficiaries, the trust fails. This strict test will tend to invalidate many trusts where vague expressions like 'good friends' are used to define the class of beneficiaries.

The fourth category is the mere power. That is, a power given to the trustees which enables them to act if they choose to do so, but which does not oblige them to act. For example, 'My trustees may pay £1,000 annually to any of my good friends.' This power is a mere power because the trustees 'may' (but are not obliged to) pay money to any of the class of beneficiaries. The trustees are able to act on their own decisions but they must be able to justify those decisions and cannot act capriciously in the decisions they make (*Re Hay's ST* (1981)). The test is the same 'is or is not' test as was outlined above (*Re Gulbenkian* (1968)). On this example, the uncertainty again surrounds the precise meaning to be accorded to the expression 'good friends'.

The fifth category is the personal power. That is, a power given to a person who is not a trustee (nor any other kind of fiduciary) to decide in their absolute discretion how to deal with trust property. It is important that this power is given to its holder in a private capacity because such a power cannot be void for uncertainty (*Re Hay's ST* (1981)). In that case Megarry VC held that the holder of the power is able to act capriciously and entirely without any of the responsibilities usually associated with trusteeship because the holder of a personal power is not a fiduciary (see Chapter 5).

Other approaches

What is important for a trusts lawyer considering the structure and analysis of express trusts is the way in which subtly different structures and analyses can alter completely the legal treatment of trusts. In the preceding section we considered the main rules relating to certainty of objects. In this section we consider in outline some alternative analyses advanced in decided cases. A good trusts lawyer will come to master these supple and subtle ways of approaching trusts so as to ensure the validity of a trust wherever possible.

First, the decision in *Re Baden's Trusts (No 2)* (1973) in which the Court of Appeal was required to consider a provision in a discretionary trust for 'relatives'. The court was required to follow the principles set out in the House of Lords in *McPhail v Doulton*. To have done so on the basis of a purely literal application of the test may well have led to the invalidity of the trust in that case. Therefore, their Lordships sought to add their own gloss to those principles. Sachs LJ upheld the literal application of the 'is or is not' test, but held that the burden of proof should be reversed, so that it fell on the person claiming to fall within the class of beneficiaries and not on the trustees to prove that she 'is or is not' within the class of objects. Consequently, *the claimant* would be required to prove that she fell within the classes of objects; if she could not prove it, then she would be deemed not to fall within the class. This is different from asking a merely hypothetical question as to whether or not it could be said of a hypothetical applicant that she is or is not within the class. Thus, Sachs LJ upheld the literal meaning of the 'is or is not' test, but changed who it was who would be required to prove whether or not she fell within the class of objects. Many trusts would thus be validated because a lot of the uncertainty can be resolved in this way. Sachs LJ did not, however, intend that this reversal should validate all discretionary trusts. Rather, his Lordship held that if the concept that defined the class was too vague (e.g. 'on trust for "nice" people, where it cannot be known what "nice" means') then it would still be found to be void.

Second, the judgment of Megaw LJ in *Baden (No 2)* preferred an approach set out in the earlier case of *Re Allen* (1953) (which had been overruled by *Re Gulbenkian*) which held that a trust should be valid for certainty if a substantial number of people fell within the test. Therefore, even though a few claimants may not be categorisable within the terms of the trust, if there would be a sufficient number of claimants about whom one could be certain, then that would be enough to render the trust valid.

Third, the judgment of Browne-Wilkinson J in *Re Barlow's WT* (1979) held that it might be possible to validate a testamentary bequest if the testator's intention could be shown to be an intention to make gifts of individual items of property rather than to impose a trust over all of that property. In *Re Barlow* the testator gave the executors power to allow the testator's friends to apply to purchase paintings from a stock of paintings left by the testator. The concept of 'friends' caused some initial difficulties (as considered above) but Browne-Wilkinson J held that the testator's intention had been to give the trustees the power to make individual gifts, not trusts, of the paintings. Therefore, a little lateral thinking saved the bequest because a gift is not dependent on the same requirement of certainty as a trust.

There is a definite lack of enthusiasm among the judiciary for holding trusts invalid if it is possible to validate that trust. This idea is pursued in more detail in relation to the beneficiary principle in Chapter 4.

Another important approach is to decide between the various forms of uncertainty that may assail a trust. As considered above, where the *concept* that describes the class of beneficiaries is uncertain, then the trust will be invalid. So, for example, if the trust terms provided that 'the trustees shall distribute £1,000 annually to any nice people I have known', the concept 'nice' would be so uncertain as to make it impossible to validate the trust. Suppose, however, a trust for 'my trustees to distribute £1,000 to each of my first cousins' would be sufficiently certain because the concept 'first cousin' is sufficiently certain. Whereas if it were merely a question of any individual claimant being unable to *prove* as a matter of evidence that she was, for example, one of the settlor's first cousins then that would not invalidate the entire trust, although it would mean that that particular claimant would not be able to demonstrate an entitlement. Similarly, if one of the first cousins could not be found because she had moved home without leaving a forwarding address, that would not invalidate the trust but it would make it impossible for the claimant to establish any entitlement.

One further concept that has arisen on the cases is that of 'administrative unworkability' (per Lord Wilberforce in *McPhail v Doulton*). This principle demonstrates the pragmatism that underpins the law of trusts. It is said that if it is impossible for the trustees to carry out the task set them by the settlor, then the trust will be declared void for uncertainty. For example, if trustees are required to distribute property to the 'inhabitants of West Yorkshire', it will be held to be an unworkable (or impracticable) task for the trustees and so the trust would be invalid (*Re West Yorks* (1986)). The law relating to express trusts has developed pragmatically in this way – only validating trusts if it is possible to do so in practice. So, if there were a trust for the benefit of 'all past and present mineworkers in County Durham' that would be an administratively unworkable task for ordinary citizens acting as trustees, but it might not be unworkable if the trustees were also trustees of the mineworkers' pension fund for County Durham because they would have access to lists of all those people who would fall within the class.

As the law of trusts encounters novel factual situations it develops commonsensically. The problem which then follows is how these pragmatic principles are to apply systematically to future situations. As ever, the tension between flexibility and certainty in the law of trusts arises.

Incompletely constituted trusts

So far we have considered how trusts are formed and how to distinguish a trust from a gift. The other problem that arises then is how to deal with trusts that have not been properly constituted. The core principle in this area is that *Equity will not assist a volunteer*. A volunteer is a person who has not given consideration or who does not have a valid trust declared in their favour. The following two sections consider some of the significant ways in which it may be possible to circumvent this general principle. As ever, for the trusts lawyer the challenge is first to identify the general rule and then to look for a means of circumventing it so that you can create a valid trust.

Perfecting imperfect gifts in some circumstances

There are three contexts in which a gift will be perfected: *donatio mortis causa*, the rule in *Strong v Bird* (1874), and the doctrine of proprietary estoppel.

The doctrine of *donatio mortis causa* relates to gifts made during the donor's lifetime, made in expectation of immediate death, and that are intended to take effect on the donor's death. For example, the Court of Appeal in *Sen v Headley* (1991) dealt with a couple who had lived together for 10 years, but had separated more than 25 years before the man's death. He died of a terminal illness but before death told his former partner (the plaintiff) that the house (with unregistered title) was hers and that: 'You have the keys . . . The deeds are in the steel box.' While it was argued against the plaintiff that she had always had keys to the house, such that the lifetime gift could have no further effect by way of gift, the claimant was successful in establishing her claim to the house because title deeds were essential in establishing title to unregistered land. There was no retention of dominion in this case because the deceased had not expected that he would return to the house nor that he would have been able to deal with it in any way before his death.

The rule in *Strong v Bird* (1874) provides that if a debtor is named by the testator as an executor of the estate of the one to whom he owed the debt, that chose in action is discharged – in effect a gift is made of the amount of the debt. The assumption is that if a person is made executor of an estate, the deceased must have intended to free the executor from any outstanding debts between them. This rule also has a pragmatic basis: the executor acquires all the deceased's rights to sue others – therefore, the executor would be required to sue herself to recover the debt. In relation to incomplete gifts, the rule in *Strong v Bird* means that, where a deceased person intended to make a gift of property to another person without ever making a complete gift of it, if that intended recipient is named as executor of the deceased's estate then the gift is deemed to have been completed. This might be considered surprising, given what is said in Chapter 5 about the obligations on a trustee to avoid conflicts of interest.

The third way in which an incomplete gift may be indirectly perfected is by virtue of the doctrine of proprietary estoppel. This doctrine is considered in detail in Chapter 8. In short, where a representation is made to the claimant in reliance on which she acts to her detriment, the court will estop the defendant from going back on that representation. The remedy available to the court is potentially very broad. So, in *Pascoe v Turner* (1979), a man left a woman with whom he had been in a relationship, but told her that the house and all its contents were hers. The woman claimed rights in the house because she had paid for decorations in reliance on the promise that she would be able to consider the house and its contents as being her own. In *Baker v Baker* (1993), an elderly man gave up his secure tenancy over property in London to live with his son and daughter in Torquay in reliance on a promise that he would be able to live in the home, which the three of them bought together, for the rest of his life. The court held that the son and daughter would be required to pay sufficient compensation to their father to secure him sheltered accommodation for the rest of his life. What proprietary estoppel demonstrates is that the court has a broad remit to reinforce the parties' intentions – primarily, to prevent the claimant suffering detriment – even where no valid trust has been created over property.

Covenants to settle property

A trust, in Moffat's phrase, is a gift made over the plane of time: in other words, the property is given in such a way that the beneficiary may take a benefit from it for a long period of time. This section considers the situation in which a settlor promises that at some point in the future she will settle some property on trust.

The particular way in which many of these cases have arisen is on the making of a covenant: that is, a contract in the form of a deed that promises to pay an amount of money to an identified person. What this indicates is another theme of trusts law: the frequent interaction between trusts and contracts that purport to govern the treatment of property. The way in which this issue might arise is the following: a settlor expects to receive some money from a relative, perhaps, at some point in the future and wishes to create a trust in favour of some other person. To achieve this the settlor enters into a covenant with a trustee to the effect that the settlor will transfer any money that is eventually received from the relative on trust for identified beneficiaries. The question is: how can the beneficiary force the settlor to receive some property acquired later if the settlor then refuses to pass it to the trustee? The answers emerge in the following ways: all are based on careful analyses of the facts of the various cases.

You need property rights to create a valid trust

First, there might be a valid trust in favour of the beneficiary. When the settlor has rights in that property at the time of making the promise there may be a valid trust (*Re Ralli's WT* (1964)); but where the settlor has no rights in that property *at the time of making the promise* then there will not be a valid trust created (*Re Brook's ST* (1939)). That basic distinction runs through this area of the law. So, in *Re Brook*, a son hoped that he would receive money from a power of appointment that his mother held. At the time of promising to settle any property received from his mother on trust, the son had a mere hope that his mother would pay him something and therefore had no property rights in any money at that time. In consequence, it was held that he could not have created a trust because he had no rights in property which he could have intended to settle on that trust. This is so, even though the son did later receive some money from his mother after purporting to create the trust.

That case can be compared with *Re Ralli's WT*, in which a daughter was a remainder beneficiary under a trust that meant that she would receive rights in trust property once the life tenant under the trust died. Therefore it was held that, when the daughter purported to create a trust over the money she would receive, she did create a valid trust because she did have some enforceable rights as a remainder beneficiary under the trust. The narrow distinction is as follows: a trust will only be valid if the settlor has rights in the property at the time of purporting to declare the trust.

It is important to think carefully about what this means for the law of property and the enforceability of trusts. Suppose I promise to make you a gift of precious stones for your birthday. Let us further suppose that I have bought the precious stones and that I show them to you, tantalising you with the gift that will soon be yours. On each day we see one another and one day I say to you: 'I will give you those precious stones at the end of your birthday party. Won't it be divine?' With each day, your excitement mounts. If I turn up to your birthday party and at its end I refuse to give you the precious stones, there is nothing you can do to force me at law to give you the stones. You are merely a volunteer and equity will not assist a volunteer. However, if you had given me £5 towards the purchase price of those stones, you would no longer be a volunteer; rather you would be someone who had a proprietary right in those precious stones under resulting trust (see Chapter 6) by virtue of your having contributed to their purchase price: thus, you will have given consideration. English law is not moral in this sense. It will not enforce mere promises; it will only enforce contractual bargains and trusts.

Using the law of contract

Second, the law of contract might help the claimant. The parties to the covenant are entitled to enforce the covenant under the ordinary principles of the law of contract. In the trusts context, the importance of a covenant would be an obligation entered into by a person to settle specified property on trust for the benefit of other people. On the basis that there is no trust created, the covenant itself will give the parties to the covenant the right to sue to enforce the promise at common law, without the need for resort to the law of trusts. Significantly, the claimant can only acquire a right to the property here under contract law and not under trusts law.

Similarly, the enactment of the Contracts (Rights of Third Parties) Act 1999 has the effect of introducing to English contract law the ability of a person to enforce a contract to which they are not a party if they can demonstrate that that contract was made specifically for their benefit. It is not clear how far this Act will stretch at the time of writing. If the contract is merely a promise to pay money it is unlikely that the claimant would receive specific performance because specific performance is not usually available for pure money claims. As we have seen, the absence of a property right under statute would not be sufficient in relation to a case of insolvency. There may be cases, therefore, when the claimant would rather have a right under trust than a purely contractual right.

What is more complex is knowing who else could enforce the contractual promise. What is clear is that if there is no valid trust created, the trustee cannot enforce the promise. If the settlor had created a contract with the trustee at a time when she had no rights in the property there could not be a valid trust. We might then think that the trustee would be able to rely on the contract, at first blush. As a party, why could the trustee not sue the settlor under the contract and then pass the property on to the intended beneficiary?

Unfortunately things are not this straightforward. If the settlor had no property right at the time of making the promise, there would have been no valid trust. Therefore, the beneficiary would acquire no rights in the property and would remain a mere volunteer, and equity will not assist a volunteer, as we know. It has been held in a number of cases that the trustee would therefore be prevented from seeking to enforce the contract because the trustee would not be permitted to take any beneficial interest in the property personally (having been intended only to act as a trustee) and the beneficiary would have no property rights (*Re Pryce* (1917)).

Trusts over choses in action, or contracts, equally valid

Third, there is one further form of analysis that may give the beneficiary some interest in the property under trusts law: that is, in the decision in *Fletcher v Fletcher* (1844), where a father covenanted with a trustee to settle an after-acquired sum of £66,000 (which was an enormous sum of money in 1844) on his sons, Jacob and John. The property was passed to the trustee on the father's death. In reliance on the principles set out in the line of cases culminating in *Re Cook* (1965), the trustee contended that there had been no valid trust because the settlor had had no property rights in the money at the time of making the covenant and consequently that the trustee ought therefore to be absolutely entitled to the money. The court held, however, that the surviving beneficiary, Jacob, was entitled to sue under the terms of the trust on the basis that there had been property that could have been settled on the purported trust.

The property identified by the court in *Fletcher* was *the benefit of the covenant itself*. This single idea requires some short analysis. A covenant creates obligations. A party to the covenant can transfer the benefit of the covenant to another party, or borrow money, using it as security. A covenant, in the same way as a debt, is a chose in action. A covenant can therefore be considered to be property in itself. Therefore, to enable the creation of a valid trust in circumstances where a covenant is created obliging the settlor to settle after-acquired property on trust, the settlor would be required to settle the benefit of the covenant on trust for the beneficiary, to be replaced by the tangible property in time. This was the mechanism used by the court in *Fletcher* to justify the finding that there was a valid trust and thus give the beneficiary a right to sue the trustee to force him to gather in the property to be settled on trust; in reality, to prevent the trustee's unconscionable claim to such an enormous sum of money.

In the important case of *Don King v Warren* (1998), two boxing promoters entered into a series of partnership agreements whereby they undertook to treat any promotional agreements entered into by either of them with boxers as being property belonging to a partnership that they had formed between them. It was held that this agreement disclosed an intention to settle the benefit of those promotion agreements on trust for the members of the partnership. In common with *Fletcher v Fletcher*, it was held that a contractual agreement can be held on trust if the settlor has an immediate intention to create a trust over the contract. Therefore, the point made in *Fletcher v Fletcher* that a trust can be declared over a chose in action is one with modern support.

What this discussion shows is that trusts lawyers revel in these subtle distinctions. There is no easier way of doing it than wrapping a cold towel round your head and considering the trust in front of you carefully.

What happens if the trust fails?

As is discussed in detail in Chapter 6, if a settlor purports to create a trust, but that trust is not validly created, the equitable interest in the property that was to have been settled on trust passes back on resulting trust to the settlor.

Moving on . . .

We should think of our settlor as someone who builds a ship and then sends it off across the seas in the hands of its captain: the settlor creates a trust and then leaves matters in the hands of the trustee, having no more control over the trust in her capacity as settlor. Once the trust is created, it cannot be undone. However, as we have seen in this chapter there are a number of formalities that the settlor must perform before the trust comes into existence.

The person who takes benefit from the trust arrangement is the beneficiary and it is to that person we will turn our attention in the next chapter.

Chapter 4

The beneficiary's rights

The need for a beneficiary

The beneficiary is an essential part of the trust. Quite literally, the trust property must be held by the trustee for the benefit of some person or it will be void. As we shall see in this chapter, the beneficiary has both rights against the trustee personally and also proprietary rights in the trust fund. Thus, a trust constitutes a web of complex rights and obligations between persons and in property. This chapter will focus most particularly on the nature of the rights that the beneficiary acquires. The ensuing Chapter 5 considers the obligations that are borne by the trustee and Chapter 10 will consider what forms of remedy are available in a case of breach of trust.

The most important point to understand about the rights of beneficiaries in express trusts is that the settlor is able to fashion almost any form of right for the beneficiary, provided that it complies with the *beneficiary principle* considered immediately below. Trusts lawyers are a subtle breed and their role in relation to the creation of express trusts is really twofold: first, to structure the terms of the express trusts so that the settlor's non-legal goals are achieved: whether that be preserving property for future generations, to use property as part of a commercial transaction, or to reduce liability to tax; and, second, to avoid those rules considered in this chapter which will invalidate trusts in particular circumstances. Our goal in this chapter is to identify those rules of the law of trusts which would invalidate a trust and to work out how to structure our arrangements appropriately so as to make the trust valid.

The beneficiary principle

To begin at the beginning: there must be someone in whose favour the court can decree performance of the trust or else the trust will be invalid (*Morice v Bishop of Durham* (1805)). That statement encapsulates a fundamental aspect of the trust: unless there is a beneficiary for whose benefit some property is held on trust, there cannot be a valid trust. This observation follows on from the discussion in Chapter 3 as to the need for there to be certainty of objects: that is, those rules requiring that the identity of the beneficiaries be made sufficiently clear by the settlor. The point we are considering here is slightly different. In relation to certainty of objects we were concerned to ensure that the identity of the benefici- aries would be sufficiently certain so that the trustees could know (and also so that the court could know) for which persons the trustees were holding the property on trust. The issue here is more fundamental than that: without there being a person expressed as being a beneficiary there cannot be a valid trust at all.

So, the simple proposition is this: no beneficiary, no trust. What the trusts lawyer must be careful to avoid is the situation in which property is purportedly held on trust for some abstract purpose that does not benefit any human being (e.g. a trust to maintain a much-loved pet cat, or a trust to polish the gravel in the grounds of Buckingham Palace). In neither of these cases is there a human beneficiary who would take a *direct* benefit from the trust purpose.

That much seems simple enough, but there are a number of cases on the margins of these rules. Most of the trusts which we have considered so far have been created for the benefit of identified individuals. We have come across some situa- tions in which the settlor had ulterior motives: to prevent a child acquiring rights in a property until she is old enough to be responsible, to pay for a child's medical care, and so forth. So where is the line between having a desire to benefit a person and having a desire to carry out some abstract purpose that is not directly for the benefit of any person?

Illustrations of the beneficiary principle

The traditional approach

The approach that the law takes is to provide that where the settlor intended only to carry out some abstract purpose (e.g. 'constructing some useful memorial to myself' – *Re Endacott* (1960)), which does not directly benefit any individual beneficiary, then that trust will be void and unenforceable. The most useful leading case on establishing the boundary here is that of *Leahy v Attorney General for New South Wales* (1959), which concerned a bequest to be held by trustees, amongst other things, for 'such order of nuns' as the trustees should select. The property to be left on trust was a sheep station (that is, a very large plot of agricul- tural land) that consisted of a large amount of grazing land for sheep and a single homestead in New South Wales, Australia. The question arose whether that purpose was an abstract purpose (and so void as a trust) or a purpose that would benefit some people as beneficiaries.

Viscount Simonds gave the leading opinion in the Privy Council and held that the bequest created only a void purpose trust. There were two main planks to his reasoning. First, the terms of the bequest were to 'such *order* of nuns' as the trus- tees should select. In his Lordship's view, giving the bequest to an order of nuns rather than to any individual nuns meant that the property could be held on trust for future members of the order as well as present members. Therefore, there was a risk that the trust would continue indefinitely and offend the rules against perpetuities (considered below). Furthermore, the gift to the order of nuns, as opposed to any individual members of the order personally, meant that it would be the abstract purposes of the order that would benefit and not individual beneficiaries. For example, none of the nuns would have been entitled to take any property away personally.

Second, there was a practical point that concerned the fact that the homestead would sleep only seven or eight people, whereas the order of Carmelite nuns selected by the trustees was made up of many thousands of nuns around the world. In consequence, Viscount Simonds could not see how it could possibly have been the testator's intention that the individual members of the order take individual, beneficial rights in the property. His Lordship considered that a beneficiary was a person who would go into 'immediate possession' of his rights, and not someone who only had an indirect right.

The rationale behind this rule is to prevent trusts lasting in perpetuity. For example, the courts in the Victorian era became concerned that the vibrant and explosive British economy, in the white heat of the Industrial Revolution, would be starved of capital while it was possible for money and other property to be bound up in trusts for abstract purposes without ever being spent and thus passed back into the economy. Therefore, it was thought, if money was tied up for the maintenance of a 'useful memorial' it was not being used for the benefit of people as part of the economy. It was thought that an efficient economy required that capital should circulate and be used by whoever would make the best use of it.

The perpetuities rules

As a consequence, the rules on perpetuities and accumulations were developed to require that property could not be dedicated to abstract purposes so that no individual could take a benefit from it (the so-called 'rule against inalienability') and also to require that property held on trust must vest in some beneficiary within an identified period of time (the so-called 'rule against remoteness of vesting'). The purpose of this principle is to prevent property from being tied up in perpetuity without being able to be used for any other purpose. If a trust operates beyond the perpetuity period, then it will be void. The old case law would find that any trust without a perpetuity period would simply be void from the outset. The Perpetuities and Accumulations Act 1964 was introduced to save such trusts.

The perpetuities rules for the future are governed by the Perpetuities and Accumulations Act 2009. The 2009 Act saves trusts without a perpetuity period by creating a statutory perpetuity period of 125 years (s 5(1)) which applies if the trust does not terminate before that date (s 7). If the trust is still in existence at the end of that period then the 2009 Act closes the class of beneficiaries at that point in time so that no one else can become entitled to the trust property (s 8).

The 2009 Act takes effect in relation to trusts created on or after 6 April 2010. For trusts created before that date the Perpetuities and Accumulations Act 1964 applies, with its statutory period of 80 years in most circumstances; with trusts created before 16 July 1964 being governed by the case law principles which construed trusts strictly and tended to invalidate them for any possible breach of perpetuity (e.g. *Re Wood* (1894)).

The modern approach to the beneficiary principle

To return to the case law on the beneficiary principle, a different generation of judges took a different approach to these rules – although they were similarly concerned to maintain the same economic freedoms. In *Re Denley* (1969), Goff J was faced with an ostensibly similar situation to that in *Leahy*. A testator had left property for trustees to create and maintain a sports ground for the benefit of employees of a specific company. At first sight it would appear that the facts are very similar to *Leahy*. The sports ground could not have been intended to be owned and used by all of the employees simultaneously. Further, it would have been available to future employees as well as to the present employees. However, Goff J upheld the trust as a valid trust under the beneficiary principle. He returned to the precise words used in the old authority of *Morice v Bishop of Durham* (1805) and found that the mischief of this rule was to ensure that there would be someone who could act as a claimant to bring matters to court if ever there was a dispute as to the trustees' actions. On the facts of *Denley*, Goff J found that there would always be some employees who could bring an action against the trustees and therefore that satisfied the beneficiary principle.

In *Re Lipinski* (1976), Oliver J went further and held that the dividing line between valid trusts for the benefit of people and void trusts for abstract purposes should not be located where Viscount Simonds had drawn it. Goff J in *Re Denley* had expressed a view that trusts that provide for a direct or even an *in*direct benefit to some beneficiaries ought to be held valid, and Oliver J built on that idea to hold that only trusts that were clearly only for abstract purposes, such as the maintenance of a monument to a favourite pet, should be declared invalid. In short, the new generation of judges was prepared to uphold the validity of trusts provided that there was some person capable of taking a benefit. This contrasted with the strict, literalist approach of judges such as Viscount Simonds, who would find trusts invalid if there was even a possibility that the precise drafting of the trust would mean that the property would not necessarily pass to some identified person (see, however, *Re Grant's WT* (1979)).

In short, there is a new pragmatism in the courts. Their concern is to find a trust valid wherever possible, unless the trust offends some public policy (e.g. where it is formed for an illegal purpose) or is clearly intended only for an abstract purpose. In *Re Lipinski*, for example, Oliver J was prepared to hold that a trust that was expressed to be 'held on trust . . . for the purpose of constructing buildings' (and which would therefore have been read by Viscount Simonds as clearly effecting a void purpose trust) could be interpreted as a gift of the money because the recipient association had complete control over the manner in which the capital was used – and therefore were said to be effectively the recipients of a gift. This means that settlors now have greater flexibility in the trusts that they create, but there is still a need for some beneficiary to be identified. Without a beneficiary, there cannot be a trust. Albeit that *Re Denley* suggests that an indirect benefit is sufficient to render you a beneficiary. It is only abstract purposes – such as erecting a memorial to a favourite pet – which will be void because no person would take a meaningful benefit from such a purpose.

The problem of unincorporated associations

Associations abound in our ordinary lives. An example of an unincorporated association would be a social club in which the members pay a subscription to join and are then bound by the club's constitution. That the association is said to be 'unincorporated' means that it has not been organised and registered as a company – and thus not made subject to company law. Aside from the many sporting and social clubs that exist there are also cooperatives, credit unions, friendly societies, benevolent societies and so forth, which play an important part in the social fabric of the nation.

As late as 1897, ordinary trading companies were still organised as associations of members with rights in partnership law, in trust and under the 'joint stock companies' legislation. It was in 1897 that the House of Lords gave companies the separate legal personality which they still enjoy today (*Saloman v Saloman* (1897)). Trade unions and other working-class groups all began life as what we would now call unincorporated associations; it is a structure with a long legal pedigree. Significantly, though, unincorporated associations do not have separate legal personality and therefore cannot be owners of their own property; rather, someone must be the owner of such property on their behalf.

The problem for trusts lawyers is this: when property is held by an association (e.g. the tennis rackets at the tennis club) how do we explain the ownership of such property? Typically, an association will have a management committee or a treasurer who will be responsible for the association's property. Therefore, we might say that the treasurer holds all of the association's property on trust for the membership. The difficulty then is that the trust might be a void trust because that property would be held for the abstract purposes of the association and not directly for the members of the association. In this regard the order of Carmelite nuns was an unincorporated association in *Leahy*, as considered above.

There is a difficult boundary to be drawn between making dispositions by way of a void purpose trust (which offends the beneficiary principle) and making a disposition to an unincorporated association in a way that does not offend against the beneficiary principle. It is possible, therefore, that dispositions to unincorporated associations might be a means of effecting purpose trusts without the use of a trust structure in some circumstances. The goal for the trusts lawyer is therefore to structure an unincorporated association so that it does not constitute a void purpose trust. The following example may help to make the point clearer.

Example

The difference between the trust for present members and the endowment capital trust is that an endowment capital trust intends that the property be locked into the trust so that income derived from the property is used to generate income for the beneficiaries. Suppose that the trust provision reads as follows: 'The football used in the 1973 Cup Final is to be held on trust so that the trustee must keep the ball on display and charge an entrance fee to members of the public to view the ball, and so that all such income generated is to be held on trust for the benefit of present and future members of the club.' There are three possible shades of interpretation here.

The first would be that the trust is a trust for people (i.e. the members of the association) which is capable of interpretation as lasting for a maximum perpetuity period so that there is certainty that the trust will be terminated; as in *Re Denley*. The second is that the trust is a trust for people, but invalid as offending the rule against remoteness of vesting. The issue is then whether or not the Perpetuities and Accumulations Act 2009 would operate to impose a statutory perpetuity period, thus validating the trust temporarily. The third is that the trust is deemed to be a trust for the purposes of the association, by virtue of supporting its present and future members. Such a trust will be a void purpose trust, as in *Leahy v Attorney General for New South Wales*.

A transfer will be interpreted as a purpose trust where it is made 'for the present and future members' of the association. The assumption is that, where future members are expressed as being entitled to the property, there cannot be an immediate, outright gift in favour of the current membership; there could only be a trust for the abstract purposes of the association. Therefore, a transfer of property 'to be held upon trust by T for the purposes of the New Sunderland AFC Supporters' Association' would be void.

For the trusts lawyer, the thought process should be the following one: 'If I cannot use a trust structure, maybe I should use a different structure, such as a gift, to effect my client's purpose but without falling foul of the law of trusts.' Therefore, we might try to structure a transfer of property to an unincorporated association as an outright gift to members as an accretion to the club's capital. So, in *Re Recher's WT* (1972), a part of the residue of will trusts was to be held on trust for an association that had ceased to exist. The issue arose as to the validity of the gift. Brightman J held that it is possible for individuals to agree to pursue a common purpose and to create a contract between themselves in the form of an association. Consequently, the use of their subscriptions and property committed under that contract could be controlled under the specific performance jurisdiction of the courts. Further, where there is no wording suggesting the creation of a trust, a transfer of property to that association should be read as an accretion to the capital collected for the association rather than creating immediate proprietary rights in favour of the members of the association.

Therefore, the interpretation that was applied to the bequest in *Recher* was that the property was transferred as an outright gift to members of the association as individuals, but held as an accretion to the capital of the association. The requisite officer of the association took possession of the property, even though it had been transferred to the members as individuals by way of a gift. The use of the gift is then as an addition to the capital held by the association.

It was accepted that the treatment of the property, once it has become part of the capital collected for the association's purposes, is governed by the terms of the contract created by the members of the association between themselves. In broad terms, the members are therefore able to rely on provisions in their mutual contract to terminate the association and distribute the property between one another, as considered below. Thus the question of the accretion to the club's funds is dealt with by contract law, not trusts law. Therefore, the beneficiary principle would not apply because that is a rule of trusts law only.

This principle of treating associations as being creatures of contract rather than creatures of trust has been pursued in the context of the division of an association's property on its termination: it is said that the property should be divided in accordance with the terms of the contract entered into between the members (*Re Bucks Fund* (1979)). Again, we see an example of contract law governing the allocation of rights in property in place of the law of trusts – a theme that will be pursued in more detail in relation to commercial trusts in Chapter 11. A trusts lawyer must analyse the terms of the trust instrument and decide whether the settlor's intention is best categorised as a trust for the benefit of people, or as a void trust for abstract or for never-ending purposes, or as an accretion to the association's property to be governed by contract law.

Thus far, we have established that a trust requires a beneficiary to be valid and we have considered the example of unincorporated associations to demonstrate how lawyers will be required to make subtle distinctions between various legal structures. We should now turn our attention to consider the precise nature of the rights that the beneficiary takes from the trust. Our first consideration is the purpose for which a beneficiary may wish to be involved with a trust structure, which is a discussion which will ground our analysis of the rights of beneficiaries.

Purposes behind the creation of the trust from the beneficiary's perspective

There is a tendency to think of the beneficiary as the hapless, helpless passenger in all of this. Frankly that is a mind-set that the law of trusts inculcates in us itself. The beneficiary has always been a species of volunteer who is given rights in equity because there is found to be sufficient intention on the part of the settlor to create a trust in her favour. In effect the beneficiary was always considered to be someone, usually a relative of the settlor, who was receiving a gift by way of a settlement. Historically, beneficiaries under trusts tended to be young members of a family who were being provided for by a patriarch who held both the family purse strings and title in the family home. As such, the law has tended to protect the beneficiary against any sort of loss which may be caused by the trustee – as considered in detail in Chapter 10.

However, that is not always the right way to think about the beneficiary. There are many situations in which the beneficiary herself will have created the trust as settlor as part of some clever ploy to avoid tax, or to structure a commercial transaction, or as part of an investment strategy to provide for a pension in her old age. It would not be right to think of the beneficiary as a hapless innocent abroad in a world run by adults. Instead, the beneficiary is often the driving force even when she is not also a settlor. For example, where the beneficiary uses powers in the law of trusts to give instructions to the trustees about how the trust property is to be managed (considered below), then perhaps that beneficiary should not be entitled to the same unthinking protection that the law on breach of trust gives to beneficiaries ordinarily.

The position of a beneficiary under a pension fund (as considered in Chapter 10) is different again. The beneficiary will have voluntarily contributed to that pension fund as a settlor to ensure her own security (and often that of her family) after retirement. In such circumstances, the position of the beneficiary is a particularly sensitive one – if the trustee defaults, that will leave a pensioner without an income in old age despite a long period of carefully saving money. In the first edition of this book, I predicted a pension mis-selling scandal of enormous proportions when all those people who have contributed to private pension plans out of economic necessity begin to realise that their pension incomes are not as high as they were led to believe they would be. Reports have shown that I was correct. The law of trusts needs to recognise that the situation of these beneficiaries is very different from the position of beneficiaries under bare trusts, which they themselves created to avoid taxation.

Never take a trust simply at face value. There is always a lot more going on under the surface.

The right of the beneficiaries in the trust property

It was said at the beginning of this chapter that the beneficiary has proprietary rights *in* the trust fund. That statement requires some elucidation. The requirement of certainty of subject matter (considered in Chapter 3) means that the law of trusts intends (in this context at least) that there be some identified property in relation to which the beneficiaries and trustees have rights and obligations. However, by itself that would not mean that the rights of the beneficiaries were necessarily rights in the fund itself. They could as easily be rights against the trustees to control their use of the property – which would be a form of property right, albeit of a looser kind.

The reason that we can say with confidence that the beneficiaries have rights *in the trust fund itself* is due to the rule in *Saunders v Vautier* (1841). The principle in that case provides that all of the beneficiaries under the trust who collectively constitute 100 per cent of the equitable interest under the trust can direct the trustees how to deal with the property if they act together to do so.

Let us explore that idea a little. This is a rule that permits a form of beneficiary democracy, but only if all of the beneficiaries agree to the direction. Therefore, any one beneficiary could object and veto the scheme. All the beneficiaries must also be acting *sui juris* (that is, they must be of sound mind and of the age of majority). If those requirements are met the beneficiaries have complete control over the trust fund, regardless of the wishes of the settlor. *Saunders v Vautier* is the ultimate expression of the power of the beneficiaries because it enables the beneficiaries to terminate the trust, or to direct the trustees to treat the trust property in a different fashion from that set down by the settlor originally.

From the perspective of the settlor this rule is potentially *unsettling* – that is, in the sense of unpicking the 'settlement', of unpicking the settlor's intentions and unmaking the settlement. In the USA, the rule in *Saunders v Vautier* does not apply, which means that settlors in the USA can create so-called protective trusts (or 'spendthrift trusts') that prevent the beneficiaries from taking control of the trust fund and frustrating the settlor's detailed intentions. Settlors often wish to create such trusts so that a profligate relative is not able simply to spend all of the trust money at once on loose living or generally having fun.

In England and Wales, the settlor has to be considerably more cunning than that. For example, a settlor wishing to prevent a beneficiary over the age of 18 from asserting *Saunders v Vautier* rights under a trust intended solely for that person's benefit would have to make it explicit that that person obtained no rights in the fund unless and until certain conditions precedent were satisfied, or to make that person one of the potential objects of a mere power of appointment so that she could have no more than a mere hope of receiving some property on the terms of the trust (*Re Brook's ST* (1939)).

Alternatively, the settlor could make herself another beneficiary so that she would not consent to an alteration of the power, or make herself the sole trustee with a power to withhold the property from the beneficiary.

In short, it is more difficult to achieve the same objective under English law precisely because the beneficiary under ordinary English law has ultimate proprietary title in the trust fund. Clearly this rule in *Saunders v Vautier* (unless obstructed by the sort of structures just considered) enables the beneficiary to frustrate the wishes of the settlor. So, in *Re Bowes* (1896), a trust fund was created for the maintenance of trees on a private estate as part of a more complex trust which benefited two human beneficiaries. The court upheld an application from those beneficiaries that in exercise of the principle in *Saunders v Vautier* the provision in favour of the trees be ignored and the money held on trust passed instead to the impecunious beneficiaries.

Variation of trusts

A further example of the law ignoring the wishes of the settlor in recognition of the desires of the beneficiaries is that of variation of trusts. The *Saunders v Vautier* principle enables the beneficiaries to terminate the trust by directing the trustees to transfer the trust property directly to them. There is a narrow dividing line between such a termination and the situation where the same trust is maintained but where its terms are merely varied. These rules therefore give more control to the beneficiaries by enabling them to change the settlor's intentions.

In general terms the trustee is required to follow the terms of the trust to the letter. However, there is an inherent power in the court to permit departure from the precise terms of the trust (*Re New* (1910)). The purpose and extent of this inherent jurisdiction is to enable the court and the trustees to manage 'emergencies' (per Romer LJ in *Re New*) that arise in the administration of the trust. The expression 'emergencies' may include anything that is not provided for in the terms of the trust.

The decision of the Court of Appeal in *Chapman v Chapman* (1954) set out four exceptions to the general principle that the trustee cannot deviate from the terms of the trust: first, cases in which the court has effected changes in the nature of an infant's property; second, cases in which the court has allowed the trustees of settled property to enter into some business transaction that was not authorised by the settlement; third, cases in which the court has allowed maintenance out of income that the settlor or testator directed to be accumulated; fourth, cases in which the court has approved a compromise on behalf of infants and possible after-born beneficiaries.

Under the Variation of Trusts Act 1958 the court is empowered to permit variations of trusts in relation to specific types of beneficiaries that are identified in the statute itself. The court's jurisdiction is then limited to variations and revocations to the extent that they interact with those categories of persons. The focus of the legislation is on infants and incapacitated persons (e.g. those suffering from mental health problems). It also includes those people who might yet become beneficially entitled under the trust fund (either because their interest has not yet been awarded to them under some fiduciary discretion or because they have not yet been born). With reference to these categories of person, the court has a discretion to permit variations of trust.

The question in relation to variations will always be whether what is proposed to the court constitutes merely a tinkering with the trust or whether it constitutes an effective termination of the original settlement and a resettlement on entirely different terms. Megarry J has said (*Re Holt's ST* (1968)) on the same subject that

> if an arrangement, while leaving the substratum, effectuates the purpose of the original trust by other means, it may still be possible to regard that arrangement as merely varying the original trusts, even though the means employed are wholly different, and even though the form is completely changed.

Therefore, it will clearly be necessary to examine the true purpose of the trust (or its 'substratum') and identify whether or not that is changed to such an extent as to constitute a resettlement on new terms. The approach to variation is explained by Lord Reid in *Re Holmden's ST* (1968) as being a consent given by the beneficiaries to the variation, rather than something imposed on them by the court – which again emphasises that the ultimate power and control lies with the beneficiaries for whom the court should be considered to be acting.

Disposition of an equitable interest

What we have not yet considered is what the beneficiary can do if she wants to dispose of her equitable interest: whether by selling it, borrowing against it, or giving it away. This issue concerns the ability of the beneficiary to dispose of her equitable interest without terminating or varying the terms of the trust. An equitable interest under a trust is itself a proprietary right and therefore is capable of being transferred (*Grey v IRC* (1960)). The problem that is raised by this facility is that the trustees may not know who the beneficiaries are at any one time if transfers of the equitable interest are permissible. Therefore, s 53(1)(c) of the Law of Property Act (LPA) 1925 was passed, which requires that all 'dispositions' of an equitable interest must be set out in writing and signed by the transferor.

This simple rule demonstrates some of the most imaginative uses of trusts on the decided cases. There are a number of situations in which the holder of an equitable interest would not want to transfer that equitable interest by signed writing. The most important is in relation to stamp duty. Stamp duty imposes a tax on any writing which transfers value property from one person to another. Consequently, tax law practitioners have sought to find ways in which title in equitable interest in particular (and in property more generally) can be passed without attracting liability to stamp duty.

The key point for the student here is to understand the subtly different approaches that are taken to attempt to avoid the need to comply with s 53(1)(c). First, we will consider the case of *Grey*, which demonstrates what will happen if the beneficiaries' actions are not structured properly, and then we will consider some alternative structures that do not fall into the same trap.

In *Grey v IRC* (1960), a man called Hunter was attempting to transfer title in 18,000 valuable shares to his grandchildren. He had created six settlements, one for each of his grandchildren, and sought a means of passing 3,000 shares into each settlement without liability to stamp duty. Therefore, he created a trust over the 18,000 shares and declared himself to be the sole beneficiary. He then directed his trustees *orally* to transfer his equitable interest in those shares under the new trust to the trusts held for his grandchildren before *subsequently writing* these instructions down with his trustees. His intention was to pass title by means of the oral instructions and not by means of the writing. However, Lord Simonds in the House of Lords held that title did not pass until the instructions to make the disposition were put into writing and therefore that it was the writing that transferred the equitable interest: in consequence stamp duty was payable.

It was key to that decision in *Grey* that the trustee remained the same and that only the equitable interest passed. In a later decision of the House of Lords in

Vandervell v IRC (1967), Mr Vandervell sought to transfer his equitable interest in valuable shares to benefit the Royal College of Surgeons. In that case Mr Vandervell instructed his trustees to pass not only his equitable interest, but also the legal title in the shares to the Royal College of Surgeons. On that point, the House of Lords held that s 53(1)(c) did not apply because Mr Vandervell had transferred both his equitable interest and the legal title together. In the opinion of the House of Lords there was no need to comply with a specific formality in relation to the transfer of the equitable title if the formality for transferring the legal title had been effected: 'the greater [the legal title] included the less [the equitable title].' Therefore, we have one means of eluding s 53(1)(c) by transferring both legal and equitable title together, rather than just the equitable title alone.

Another means of avoiding s 53(1)(c) is by deploying *Saunders v Vautier* (1841). If the beneficiary terminates the trust by calling for the trustees to transfer legal title to the beneficiary, the beneficiary becomes the absolute owner of the property and can declare new trusts without the need to comply with s 53(1)(c). This structure works because a *declaration* of a new trust is something different from a mere *disposition* of the equitable interest by itself (*Cohen and Moore v IRC* (1933)). Alternatively, the beneficiary could carry out a variation of trust in favour of another person which takes effect automatically on the court's order and does not need signed writing – so transferring the equitable interest to that other person without the need for signed writing (*Re Holt's Settlement* (1968)).

A further range of older cases provide another mechanism to avoid s 53(1)(c). Under the doctrine in *Walsh v Lonsdale* (1882), when a contract is created for the transfer of property equity deems the equitable interest in that property to pass as soon as the contract is complete. The underlying rationale for that rule is that the transferor can be compelled under the doctrine of specific performance to transfer the property (provided that the transferee has provided valuable consideration and that there is no other applicable equitable bar to specific performance on the facts). Therefore, equity deems that transfer to have taken effect because specific performance would require it to be done – thus the equitable title passes. In consequence, if the holder of an equitable interest under a trust enters into a contract with another person to transfer that equitable interest, the completion of the contract causes the equitable interest to pass automatically to the transferee without the need for signed writing under s 53(1)(c) of the LPA 1925 (*Oughtred v IRC* (1960); *Neville v Wilson* (1996)).

The cases making up the *Vandervell* litigation together with *Oughtred* and *Grey* all demonstrate the ways in which the law of trusts deals with innovative thinking to manipulate trusts law concepts. What is important at this stage is to understand the flexibility and the dynamic energy that trusts lawyers invest in attempting to produce structures that avoid potential legal problems. As with the beneficiary principle considered above, whenever the case law or statute produces an obstacle to the settlor's intentions, the good lawyer will fight to go round, over or under that obstacle – a little like a worker ant carrying food back to the nest. Of course, the physical resemblance between trusts lawyers and insects ends there.

Thinking about formalities in express trusts

The principal way in which the law of trusts seeks to impose order on chaos is by means of legal formalities. Most of the formalities relating to the creation and constitution of trusts are based on the 1677 Statute of Frauds, which was concerned to prevent fraudulent claims by people asserting rights to property.

The main problem identified by this legislation was the lack of evidence as to which person owned which rights unless claimants were required to produce written evidence of their entitlement before their claim would even be entertained by the courts. This approach was the basis for formalities as to declarations of trust over land, conveyances of rights in land, dispositions of equitable interests and the proper creation of wills.

That thinking has also informed much of the case law in this area. The rules as to certainty of intention, of objects and of subject matter (considered in Chapter 3) are all based on the courts' need to be able to understand the settlor's intentions and thus to control the trustees' actions. Similarly, the beneficiary principle was founded such that the courts would be able to enforce the trust through the claims brought before them by beneficiaries.

Indeed, for all the squabbling among the judiciary as to the precise scope of the beneficiary principle (in *Leahy*, *Denley* and *Lipinski*) the only area on which all of their Lordships could agree was the foundation of the principle on the need for there to be some person who could bring the matter before the courts.

While the courts remain wedded to principles of certainty, the use of trusts law principle highlights the inherent flexibility in the core ideas. For each potential for tax liability, or for each argument that a trust might be invalid, there are a range of ways and means of avoiding those pitfalls. So, in relation to the void purpose trust, it is possible to validate a trust intended in truth for abstract purposes by making gifts for the benefit of identified individuals (*Denley*), by passing control of capital (*Lipinski*), by making a transfer to an unincorporated association as an accretion to its funds (*Recher*) and so forth.

What is interesting is the strict adherence to formality and the spirit of the legislation in decisions by Viscount Simonds in *Leahy* and in *Grey v IRC*, when compared with more purposive approaches taken by other judges in later cases. What this illustrates is a movement away from perceiving the law of trusts as being something to do with the strict observance of age-old rules and a shift towards enabling citizens to make use of trusts law techniques to achieve socially desirable goals. It would be wrong to try to think of the distinctions between these various cases as being capable of reconciliation one with another. The approach taken by Goff J in *Re Denley* and by Oliver J in *Re Lipinski* is simply different from that taken by Viscount Simonds in *Leahy*. Two different generations of judges had different attitudes to the role of the law in exactly the same way that two generations of ordinary people would have different tastes in music. Viscount Simonds is concerned to see observance of the law for the law's sake; the later judges prefer to permit people to use trusts provided that they do not transgress certain mandatory rules about the possibility of some beneficiary being able to enforce the trust in court.

The law of trusts as it develops should be seen as a growing literature in exactly the same way that one would study developments in fiction, fashion or film. As time passes new ideas come to the fore and replace old ideas. Just as most modern directors would not use black-and-white film, we see a different approach to film-making in the 21st century to that used in the first half of the 20th century. In the same way approaches to law will adapt and change – particularly in a common law system. It is only by accepting that idea that any student of equity and trusts will be able to understand why some judgments are different from other judgments, rather than trying to reconcile one judgment with another in all circumstances.

Understanding the role of express trusts

What the student should take away from the study of trusts is an appreciation of the many pliable techniques that exist for the manipulation of trusts techniques for a number of purposes. Those purposes fall into two general categories. The first is as a socially useful means by which ordinary citizens and corporations can organise the terms of their communal use of property. Trusts and derivatives of trusts techniques are used to organise charities, pension funds, cooperatives and even (in a very particular manner) NHS trusts. Similar techniques based on the stewardship of property by a trustee for the ultimate entitlement of beneficiaries also form an important part of commercial agreements, as considered in outline in Chapter 2 and in more detail in Chapter 11.

The second is as a means of using trusts to elude or avoid problems of law. So, for example, the preceding discussion of the carrying on of dispositions of equitable interests in ways that avoid the provisions of s 53(1)(c) of the LPA 1925 have indicated the manner in which trusts lawyers are able to *structure* their clients' affairs to achieve the desired effect. The same holds true for situations in which the client is not seeking to avoid some legal rule, but rather to achieve an identified, desired effect. Therefore, a commercial contract between two multi-national financial institutions dealing in financial derivatives or between two sole traders dealing in used cars can be secured by providing that payment is held on trust until both buyer and seller are satisfied that the contract has been properly performed. The same techniques will apply, with suitable adaptations, to both circumstances.

However, equity ought to be about more than merely creating trusts-by-numbers. While the use of the express trust will become ever more institutional-ised with its deployment in commercial contracts, will trusts and so forth, it should not be forgotten that this difficult concept of 'conscience' lies in the background. It is suggested in cases such as *Westdeutsche Landesbank v Islington* (1996) that the single idea of 'conscience' will solve all of those various disputes. And yet the question as to what constitutes good and bad conscience in different circumstances remains unanswered in many situations. It is a question that falls to be answered not simply by reference to the *creation* of such trusts but certainly in relation to the *management* and *breach* of such arrangements. The available remedies and equitable responses to contravention of the trust will differ in desirability from context to context.

This ideal of good conscience is a useful way of describing the pattern that equity creates in resolving these disputes; but it is not a means by which the legal system ought to attempt to impose order on that chaos by shoe-horning different social problems into the same ill-fitting boots.

An exceptional category: secret trusts

Thus far we have focused in this chapter on very deliberate legal structures; it would be useful to remind ourselves of the flexible and responsive uses of equity. A secret trust is almost as exciting as it sounds. Suppose the following circumstances. A man expects to die and decides to write his will. He has the following problem. He is married with children but also has a mistress and an illegitimate child by his mistress. In such circumstances he might not want to mention his mistress or her child in his will so as not to hurt his wife and children, but yet will want to provide for his illegitimate child. In this situation he may make what is known as a secret trust. He would leave property in his will to his best friend on the understanding that this friend would hold that property on trust for his mistress and child. As such there would be an arrangement created in secret: a secret trust.

This arrangement would be in contravention of s 9 of the Wills Act 1837, which provides that all the terms of the will must be included in a properly attested document and, more importantly, oral evidence which contradicted the terms of the will (such as holding property on trust for the mistress and child) would not be admissible. As we have already discussed in Chapter 1, the purpose of equity is to introduce fairness in circumstances in which statute might permit unfairness. Therefore, in our example, if the best friend were entitled to refuse to observe the secret trust, that would be to allow him to use the Wills Act as an engine of fraud and to deny the mistress her property unconscionably.

The underlying purpose of the doctrine of secret trusts is to prevent statute or common law being used as an instrument of fraud (*McCormick v Grogan* (1869)), for example in situations in which the beneficiaries under a will only received the property on the understanding that they would hold it for someone else. In *McCormick*, Lord Westbury considered that the basis of the secret trust was as a means of preventing fraudulent reliance on common law or statutory rights. Thus, the legal owner of property may be made subject to a 'personal obligation' (perhaps 'proprietary obligation' imposed *in personam*) that requires that person to hold the specific property on trust for the person whom the testator had intended to receive equitable title in the property.

Fully secret trusts

Fully secret trusts arise in circumstances where neither the existence nor the terms of the trust are disclosed by the trust instrument. Oral evidence of the agreement between the testator and trustee is generally satisfactory. The settlor must have intended to create such a trust. That intention must have been communicated to the intended trustee. The trustee must have accepted the office and the terms of the trust explicitly or impliedly.

In the leading case of *Ottaway v Norman* (1972), Ottaway left his bungalow, half his residuary estate and a sum of money to Miss Hodges on the terms of his will, on the understanding that she was in turn to bequeath this property to the plaintiff. Hodges failed to do this in her will. Rather, she left the property to Mr and Mrs Norman. After Hodges's death, the plaintiff brought an action against Hodges's executors claiming entitlement to the property that had been left in Ottaway's will. Brightman J held that the elements, which must be demonstrated to substantiate a fully secret trust in this way, were an intention to benefit the plaintiff; communication of this intention to Hodges; and acceptance by Hodges of the obligation.

It was found on the facts of *Ottaway* that Hodges had known of Ottaway's intention and had acquiesced in it. Therefore, it was held that the bungalow and residuary estate should pass to the plaintiff. However, the money was not subject to the same obligation because the court found it difficult to see how this could have been done if Hodges was entitled to use the money during her lifetime, unless there was an implication that she had to keep Ottaway's money separate from her own.

Perhaps the easiest conceptualisation of what the court is really looking for, beneath the three-stage test set out in *Ottaway*, appears in *Wallgrave v Tebbs* (1855), where it was held by Wood VC that where the secret trustee–legatee 'expressly promises' or 'by silence implies' that he is accepting the obligation, he will be bound by it. The Wills Act will not interfere with the working of secret trusts in this way.

Time of the creation of the fully secret trust

It is generally assumed that a fully secret trust is created at the point of the testator's death. This assumption is sensible. The trust must come into existence at some point in time. It must be possible to know at what moment the trustee becomes subject to the fiduciary duties of trusteeship. The sensible approach to providing for the date of death means that the most recent version of the will applies, passing legal title in the property to the secret trustee. Before that time, the trustee has no title in the property. (If the trustee had had title in the property, that would raise the question whether the trust was a normal *inter vivos* express trust, rather than a testamentary secret trust.)

However, there is an alternative authority of *Re Gardner* (1923) under which Romer J held, controversially, that the gift is created at the date of the will, rather than at the date of death. It is suggested that the decision in *Re Gardner* cannot be correct in principle because the will could have been altered subsequently, thus revoking the gift.

Half-secret trusts

A half-secret trust is a trust under which the *existence* of the trust is disclosed in a document, such as a will, but the *terms* of the trust remain secret. In short, it is the situation in which the existence of the trust is disclosed by the will, or other instrument, but the terms are not. The requirements for a valid half-secret trust were set out in *Blackwell v Blackwell* (1929) by Lord Sumner, who held that there must be 'intention, communication and acquiescence' between settlor and trustee. Therefore, the test for a half-secret trust is very similar to that for a fully secret trust. It was also held that there is no need for the plaintiff to prove actual fraud on the part of the defendant (the secret trustee).

Communication of the trust to the secret trustee must be before or at the time of the execution of the will. Lord Sumner held in *Blackwell* that '[a] testator cannot reserve to himself a power of making future unwitnessed dispositions by merely naming a trustee and leaving the purposes of the trust to be supplied afterwards'. The rationale for this rule is that the trustee must know of the terms of the trust and be able to disclaim the obligations of trusteeship. Where communication occurs after the will, the trust will fail and the legatee will hold any property on resulting trust for residuary estate (*Re Keen* (1937)).

Therefore, there is a distinction between half-secret trusts and fully secret trusts in that the settlor must communicate before the execution of the will in the former, but need not communicate the existence or terms of the trust until the time of death in the latter (*Re Spence* (1949)), although, as with fully secret trusts, the intended trustee must accept the office of trustee and acquiesce in the terms of the trust. Similar issues arise as to the necessity of all trustees being aware of their obligations under the trust, as considered above.

The point of secret trusts

In the case of *Re Young* (1951), the juxtaposition between the requirements of the Wills Act 1837 and the rules as to secret trusts was made most clear. In the case of *Re Young*, a secret trust was referred to in the will. The terms of that secret trust were that the chauffeur would receive a legacy. The formal difficulty was that the chauffeur had witnessed the will and therefore ought to have been precluded from taking beneficially under that will in accordance with s 15 of the 1837 Act. It was held by Dankwerts J that the chauffeur could take validly in accordance with the terms of the secret trust. The underlying rationale is that the 1837 Act necessarily has no part to play in the decision whether or not there is a secret trust, given that the rationale that underpins the doctrine of secret trusts operates in the face of the requirements of that statute. The stated rationale was that, when considering s 15 of the Wills Act with reference to a legatee who has witnessed the will, it might be that the beneficiary is actually taking as trustee under a secret trust so that the policy under the 1837 Act is not necessarily contravened.

So, what is a secret trust?

There is a problem of categorising the secret trust. This book has left secret trusts among the express trust material because that is how the majority of commentators and judges seem to categorise them. But, to be honest with you, my heart is not in it. Some writers do maintain that secret trusts (particularly half-secret trusts) are a form of express trust, whereas the traditional view revolves around the doctrine in *Rochefoucauld v Boustead* (1897), which precludes a person from relying on their common law rights to perpetrate a fraud.

All forms of secret trusts should be considered to be constructive trusts because they are imposed on the recipient of the testamentary gift where that person knows in good conscience that she is required to hold that property on trust for someone else. As outlined above, the secret trust cannot be considered to be an ordinary express trust because it does not obey the formalities for testamentary trusts, nor does it necessarily obey the formalities set out in cases such as *Milroy v Lord* (1862) or *Morice v Bishop of Durham* (1805) as considered above and in Chapter 3.

Moving on . . .

Having considered the rights attaching to the beneficiary, it is time to consider the onerous burdens assumed by the trustee.

Chapter 5

The trustee's duties

Foundations of the duties of trustees

This chapter considers the obligations borne by trustees either under the trust instrument (if there is one) or under the general law of trusts. While this chapter will focus on those rights and duties that statute and the case law have developed, what should not be forgotten is that the detailed terms of the trust will be decisive of most of these issues as to the duties of the trustees on a case-by-case basis. By considering both the case law and the statutes dealing with the obligations of trustees we will be able to form a more complete picture of the nature of a trust.

Cotterrell (1993b) identifies one peculiar feature of the trust as developed by equity as opposed to the ordinary meaning of the word 'trust' in everyday speech. Ordinarily, if I place trust in someone then I am in a position of weakness because I am dependent on the person in whom I place trust to act in my interests or to treat me well. What trusts law does is to reverse the power relationship here by putting the beneficiary in a position of strength over the trustee by giving that beneficiary a means of enforcing the trustee's obligations to act in the beneficiary's best interests.

The general duties of trustees

The duties of the trustee are built around concepts of loyalty and good conscience (as in *Westdeutsche Landesbank v Islington* (1996)). Beyond that general principle, Chapter 8 of *Equity & Trusts* (Hudson, 2014) identifies thirteen key duties which are incumbent on trustees in ordinary circumstances under the general law of trusts. Those obligations are summarised here and then the principal obligations are discussed in greater detail in the remainder of this chapter, together with the principles governing exclusion of trustees' liability and the principle in *Hastings-Bass*.

First, trustees are obliged to familiarise themselves with the terms, conditions and history of the management of the trust. Second, trustees are obliged to obey the terms of the trust unless directed to do otherwise by the court. Third, trustees are required to safeguard the trust assets, which includes duties to maintain the trust property in accordance with the terms of the trust. Fourth, trustees are obliged to act impartially between beneficiaries and to avoid conflicts of interest, as considered below. Fifth, trustees bear a duty to act with reasonable care, meaning generally a duty to act as though a prudent person of business acting on behalf of someone for whom one feels morally bound to provide, as considered below. Sixth, trustees bear duties in relation to trust expenses.

Seventh, trustees have obligations related to the investment of the trust, as considered below. Eighth, trustees bear a duty to distribute the trust property in accordance with the terms of the trust. Ninth, trustees (and all other fiduciaries) are obliged to avoid conflicts of interest, not to earn unauthorised profits from the fiduciary office, not to deal on their own behalf with trust property on pain of such transactions being voidable, and to deal fairly with the trust property, as considered below. Tenth, trustees must preserve the confidence of the beneficiaries. These two types of duty give rise to constructive trusts, considered in Chapter 7. Eleventh, trustees are obliged to act without payment, unless they are permitted to do otherwise by the trust instrument or by the general law. Twelfth, the trustees are obliged to account to the beneficiaries and to provide information in the qualified manner considered below. Thirteenth, trustees bear a duty to take into account relevant considerations and to overlook irrelevant considerations; failure to do so may lead to the court setting aside an exercise of the trustees' powers if they have committed a breach of trust in so doing, as considered below in relation to the principle in *Hastings-Bass*. The nature of the trustees' liabilities for breaching any of these duties are considered in Chapter 10.

Fiduciary duties in general terms

The trustee is one example of a more general concept of English law: the fiduciary. Thus, it is often said that trustees bear 'fiduciary duties'. For our purposes the terms 'trustee' and 'fiduciary' can be read as being synonymous. It is useful to understand, though, that there are four classic categories of fiduciary relationship: trustee and beneficiary; partners between themselves; company director and company; and agent and principal. The common link is an obligation of loyalty owed by the fiduciary to the beneficiary in each relationship. The term fiduciary itself is derived from the Latin *fiduciarius*, meaning 'faithful'. The categories of fiduciary are not closed; rather, it is a flexible category which English law will add to whenever it encounters a situation that it considers appropriate for extension. In short, the label 'fiduciary' will be applied whenever there appears to be a context in which one person is required to act in the interests of another in a way that requires that actions be undertaken in the utmost good faith.

As will emerge in this chapter and in Chapter 10, it is very advantageous to a claimant to be able to demonstrate that the defendant is a fiduciary because that person is consequently prevented from making unauthorised profits from the relationship, from acting otherwise than in the beneficiary's best interests, and from permitting any conflict of interest. The remedies that are available for breach of a fiduciary duty include the whole range of trusts implied by law as well as the general, almost strict liability to account to the beneficiary for any loss suffered by the beneficiary, whether or not caused entirely by the fiduciary's actions.

Liability for breach of trust

Chapter 10 considers the remedies available in cases of breach of trust, whereas this chapter will focus on the nature of the trustee's general obligations. A breach of trust may arise when there is a breach of the specific terms of a particular trust instrument or a breach of the duties of trustees under the general law of trusts. A trustee will be liable to account to the beneficiaries for any loss suffered by the trust which was caused by their breach of trust (*Target Holdings Ltd v Redferns* (1995)). In essence, the trustee's obligations are to restore any property taken from the trust; or if that is not possible, to restore the value of the fund in cash and to compensate the beneficiaries for any other consequent loss. The trustee bears full liability out of their own property.

The duty to act impartially between beneficiaries

The trustee is obliged to act impartially as between all of the beneficiaries (*Nestlé v National Westminster Bank plc* (1994)). At one level this requires the trustee to exercise fairness as between each beneficiary, showing no favour to any one beneficiary. At another level, this requires the trustee to act evenly as between different classes of beneficiaries. It is suggested that the duty of impartiality is akin to the duty not to permit conflicts of interest, considered above, in that the trustee is expected to stand apart from and above partisan considerations as to entitlement to the fruits of the trust fund and to the fund itself. As a fiduciary, the trustee is required to act in relation to each of the beneficiaries without any grace or favour, in the same way that the trustee must not take any personal advantage from the trust.

So, in *Nestlé v National Westminster Bank plc*, it was held that a trustee must act fairly where there are different classes of beneficiaries. As between life tenant and remainderman, the trustee must be aware of the interests of the remainder beneficiary. However, it was held that 'it would be an inhuman rule which required trustees to adhere to some mechanical rule for preserving the real value of the capital when the tenant for life was the testator's widow who had fallen upon hard times and the remainderman was young and well-off'. Therefore, it does appear that there is some flexibility in the operation of this principle. Again, it will depend on the context of the particular trust in question.

To illustrate this principle one might consider the following example. A trustee is obliged not to focus the investment and distribution of the trust fund on the generation of short-term income for the life tenant when that would be to the detriment of the remainder beneficiaries who would depend on there being capital left in the trust fund (*Re Barton's Trust* (1868)). Therefore, additions to the trust capital are to be treated as additions to capital, rather than as further sources of income to be applied to the life tenant's benefit. However, where the property has only taken the form of mere income (as with a bonus dividend paid on a share) it falls to be treated as income (*Re Bouch* (1885)). In contradistinction to that, the addition of capital amounts to the account of a trustee, such as a reduction of capital by a company paid out to its shareholders, will be taken to form part of the capital of the fund (*Hill v Permanent Trustee Co of New South Wales* (1930)). The more difficult situation will be the in-between one, where profits are generated which would appear to be in the grey area between clear capital gains and the generation of a large amount of income. Therefore, the precise application of these principles will vary from situation to situation. The key point is that the trustee must always have acted faithfully and impartially.

The further question, beyond entitlement to various cash and other proprietary benefits from the trust fund, is the exercise of the trustee's powers of discretion. Thus, aside from the decisions as to the payment of items of property from the fund, there are issues such as the exercise of powers as to which beneficiaries are entitled to benefit from the trust at all, as with discretionary trusts. The question then is as to the form of power that the trustee is exercising. In relation to merely personal powers, the holder of the power is entitled to act capriciously, whereas fiduciaries are required to consider formally the exercise of mere powers and to act in a proper manner in relation to full trust powers (*Re Hay's ST* (1981)).

This impartiality will be required of trustees by the courts unless there is some provision to the contrary in the terms of the trust itself, which require that there be some different treatment. That policy is clearly in line with a broader policy of applying the wishes of the settlor as manifested in the terms of the trust. Therefore, the case law rules are really a default setting in the absence of any express provisions set out by the settlor as to the treatment of the trust fund. It will frequently be difficult for trustees to treat all beneficiaries equally; indeed, this principle requires only 'even-handed' and not 'equal' treatment. In relation to discretionary trusts the trustees' job is precisely to choose between beneficiaries. Therefore, the trustee's obligation boils down to an obligation to consider her fiduciary powers carefully and to be able to justify her actions (*Edge v Pensions Ombudsman* (2000)).

The general duty of trustees to act reasonably under the Trustee Act 2000

The Trustee Act 2000 introduces a code of provisions that relate primarily to the appointment of agents, nominees and custodians by trustees and particularly introduces provisions in relation to the investment of trust funds. (The Trustee Act 2000 does not apply generally to pension funds and does not apply to authorised unit trusts, both of which have statutory and regulatory regimes of their own – as considered in Hudson, 2014.) The Trustee Act 2000 provides for a statutory duty of care which imposes a duty of 'such skill and care as is reasonable in the circumstances' on trustees (s 1(1)). That 'duty of care' is relative to the context in which the trustee is acting. Where the trustee has, or holds himself out as having any particular 'special knowledge or experience', then the trustee's duty of care will be inferred in the light of those factors: for example, a trustee who is a stockbroker or lawyer will be expected to maintain a higher standard than someone who has no formal qualifications. So, if the duties of trustee are performed 'in the course of a business or profession', then the duty of care is applied in the context of any special knowledge or experience that such a professional could be expected to have.

The provisions of the 2000 Act can be expressly or impliedly displaced by the trust instrument. In consequence this duty of care may be limited by the express provisions of the trust, or even by a construction of those provisions which suggests that the settlor's intention was to exclude such a liability.

The principal context in which the statutory duty of care applies is in relation to a trustee exercising a 'general power of investment' (s 3) under the Act or any other power of investment 'however conferred'. Alternatively, the duty of care applies when trustees are carrying out obligations under the Act in relation to exercising or reviewing powers of investment. The duty of care also applies in relation to the acquisition of land, which would logically appear to cover the use of appropriate advice and appropriate levels of care in selecting the land, contracting for its purchase and insuring it. It applies in general terms in relation to the appointment of agents, custodians and nominees, which would include the selection of reasonable agents with appropriate qualifications for the task for which they were engaged.

The investment of trust funds

Investment under the Trustee Act 2000

In a break with the formalism imposed by the previous legislative code under the Trustee Investment Act 1961, the Trustee Act 2000 provides that 'a trustee may make any kind of investment that he could make if he were absolutely entitled to the assets of the trust'. This is referred to in the legislation as a 'general power of investment'. Therefore, the trustee is not constrained as to the investments that are made by reason only of his trusteeship. It should be remembered that the trust instrument may impose restrictions on the trustee's powers to make investments, and financial regulation may, in effect, preclude certain types of investment by persons who are considered to be insufficiently expert to make them. There remain restrictions on the power of trustees to make investments in land unless by way of loans secured on land (such as mortgages).

In creating a general power of investment, the Trustee Act 2000 also provides that that power is both in addition to anything set out in the trust instrument and also capable of being excluded by any such trust instrument. Therefore, the settlor could preclude the trustees from making particular forms of investment. In contradistinction to the now-repealed 1961 statutory code, this means that the trustee is presumed to be free to make any suitable investments in the absence of any express provision to the contrary, whereas the trustee was previously presumed to be capable only of making a limited range of investments in the absence of any provision to the contrary. The 1961 code is now replaced by the Trustee Act 2000 in this regard.

The movement from 'prudence' to 'reasonableness'

The old case law required that trustees must act prudently. That is, the trustees were required to act with caution and they were required to act carefully. Naturally, this duty had the effect that trustees would tend to invest very cautiously and so would not make large profits for trusts, unless their liabilities were excluded by the trust instrument. The purpose of the Trustee Act 2000 was therefore to liberate trustees and to enable them to act appropriately in the context of the trust that they are managing. Thus, a standard of acting 'with reasonable care and skill' means that trustees can take greater risks than before, provided that the level of risk that they take is reasonable in the context of the trust that they are managing. For example, a trustee holding the only savings of an elderly widow on trust would need to invest in a way that does not take too much risk if she is to be considered to be acting reasonably in that context; whereas a trustee employed as a professional stockbroker to invest £50 million on behalf of a billionaire, with express instructions to earn as much profit as possible, would be expected to make investments in risky and progressive markets so as to make sufficient profit for the billionaire beneficiary. This movement from 'prudence' to 'reasonableness' has therefore had an enormous impact on the conceptualisation of trustees' obligations in general terms.

Standard investment criteria

The 2000 Act requires that the trustees have regard to something described in the statute as the 'standard investment criteria' when exercising their investment powers: that is, it is suggested, whether making new investments or considering their existing investments. The 'standard investment criteria' to which the trustees are to have regard are two core principles of prevailing investment theory that relate, first, to the need to make 'suitable' investments, and second, to the need to maintain a diverse portfolio of investments to spread the fund's investment risk. We shall take each of these in turn. The trustees are required to consider '. . . the suitability to the trust of investments of the same kind as any particular investment proposed to be made or retained and of that particular investment as an investment of that kind' (s 4(2)).

The expression 'suitability' is one familiar to investment regulation specialists, which requires that, in general terms, investment managers are required to consider whether or not the risk associated with a given investment is appropriate for the client proposing to make that investment. In consequence the investment manager could not sell, for example, complex financial products to inexpert members of the general public who could not understand the precise nature of the risks associated with such a transaction. Under the terms of the Trustee Act 2000 the trustee is required to consider whether the trust fund for which she is making an investment would be dealing in a suitable manner in making the proposed investment. It is presumed that the trustee would be liable for breach of trust in the event that an unsuitable investment was made which caused a loss to the trust.

Second, the trustees must pay heed to 'the need for diversification of investments of the trust, in so far as is appropriate to the circumstances of the trust' (s 4(2)). Two points arise from this provision. First, the question as to the amount of diversification necessary is dependent on the nature of the trust. A trust that requires the trustees to hold a single house on trust for the occupation of a named beneficiary does not require that the trustees make a range of investments; rather, the trustees are impliedly precluded from making a range of investments by the duty to maintain that one house. Similarly, a trust with only a small amount of capital could not afford to buy a large number of investments. Second, the need for diversification itself is bound up with the need to dilute the risk of investing in only a small number of investments. This is frequently referred to as 'portfolio theory' (*Nestlé v National Westminster Bank plc* (1994)) and is predicated on the theory that if an investor invests in a number of investments in different markets the impact of any individual market or investment suffering from a fall in value is balanced out by the investments made in other investments, which will not have suffered from that particular fall in value.

The Trustee Act 2000 imposes a positive obligation on the trustees to seek out professional advice on the investments to be made (s 5). Similarly, when considering whether or not to vary the investments that the trust has made, the trustees are required to take qualified investment advice unless it appears reasonable to the trustee in the circumstances to dispense with such advice.

The type of advice that the trustee must acquire is 'proper advice', being advice from someone who the trustee reasonably believes is qualified to give such advice.

Investment powers under case law

What is most significant about the Trustee Act 2000 is that the settlor may choose not to have it apply to her trust. In such circumstances, the settlor would typically create her own code of investment powers. In such situations, disputes about the management of the trust would fall back on the principles set out in the case law. An express power on a trustee to make an investment may be general, giving the trustees power to invest in whatever they wish, or limited to specific types of investment. The trustee will nevertheless be subject to certain limitations. Although in *Re Harari's ST* (1949) it was held that such a power would not be interpreted restrictively, the case of *Re Power's WT* (1951) established that the word 'invest' implied a yield of income; thus, property which did not generate income would not be permissible as an investment. Therefore, while there is a permissive approach to interpreting investment clauses, it is important that it is 'investment' that is taking place. In *Re Power*, the trustee was relying on the investment provision to justify the acquisition of a house for the beneficiaries to live in. It was held that this acquisition did not include the necessary element of income generation for the trust. Thus, in *Re Wragg* (1919), it was permitted to acquire real property on the basis that that property was expected to generate income. It should be remembered that the trustee will have powers of investment both under the express power and under the Trustee Act 2000 if the latter is not excluded.

The trustee's duty to act prudently and safely under the case law

What will emerge from the following sections is that the case law imposes seemingly contradictory duties on the trustee: first, an obligation to avoid hazardous investments, and second, a counter-balancing duty to generate the best possible return from the trust property in the circumstances (*Cowan v Scargill* (1985)). The trustee's general duties of investment under the pre-2000 case law can be summarised in the following three core principles: to act prudently and safely; to act fairly between beneficiaries; and to do the best for the beneficiaries financially. Each will be considered in turn. After 2000, these principles can be best understood as aids to the interpretation of the Trustee Act 2000.

Under the old authority of *Learoyd v Whiteley* (1887), when the trustee is investing trust property she must not only act as a businessperson of ordinary prudence, but must also avoid all investments of a hazardous nature. The difficulty with this approach is that all investment necessarily involves some risk and therefore it is impossible for the trustees to make investments that are completely risk free. A trustee can invest in less risky securities, or other property, such as deposit bank accounts, but that is still not entirely free of the risk that the bank would go into insolvency. Therefore, the old approach was modified slightly in *Bartlett v Barclays Bank* (1980), in which a distinction was drawn between a prudent degree of risk and something that amounted to 'hazard'. The former prudently taken risk would be acceptable, whereas to put the trust fund in hazard would be unacceptable. Of course, it will typically be the case that it is only possible to decide with hindsight whether an investment constituted a brilliant piece of investment or a hazardous exposure to financial market movements.

In the context of delegating authority to invest to some other person, the classic statement of the trustee's obligation is set out in *Speight v Gaunt* (1883) in the decision of Lord Jessel MR:

> It seems to me that on general trust principles a trustee ought to conduct the business of the trust in the same manner that an ordinary prudent man of

business would conduct his own, and that beyond that there is no liability or obligation on the trustee.

Clearly, this is a difficult test for a trustee to observe – particularly if that trustee is not a professional investment advisor. What complicates the picture further, however, is the concomitant obligation of the trustee to make the most profit possible for the beneficiaries. That obligation is considered in the following section.

The trustee's obligation to do the best for the beneficiaries financially

This principle is probably more elegantly expressed as an obligation to make the optimum return for the trust. This issue arose in the case of *Cowan v Scargill* (1984), in which the defendant was one of the trustees of the miners' pension fund and also President of the National Union of Mineworkers. The board of trustees was divided between executives of the trade union and executives from the Coal Board. The most profitable investment identified by the trustees was in companies working in oil and also in South Africa. The defendant refused to make such investments on the grounds that it was ethically wrong for the fund to invest in apartheid South Africa and also contrary to the interests of the beneficiaries to invest in an industry that competed with the coal industry, in which all the beneficiaries worked or had worked previously.

Megarry VC held that: 'When the purpose of the trust is to provide financial benefits for the beneficiaries, the best interests of the beneficiaries are their best financial interests.' Therefore, the duty of the trustees to act in the best interests of the beneficiaries is to generate the best available return on the trust fund regardless of other considerations. The scope of the duty of investment was summarised by his Lordship as the need to bear in mind that 'the prospects for the yield of income and capital appreciation both have to be considered in judging the return from the investment'.

His Lordship therefore focused on the objections that the defendant trustee had raised in respect of the particular form of investment that had been suggested. He held that 'the trustees must put on one side their own personal interests and views', and later that 'if investments of this type would be more beneficial to the beneficiaries than other investments, the trustees must not refrain from making the investments by reason of the views that they hold'. The irony is that, in relation to the moral nature of the obligations on the trustee to deal equitably with the trust fund, the trustee is not permitted to bring decisions of an ethical nature to bear on the scope of the investment powers. As his Lordship put it: 'Trustees may even have to act dishonourably (though not illegally) if the interests of their beneficiaries require it.' This may seem surprising to us given that the primary duty of the trustee was said in Chapter 2 to be a duty of conscience. It may seem to us strange that good conscience means generating the most money regardless of ethics or morals. Or perhaps that is just a symptom of our age.

The duty to avoid conflicts of interest

In general terms, fiduciaries are obliged to avoid conflicts of interest of any kind. If any unauthorised profits are taken from the fiduciary office then those profits must be held on constructive trust for the beneficiaries. As considered in Chapter 7, this principle means that even if a fiduciary (such as a solicitor advising trustees) invests his own money in a transaction which also involves trust property, without authorisation to do so, then any profits which the fiduciary takes will be held on constructive trust for the beneficiaries of that trust (*Boardman v Phipps* (1967)). Two minor forms of this general principle are the self-dealing principle and the fair-dealing principle.

The self-dealing principle

The self-dealing principle restricts the ability of a trustee to deal with trust property in a personal capacity. So strict is the restriction on trustees benefiting, or even appearing to benefit, from trust property that the trustee is restricted from dealing with trust property even on a commercial, arm's length basis. For example, if land were held on trust and the trustee sought to buy that property from the trust, the trustee would be acting on behalf of the trust as well as acting on her own behalf in the sale. Such a transaction would bear the risk that the trustee would acquire the property from the trust at an artificially low price and thus exploit the beneficiaries. By the same token it might be that the price that the trustee obtains would have been the same price that the beneficiaries would have obtained on the open market.

The self-dealing principle entitles the beneficiary to set aside any such transaction on the basis, set out in *Keech v Sandford* (1726), that even the possibility of fraud or bad faith being exercised by the trustee is to be resisted: this is often referred to as the principle in *Ex p Lacey* (1802). Megarry VC in *Tito v Waddell (No 2)* (1977), enunciated the self-dealing principle in the following terms: 'if a trustee purchases trust property from himself, any beneficiary may have the sale set aside *ex debito justitiae*, however fair the transaction.' There is no defence for the trustee against the exercise of such a right of set-aside that the transaction was entered into as though between parties at arm's length. It is only where the beneficiary has expressly authorised the transaction that the trustee can rely on the transaction – which again demonstrates that ultimate control of trust affairs rests with the beneficiary.

The fair-dealing principle

The fair-dealing principle is similar to the self-dealing principle considered immediately above. The fair-dealing principle validates acquisitions by trustees of the interests from the trust provided that the trustee does not acquire any advantage attributable to his fiduciary office. This principle also applies to fiduciary relationships such as acquisitions by agents of the interests of their principals.

To demonstrate that the transaction was not procured as a result of any abuse of position the trustee will be required to demonstrate that no details were concealed from the beneficiaries, that the price obtained was fair and that the beneficiary was not required to rely entirely on the trustee's advice.

The fair-dealing principle is necessarily less strict than the self-dealing principle because the trustee is able to seek justification of the former by demonstrating that the transaction was not procured in bad faith. It is an unconscious aspect of the principle, nevertheless, that the beneficiaries are required to authorise the transaction rather than permitting the trustee to act entirely alone. However, where the beneficiary is an infant the trustee will not be able to demonstrate that the beneficiary made an informed decision.

The principle in *Hastings-Bass*: setting aside trustees' decisions

The key principles

In circumstances in which trustees have a power or are trustees over a discretionary trust, and if the trustees fail to take into account a relevant consideration or if they take into account an irrelevant consideration, then that exercise of the trustees' decision is voidable (and so may be set aside by the court so that they can make it again), provided that the trustees' original decision constituted a breach of trust. This proviso requiring that there must have been a breach of trust was confirmed by the Court of Appeal in *Pitt v Holt* (2011) and was approved by the Supreme Court in *Pitt v Holt* (2013). This development has had the effect of narrowing the principle. It is no longer sufficient simply to claim that professional advisors advising the trustees made a mistake; rather, there must also have been a breach of trust. Previously, trustees needed only to claim that they had failed to take into account a relevant factor (such as failing to appreciate that the trust would have suffered a charge to tax), or something similar, for the doctrine to apply.

Introduction

Imagine for a moment how wonderful your life would be if you had a 'magic eraser' with which you could wipe out all of your poor choices in life, before going back and making those choices again. In the law of trusts, the 'principle in *Hastings-Bass*' had once seemed to offer trustees and their advisors just such a magic eraser. This principle meant that the trustees of a discretionary trust, or trustees with a fiduciary power, could ask the court to set aside any inappropriate exercise of their powers or discretions so that they could make their choices again. This was particularly useful where the trustees and their advisors had inadvertently made a decision which had an unfortunate tax or other consequence for the trust.

The principle in *Hastings-Bass* had acquired a life of its own in recent years as the judgment of Buckley LJ in the case of *Re Hastings-Bass* (1975) was broadened beyond its original shape, particularly as a result of the judgment in *Mettoy Pension Fund Trustees Ltd v Evans* (1990). The decision of the Supreme Court in the joined cases of *Pitt v Holt* and *Futter v Futter* (2013) effectively overruled *Mettoy* and changed the law to a narrower model. The discussion to follow surveys the law before *Pitt v Holt*, before analysing the principles which were set out by Lloyd LJ in the Court of Appeal in *Pitt v Holt*, which Lord Walker approved in the Supreme Court in that case.

The road from Hastings-Bass to Pitt v Holt

In the judgment of Buckley LJ in the Court of Appeal in *Hastings-Bass* (1975) it was held that the court should not interfere with the trustees' decision unless:

> (1) what he had achieved is unauthorised by the power conferred upon him, or (2) it is clear that he would not have acted as he did (a) had he not taken into account considerations which he should not have taken into account, or (b) had he not failed to take into account considerations which he ought to have taken into account.

This formulation of the test was a 'negative' formulation in that the court would not interfere unless those elements were present.

However, Warner J held in *Mettoy Pension Fund Trustees Ltd v Evans* that the court would intervene if the trustees 'did not have a proper understanding of the effect of their act', without the need for a breach of trust. This had the effect of broadening the availability of this principle markedly because it meant that the court would undo a decision of the trustees if they had not understood, for example, that the trust would suffer a tax charge as a result of their decision. This was very popular among trusts law practitioners and trustees because it made it easy to unpick trustees' decisions and to make them again in a more advantageous way. In effect, trusts lawyers had been given a magic eraser by Warner J.

Nevertheless there were judgments, such as that of Lightman J in *Abacus Trust v Barr* (2003), which held that the doctrine should only be available if there had been a breach of trust. This meant that the trustees would only be able to reverse their decisions if they could show that they had actually committed a breach of trust when making that decision; otherwise, the decision would stick because it would be within their powers. There were other decisions, such as that of Lloyd LJ in *Sieff v Fox* (2005), which disagreed with this approach and which wanted effectively to continue with the approach set out in *Mettoy*.

The principle set out in Pitt v Holt

The decision of the Supreme Court in *Pitt v Holt* (2013) was centred on the judgment of Lord Walker. That judgment had the advantage of the very thorough judgment of Lloyd LJ in the Court of Appeal which was approved in general terms in relation to this principle (although it was doubted in relation to the law on mistake, which is considered below).

The judgment of Lloyd LJ in *Pitt v Holt* and *Futter v Futter* traced the original principle in *Hastings-Bass* back into its narrow form on the basis of a close reading of the judgment of Buckley LJ in that case. Lloyd LJ held that it is required that the trustees have committed a breach of trust before the principle can be invoked. Therefore, there must be some breach of the trust instrument or some breach of the general law of trusts before the principle can be invoked. Furthermore, the trustees must be demonstrated to have taken into account an irrelevant consideration or to have failed to take into account a relevant consideration, provided that in either case consideration was of an appropriate sort. (Thus, for example, the colour of the trustees' socks would not be appropriate because it would be unimportant to the operation of the trust, whereas the tax effect of their decision would be appropriate because that is clearly important to the operation of the trust.) Significantly, it was also confirmed that even if the principle applies, the trustees' decision is not automatically void, but rather it is merely voidable at the discretion of the court.

The remedy following the Hastings-Bass principle

To summarise, if the trustees have a power or the trust is a discretionary trust, and if the trustees fail to take into account a relevant consideration or if they take into account an irrelevant consideration, and if the trustees' original decision constituted a breach of trust, then the trustees' decision is voidable. That the decision is voidable means that it may be set aside by the court, if the court considers that to be appropriate, so that the trustees can make their decision again. The decision is not automatically void.

So, if the trustee failed to take into account the fact that the trust and its beneficiaries would suffer a large capital gains tax or inheritance tax charge, then that would be an example of a trustee failing to take into account a relevant consideration (*Green v Cobham* (2002), *Burrell v Burrell* (2005)). The effect would be that the trustee's decision would be set aside as though it had never been exercised in that way, with the happy result that the action that invoked the tax charge would be similarly revoked (*Re Hastings-Bass* (1975)).

Mistakes by trustees

There is a different doctrine from the *Hastings-Bass* principle which relates to mistakes which are made by trustees. The Supreme Court in *Pitt v Holt* (2013) cleared away the earlier case law in this area. Lord Walker in *Pitt v Holt* held that the court can set aside the exercise of a trustee's powers on grounds of mistake by reference to the following principles:

> The court cannot decide the issue of what is unconscionable by an elaborate set of rules. It must consider in the round the existence of a distinct mistake (as compared with total ignorance or disappointed expectations), its degree of centrality to the transaction in question and the seriousness of its consequences, and make an evaluative judgment whether it would be unconscionable, or unjust, to leave the mistake uncorrected. The court may and must form a judgment about the justice of the case.

Therefore, an exercise of the trustees' powers can be set aside on grounds of mistake if it would be unconscionable to leave that mistake uncorrected, and if the nature and significance of the mistake required that it be set aside.

Judicial review of trustees' actions

There is also a doctrine permitting the judicial review of trustees' decisions. In *Re Beloved Wilkes's Charity* (1851), Lord Truro held that there is a duty of supervision on the part of the court which will consider whether or not the trustees have acted with 'honesty, integrity, and fairness' in the exercise of their powers. If there was insufficient honesty, integrity or fairness then the trustees' decision may be set aside.

Provision of information

This section considers the ways in which beneficiaries are able to exert control over the administration of the trust. Typically, control will be exercised by petition to the court seeking a declaration as to the manner in which the trustees are required to act.

Control of the trustees by the beneficiaries

As has been made clear already, the most complete form of control for absolutely entitled, *sui juris* beneficiaries acting together is that they are able to terminate the trust by directing that the trustees deliver the trust property to them (*Saunders v Vautier* (1841)). What is less clear is the basis on which the trustees can be controlled during the life of the trust, that is, without calling for termination of the trust by delivery of the property to the beneficiaries. It is clear that the trustee cannot decide the terms of the trust (*Re Brook's ST* (1939)). Therefore, the trustee is necessarily bound by the terms of the trust, entitling the beneficiary to petition the court to have the trust administered in accordance with the terms of the trust. In *Re Brockbank* (1948), it was held that where the court is unable to interfere in the selection of trustees, the beneficiaries are similarly unable to act. *Tempest v Lord Camoys* (1882) illustrates the principle that the court will not interfere in the appointment of a new trustee, provided that it is done in accordance with the terms of the trust and not in contravention of public policy.

Control of the trustees by the court

The extent of the court's control of the trustees will depend upon the precise nature of the trust and whether the power given to the trustee is a personal power or a fiduciary power. Trustees are required to consider the exercise of fiduciary powers: they cannot exercise them entirely capriciously (*Re Hay's ST* (1981)). A trustee can act by personal choice where it is a personal power. In this latter circumstance the court will not interfere with the bona fide exercise of the power. Where trustees have a power of appointment, they are required to consider the exercise of their discretion and the range of the objects of their power (*Re Hay's ST; Turner v Turner*). However, the exercise of a discretion was set aside in *Turner v Turner* (1978), where the trustees failed to examine the contents of deeds before signing them.

Where a company has a power to distribute the surplus of an employee pension fund (where that fund is actually held by a trust company) the company has a fiduciary duty to distribute the proceeds of the pension fund (*Mettoy Pension Trustees Ltd v Evans* (1990)). This power is incapable of review by the court unless it is exercised capriciously or outside the scope of the trust. However, in *Mettoy*, because the power was held to be a fiduciary power, it was held that it could not be released or ignored by the fiduciary.

This meant that the company was always trustee of that power, with no beneficial interest in the fund. Therefore, when the company become insolvent, the liquidator could not take possession of the content of the trust fund and use it to pay off ordinary creditors of the company on the basis that the employee–contributors to the fund were not volunteers but rather beneficiaries under a trust.

Trustees must give informed consideration to the exercise of their discretion. The trustees may need to have reference to actuarial principles to come to a particular decision (*Stannard v Fisons* (1992)). The exercise of the decision of the trustees in *Stannard v Fisons* was found by Dillon LJ to be capable of review where such knowledge 'might materially have affected the trustees' decision'. One further argument in this context would be that a beneficiary is entitled to see documents with reference to the trust as part of the trustee's duty to account to the beneficiary of the trust, considered next.

The duty to give accounts and information

An important part of the ability of the beneficiaries to control the trustees is their ability to force the trustees to give accounts to them and also to give information as to the administration of the trust. As will become clear from the decided cases, there is a distinction drawn between cases of necessary confidentiality between trustee and settlor, cases concerning the trustees' exercise of their discretion as to the entitlement of beneficiaries to have interests in specific trust property, and cases concerning information as to the day-to-day management of the trust. The trustees are not, however, required to give all information to all beneficiaries, as will emerge from the following discussion. The various categories of information which might need to be given are considered in the sections below.

The extent of the requirement for trustees to give reasons for their decisions

Where trustees fail to explain the reasons for their decision to exercise their discretion in a particular way, the court may set aside that decision or require reasons to be given (*Re Beloved Wilkes Charity* (1851)). In that case, the trustees were required to select a boy from among a list of boys of given parishes. They chose a boy, not from one of those parishes, but rather one who was the brother of a minister who had sought help for his brother from one of the trustees. Lord Truro set aside the trustees' selection on the basis that it was done solely to benefit a person who had a nexus to the trustee and therefore was not a proper exercise of that power.

The court will look at the adequacy of reasons where they are given (*Klug v Klug* (1918)). Written material which gives minutes of management of trust property should be disclosed to beneficiaries but material relating to the exercise of discretions need not be (*Re Londonderry's Settlement* (1965)). It might be wondered why there is a difference in these two contexts. The rationale is that the former rule (concerning management of the trust fund) relates to professional management of the beneficiary's entitlement to the trust property, whereas the latter principle (concerning the exercise of discretion in connection with a discretionary trust) relates to a more fundamental question in that such exercise of the trustees' discretion decides whether or not the beneficiary will have an interest in the trust in any event. One issue deals with the competence of the trustees' management, whereas the latter relates to bias and the very entitlement of the beneficiary. The beneficiaries are entitled only to information about management and not about the fundamental nature of their rights – which, again, may seem strange in an era of expanding human rights law.

The duties of trustees in relation to confidential information

A further question might arise: are beneficiaries entitled to see a memorandum set out by the settlor giving her intentions with reference to the fund? Suppose the following set of facts: the settlor gave the trustees a memorandum setting out the settlor's intentions with reference to a power of appointment under the fund. The trustees then told the claimant's sister that they would not make an appointment to her because of the terms of the memorandum. In just such a case in New South Wales, the majority of the court followed the *Londonderry* decision in holding that the memorandum itself need not be shown to the beneficiary because it related to the exercise of the trustees' discretion (*Hartigan v Rydge* (1992)). Rather, there is an implied obligation of confidentiality between trustee and settlor, which would prevent the trustees from being obliged to disclose any such information.

In the Cayman Islands case of *Lemos v Coutts and Co* (1992), the *Londonderry* decision was also followed. Although a beneficiary has proprietary rights to trust documents, it was held not to be an absolute right. The court held that there may be categories of document that it is right to exclude from the beneficiaries. The right to see documents will be granted where they are evidentially important to the beneficiaries' case. The question that is not answered by that is whether the beneficiary should be allowed to see documents where there is no litigation pending.

The duty to give accounts

Trustees are required to give accounts and to provide details as to the decisions that have been made in accordance with the management of the trust (*Re Londonderry* (1965)). The beneficiaries, or the class of objects of a power, are entitled to be informed of a decision, but are not entitled to be given the reasons as to why that decision was taken, as considered above. In similar vein, the beneficiaries are entitled to accounts that disclose the investment policy of the trust and to minutes of meetings not related to confidential matters. As Lord Wrenbury held in *O'Rourke v Derbishire* (1920):

> A beneficiary has a right of access to the documents which he desires to inspect upon what has been called in the judgments in this case a proprietary right. The beneficiary is entitled to see all trust documents, because they are trust documents, and because he is a beneficiary. They are, in this sense, his own.

The question is then as to the nature of documents that can properly be described as 'trust documents'. The contents of that category have been found to be incapable of precise definition (*Re Londonderry* (1965)). This obligation to provide information (albeit of limited types) is an important part of the control of the conscience of the trustee by the court and by the beneficiaries. Without such information it would be impossible in many circumstances to commence the type of litigation dealt with in Chapter 10.

The opinion of Lord Walker in the Privy Council in *Schmidt v Rosewood Trust Ltd* (2003) suggested a different approach to trustees' obligations to provide information to beneficiaries. Lord Walker held that the courts have a general discretion as to whether or not disclosure of information should be ordered, and thus that the courts should not be bound by the approach in *O'Rourke v Derbishire*. In that case Lord Walker broached an interesting and difficult problem. A member of the class of objects under a discretionary trust does not own outright any part of the equitable interest in any part of the trust property unless and until the trustees exercise their discretion in his favour – until that time he is simply entitled to ensure that the trustees exercise their powers appropriately. Consequently, a member of the class of objects under a discretionary trust has no distinct property rights that under the doctrine in *O'Rourke v Derbishire* would entitle her to disclosure of information. As Lord Walker held, such a person would have no necessary right to disclosure of information.

The result of the approach in *Schmidt v Rosewood*, it is suggested, will increase litigation by requiring beneficiaries to approach the courts to find out whether or not they are entitled to disclosure of information. Furthermore, it is difficult to commence litigation for breach of trust as a beneficiary if you are not permitted any information on which to base that claim. For example, how can an object under a discretionary trust know whether or not to commence litigation for an inappropriate exercise of the trustees' discretion if she is not entitled to any information about the basis on which that decision was made? The answer presented to this question on the cases is that the other objects of the trust are entitled to their privacy but, it is suggested, if the beneficiary principle is of paramount importance (requiring that there be someone in whose favour the court can decree performance) then it is necessary that all of the objects have access to as much information as possible.

The problem which remains from these limitations in the obligation to give information is that it will be impossible for the beneficiaries to sue the trustees for breach of trust if they do not have the information to demonstrate their claim. This issue was considered by Briggs J in his very full judgment in *Breakspear v Ackland* (2008). In that case a beneficiary sought disclosure of a settlor's 'letter of wishes', which is a non-binding letter to the trustees indicating how the settlor would like the trustees to exercise their powers. Briggs J ordered disclosure of the letter of wishes on the facts of the case before him. His Lordship acknowledged further to *Re Londonderry* that the trustee's 'discretionary dispositive powers' remained 'inherently confidential', with the result that the letter of wishes was similarly confidential in ordinary circumstances. However, on the facts of that case, Briggs J considered that the circumstances and the best interests of the beneficiaries required it.

His Lordship identified a weakness in the decision in *Schmidt v Rosewood* in that if the resolution of the question depended on the court's discretion, then trustees would be required to bring litigation on every occasion, which would be very expensive. Briggs J identified a key tension in this area: on the one hand, there is a traditional preference for confidentiality (which is likely to find favour among trustees), while on the other hand, modern mores prefer openness in financial dealings as opposed to secrecy. His Lordship was bound by precedent and the confidentiality in *Re Londonderry*, but was evidently in favour of greater transparency in trust dealings. The principle remains that the trustees are advised to seek a court order before bringing or defending proceedings. It was held in

Wilson v Law Debenture Trust Corporation plc (1995) that the trustees of a pension fund who had been given a discretionary power ought not to be required to disclose the reasons for their decisions precisely because the creators of the pension scheme intended to prevent that so as to minimise litigation.

The exclusion of trustees' liabilities

A provision in a trust instrument which restricts the liability of the trustee for breach of trust will be valid, unless it purports to exclude liability for dishonesty or unless it purports to exclude that person's core fiduciary liability. The case of *Armitage v Nurse* (1998) (decided before the enactment of the Trustee Act 2000 discussed above) held that a clause excluding a trustee's personal liability for breach of trust would be valid, even where it purported to limit that trustee's liability for gross negligence. In explaining the limit of the trustee's obligations, Millett LJ held that:

> [T]here is an irreducible core of obligations owed by the trustees to the beneficiaries and enforceable by them which is fundamental to the concept of a trust. If the beneficiaries have no rights enforceable against the trustees there are no trusts. But I do not accept the further submission that their core obligations include the duties of skill and care, prudence and diligence. The duty of trustees to perform the trusts honestly and in good faith for the benefit of the beneficiaries is the minimum necessary to give substance to the trusts, but in my opinion it is sufficient . . . a trustee who relied on the presence of a trustee exemption clause to justify what he proposed to do would thereby lose its protection: he would be acting recklessly in the proper sense of the term.

Therefore, a trustee may have her liability for breach of trust excluded by an express provision in the trust instrument. In this case, the trustees were thus able to exclude their liabilities for gross negligence. However, the clause would have been invalid if it had purported to exclude the trustees' liability for a breach of trust which they had caused by acting dishonestly or fraudulently, and if the trustees had indeed been dishonest or had acted fraudulently. In *Barraclough v Mell* (2005) it was held that trustees could also exclude their liability for recklessness. It is not an objection to such an exclusion clause that the trustee was a solicitor who drafted that provision (*Bogg v Raper* (1998/99)).

The problem with the approach in *Armitage v Nurse* and the cases which have followed it is that, in practice, it means that professional trustees who will know to include a term in the trust instrument to exclude their liability will escape liability for negligence; whereas non-professional trustees who do not know to have such a clause included in the trust instrument will therefore be fully liable for any breach of trust, including a negligent one. This puts professional trustees at an illogical advantage when compared to people who never claimed to have any professional skills to act as a trustee. Furthermore, if trustees are required to act in good conscience (as in *Westdeutsche Landesbank v Islington* (1996)) then allowing trustees to be careless or negligent (if not dishonest) appears to be contrary to that obligation of good conscience.

The Privy Council considered the law relating to the exclusion of liability of trustees in an appeal from Guernsey in *Spread Trustee Company Ltd v Hutcheson* (2011). A statute enacted in 1989 in Guernsey permitted liability to be excluded for negligence and gross negligence but not for fraud nor for wilful default. It was accepted by Lord Clarke (speaking for the majority) that there were instances in which English law does differentiate between ordinary negligence and 'gross negligence', contrary to what Millett LJ had held in *Armitage v Nurse*. Nevertheless, it was accepted that under English law, since *Armitage v Nurse*, liability could be excluded for gross negligence. Nevertheless, the point was not without some difficulty. Lady Hale doubted that English law had always been clear about the treatment of grossly negligent breaches of trust. Most interestingly, Lord Kerr made the following pertinent point, at paragraph 180:

> If . . . the placing of reliance on a responsible person to manage property so as to promote the interests of the beneficiaries of a trust is central to the concept of trusteeship, denying trustees the opportunity to avoid liability for their gross negligence seems to be entirely in keeping with that essential aim.

His Lordship meant that a trustee ought not to be able to exclude liability for gross negligence. A trustee is a fiduciary who is required to act selflessly in the interests of her beneficiaries, or to take proper advice where that is not otherwise possible. It is not too high a standard to set for that person to avoid grossly negligent performances of those duties. The decision in *Armitage v Nurse* is both an opiate on the professionalism of trustees and an opiate on their consciences.

What is the core of a trustee's obligations?

The question 'What is the core of a trustee's obligations?' remains unanswered on the authorities in the sense that there is no single comprehensive list of the obligations that all trustees will owe to all beneficiaries. In this chapter we have identified some of the key obligations incumbent on trustees, such as avoiding conflicts of interest and providing identified forms of information to the beneficiaries, but we have not produced a definitive list that will apply in equal measure to all trusts. One reason for this is the ability of trustees to limit their liability for negligence and other wrongs in a contract with the settlor (*Armitage v Nurse* (1998)); another reason relates to the large number of trusts in relation to which there are specific statutory codes, such as pensions and unit trusts, which identify the limit and extent of the obligations of trustees in those particular contexts. Trustees may not act dishonestly, even if a contract governing their obligations purports to exclude their liability for dishonesty in the course of their duties (*Walker v Stones* (2001)). However, to say that trustees may not act dishonestly in the discharge of their duties is hardly progressive, nor is it sufficient to help us know what marks out a trustee in contradistinction to people holding other types of office.

To understand the nature of trusteeship, we need to begin at the beginning. Trusteeship is imposed on a person who is required by ties of conscience to recognise the rights of others in equity to that property (*Westdeutsche Landesbank v Islington* (1996)). In relation to express trusts, the express declaration of trust by the settlor is sufficient to create that obligation. As considered in Chapters 6 and 7, it is also possible that the courts will infer from the circumstances an obligation on that trustee to hold the property on trust for the benefit of another person, not due to some declaration of trust, but rather because good conscience requires that person so to do.

The express exclusion of the trustee's obligations by means of contract could be thought of as a problematic test of the extent of a trustee's obligations. On the one hand, it could be said that it would be wrong to impose obligations on a trustee if the only basis on which she agreed to act was that her liability to account to the beneficiaries for breach of trust would be limited as set out in the contract. On the other hand, it could be said that no trustee should be allowed to act negligently in relation to the treatment of the trust fund, if one is to observe the strict obligations of a trustee to account to the beneficiaries for any reduction in the value of the trust fund (see Chapter 10).

To understand these questions a little better, we will need to consider the potential for the imposition of trusts by the courts in the coming chapters.

Moving on . . .

The foregoing gives a flavour of the obligations of the trustee, although the remainder of the book remains concerned with the situations in which the obligations on a trustee will be imposed on a defendant – whether by the voluntary act of a settlor or by the operation of law. Chapters 6 and 7 consider those forms of trust that are implied by law.

Chapter 6

Resulting trusts

What is a resulting trust?

The resulting trust is a means by which equity resolves problems as to the ownership of property where transfers are not effected properly or where people buy
property together. A resulting trust arises in either of two circumstances
(*Westdeutsche Landesbank v Islington* (1996)). First, a resulting trust will arise
where a settlor has sought to transfer property or to declare a trust but has failed
to make clear who is intended to take those rights, with the result that any rights
left unallocated pass back to the settlor on resulting trust. Second, where the
claimant has contributed to the purchase price of property, the claimant acquires
an equitable interest in the property on resulting trust in proportion to the size of
her contribution.

The details of each of these forms of resulting trust are considered below. It is
worth considering the purpose of resulting trusts first, however. The resulting
trust is a form of trust implied by law: that is, a resulting trust is imposed by the
court in the circumstances considered below without any of the parties having
intended that such a trust be created. Rickett and Grantham (2000) have argued
that the resulting trust is therefore best thought of as a means of allocating ownership in property where that ownership is unclear, and nothing more than that. It
connects with the basic notions of 'trust' in that the common law owner would not
be entitled to assert beneficial ownership but rather would be bound to hold that
property on trust for the previous owner. As considered towards the end of this
chapter, arguments advanced by a range of academics for a broader role for the
resulting trust were rejected in the leading case of *Westdeutsche Landesbank
v Islington* (1996) in favour of the two limited categories set out above: we shall
consider each of those categories in turn.

Automatic resulting trusts

The automatic resulting trust operates a little like a ball on a piece of elastic. If the
settlor attempts to throw the ball away – either by transferring the property to
somebody else or by purporting to declare a trust over it – but fails to make clear

who is to take the beneficial interest in that property, then those unallocated beneficial rights will bounce back to the settlor just as a ball on a piece of elastic would. The problem that property law faces is the following one: it is said that property cannot be without an owner. The law of property requires that all rights in property are owned by someone. As such, it is impossible (in theory) to abandon property because someone must agree to assume the rights and the obligations of its owner. Therefore, if the settlor fails to identify the intended owner of property, the law requires that someone be its owner. The answer that equity has developed is to hold that the equitable interest in the property passes back to its previous owner on resulting trust.

This principle can be best explained by means of some examples from case law. The case of *Vandervell v IRC* (1967) was considered in Chapter 4. In that case, Mr Vandervell sought to transfer shares that were held on trust for him to the Royal College of Surgeons. His intention was to recover the equitable interest in those shares once a dividend had been paid to the Royal College. This convoluted stratagem enabled Mr Vandervell to make a tax-efficient donation to the College. To recover the shares, Mr Vandervell created an option to buy the shares back from the College. However, what Mr Vandervell did not do was to explain who was to be the owner of the option to repurchase the shares. The option was found to constitute an equitable interest in the shares. Therefore the court was faced with a situation in which there was an equitable interest in existence without an owner. Equity deals with such a situation by holding that the equitable interest returns on resulting trust to its previous owner. On these facts that meant that the equitable interest in the shares returned to Mr Vandervell on resulting trust.

Similarly, if the trust fails for some reason, the equitable interest will return to the settlor on resulting trust. So, in *Re Cochrane's ST* (1955), the entire estates of two spouses were settled on trust for those spouses as beneficiaries provided that they remained married. The wife left her husband; the husband subsequently died. The wife claimed to be entitled to her husband's estate; whereas the husband's other relatives contended that the termination of the marriage ought to constitute a failure of the settlement. The court agreed that the failure of the marriage constituted a failure of the trust. Therefore, all of the property that the husband had contributed to the settlement returned to the husband on resulting trust and was consequently distributed among his relatives in accordance with his will. Similarly, in *Re Ames' Settlement* (1964), where a marriage was declared to have been null and void, it was held that the marriage settlement predicated on that marriage was similarly ineffective. The property settled on trust was held on resulting trust for its settlors.

In these circumstances, the resulting trust operates simply to fill a gap in the title over property. The simplest, common-sense approach to the question 'Who owns this property?' is to decide that 'the property should belong to whoever had it last'. There is one logical problem with this doctrine, however. The problem is with the assertion that the title goes *back* to the settlor. That would require that the property leaves the settlor before going back. In the case, for example, of

Vandervell, it is not at all clear that the property ever left Mr Vandervell. It would seem that if no new owner of the equitable interest was ever identified then the equitable interest should be treated as having *remained* with Vandervell throughout.

An alternative explanation which was advanced by Harman J in *Re Gillingham Bus Disaster Fund* (1958) was that the resulting trust should be understood as being a form of trust which arises *sub modo*. That means, each type of resulting trust could be understood as arising on its own terms – therefore, the *Vandervell* trust could be understood simply as occupying a category of its own in resolving the ownership of that property.

Again, this is an example of the logic of trusts law finding difficulties in adapting to novel factual situations, as discussed in Chapter 2.

Purchase price resulting trusts

The second form of resulting trust identified by Lord Browne-Wilkinson in *Westdeutsche Landesbank v Islington* (1996) arises in the following situation:

> Where A makes a voluntary payment to B or pays (wholly or in part) for the purchase of property which is vested either in B alone or in the joint names of A and B, there is a presumption that A did not intend to make a gift to B: the money or property is held on trust for A (if he is the sole provider of the money) or in the case of a joint purchase by A and B in shares proportionate to their contributions.

What these *dicta* indicate are the following ideas. Traditionally, there is a presumption that where two people contribute to the purchase of property, that property is intended to be held on trust for those contributors by whoever is the common law owner of the property. So, if Xena buys the freehold over a small workshop for the designer clothes business which she runs together with Yasmin for £800,000 with £400,000 of her own money and with £400,000 belonging to Yasmin, but if Xena had the property registered in her sole name at the Land Registry, then it would be *presumed* that the property is held on resulting trust by Xena as trustee for Xena and Yasmin in equal shares. That presumption can be displaced if some other intention can be proved. So, for example, if it can be proved that Yasmin was only intended to make a loan of money to Xena which Xena was to repay, then the workshop would not be held on resulting trust because Yasmin would not be intended to take any equitable interest in it.

Latterly this presumption has been displaced specifically in relation to disputes as to the equitable ownership of the home between unmarried couples. It was held in *Stack v Dowden* (2007), and in *Jones v Kernott* (2011), that the resulting trust should not arise automatically in cases relating to the home and that instead the presumption should be that the equitable ownership mirrors the legal title (as considered in the next section of this chapter).

Presumptions and resulting trust

There were a number of situations in which presumptions have operated histori-cally in relation to resulting trusts. Those presumptions require some explanation. There will be situations in which it is not possible for the court to have it proved conclusively what two parties' intentions were in relation to property. For example, Xena may purport to transfer a valuable painting to her son Xavier on his birthday but with the sole intention of making it appear to her creditors that she does not have any property rights in that painting. In that situation, when the creditors have been paid off, Xena would seek to recover the painting but Xavier may refuse to return the painting. Both parties will advance contradictory argu-ments: Xena will argue that she did not intend to make a gift of the painting whereas Xavier will argue that it was a birthday present. In that situation, the court would not know which argument to prefer. Therefore, the court will rely on presumptions in some cases to decide how to allocate title in such cases where the evidence is not conclusive.

So, what are these presumptions? It was presumed by the courts of equity that there were certain situations in which men, and only men, would be assumed to have intended to transfer property to their children and to their wives. The basis for these presumptions was that only men/husbands owned property and that, as a consequence, those men should provide for the maintenance of their wives and chil-dren who had no property of their own. Clearly, these assumptions are something of an anachronism now. The House of Lords, in *Pettitt v Pettitt* (1970), suggested that these presumptions ought not to be applied in cases relating to rights in the family home any more. The Equality Act 2010 has abolished the presumption of advance-ment prospectively. So, under s 199 of that Act, it is provided that 'the presumption of advancement is abolished' but that abolition applies only to 'anything done' after the Act has come into effect. Under s 198 of the Act it is provided that '[t]he rule of common law that a husband must maintain his wife is abolished'.

As discussed in Chapter 9, in relation to trusts of homes there will be a presump-tion that if the legal title over the home is held in joint names then the equitable ownership of the home is presumed to be held jointly, whereas if the legal title is in the name of one only of the parties then it is presumed that the equitable interest is held by that same person alone (*Jones v Kernott* (2011)).

When a presumption does operate, it is nevertheless open to the defendant to seek to rebut that presumption. In short, the defendant must convince the court that he did not intend to make a gift of the property (*Fowkes v Pascoe* (1875)). The presumption in *Jones v Kernott* may be rebutted by cogent evidence which suggests that the common intention of the parties was something different. If the defendant is successful in demonstrating that his purpose was not to make a gift of the property to the other party, then that property will be held on resulting trust for the defendant. The real difficulty has arisen where the defendant has had an illegal purpose in placing the property in the other person's hands; that issue is considered next.

Illegality and resulting trust

The problem of illegality in trusts based on good conscience

We live in a cruel world in which people often seek to do unlawful things. For example, we mentioned in the previous section that Xena was transferring property to her son Xavier to avoid her creditors. What this means is that Xena owes money to people and faces the prospect of being made bankrupt if she does not pay. In that situation it is common for the person fearing bankruptcy to try to hide all of their assets (their home, car and movable property) by putting them in the name of a friend or relative and claiming not to have any rights in them. This is an illegal act under insolvency law. The difficulty in this situation is that to rebut a presumption of advancement, or simply to prove her entitlement to a resulting trust, Xena must tell the court, 'I can prove that I did not intend to make a gift because what I was really doing was trying to commit an illegal act.' It was an old principle of equity that a claimant cannot have committed an illegal act and also be entitled to an equitable remedy (*Gascoigne v Gascoigne* (1918)).

An example of this occurred in *Tinker v Tinker* (1970) in which Mr Tinker was attempting to put his property unlawfully out of the reach of his creditors, ostensibly by transferring that property to his wife. Subsequently, his marriage broke down and Mr Tinker sought to convince the court that this particular property did not belong to his wife but rather ought to be considered to be held on resulting trust for him. His wife contended that the presumption of advancement applied (because it was a case of a husband transferring possession of property to his wife) and that her husband was therefore required to rely on evidence of his own illegality (i.e. that he was unlawfully avoiding his creditors). Lord Denning held that Mr Tinker could not claim to his creditors that this property belonged to his wife and simultaneously wish to convince the court that the property remained his on resulting trust. Therefore, the property was declared to belong absolutely beneficially to Mrs Tinker.

The preference for logic over ethical behaviour

So far so good. Unfortunately, as was said at the very beginning of this book, while legal systems may seek to develop certain rules, the factual situations that are thrown up in front of them will always challenge the desirability of such rules. So, it became clear that there would be situations involving illegality in which the courts would wish nevertheless to use an equitable remedy. The House of Lords had to consider the following situation in *Tinsley v Milligan* (1993). Kathleen Milligan and Stella Tinsley were a couple who had acquired a guesthouse together. They ran the guesthouse as a joint business venture. It was decided between them that the property would be put in Tinsley's sole name so that Milligan could attempt to defraud the social security system by claiming entitlement to housing benefit on the basis that she had no rights in any property. Milligan was convicted of a criminal offence as a result of this illegal act. A dispute arose between the two, whereby Tinsley claimed to be absolutely entitled to the house. Milligan contended that her agreement to the house being placed in the sole name of Tinsley was not intended to constitute a gift to Tinsley but was intended only to facilitate her illegal act; therefore, she claimed to be entitled to half of the equitable interest in the property on the basis of a purchase price resulting trust. Tinsley argued that Milligan could not be entitled to a resulting trust because she had committed an illegal act.

Tinsley's argument was accepted by Lord Goff in a strong dissenting judgment on the basis that one should 'come to equity with clean hands'. Being a convicted criminal in relation to this scheme, it was held by Lord Goff that Milligan could not do that. Lord Browne-Wilkinson, however, spoke for the majority of the House of Lords in finding that Milligan ought to be entitled to a right under resulting trust principles. His Lordship's approach was strictly logical – indicating a great difference of approach from Lord Goff's general ethical approach. It was held that Milligan's right in the house stemmed from the fact that she had contributed to the purchase price of the property and had thus acquired an equitable interest in the property on resulting trust. That she had committed an illegal act did not affect the fact that her contribution to the purchase price had already granted her that right. Therefore, the old rule in *Gascoigne v Gascoigne* was abrogated. She was held to be entitled to a right on resulting trust principles because her right flowed from her cash contribution to the purchase price and not from her illegal act in defrauding the social security system.

In a further example of this preference amongst the judiciary for logic over ethics, in the case of *Tribe v Tribe* (1995) it was held that it was permissible for a person to intend to commit an illegal act but not actually to carry it out, and still acquire rights under resulting trust. Mr Tribe was convinced that he would be made bankrupt as a result of a large amount of work needing to be done to property over which he held a lease. Therefore, he committed the illegal act of putting his shares in a family company beyond the reach of his creditors by transferring them to his son. Mr Tribe was very fortunate because the lessor agreed not to force him to pay for the work on the property and instead agreed simply to terminate the lease. Therefore, Mr Tribe did not go into bankruptcy. However, the son refused to return the shares to his father, claiming that they were the subject of a presumption of a gift to him. Millett LJ held that Mr Tribe was entitled to rely on his illegal purpose to prove that his intention was to reserve the equitable interest in the shares to himself because that illegal purpose had not been carried out; by Mr Tribe not going into bankruptcy there were no bankruptcy creditors who could be said to have been defrauded, therefore, technically, no illegal act had been performed. What is remarkable is that Mr Tribe was entitled to rely on a remedy of good conscience in equity despite having intended to commit an illegal act if he had been made bankrupt.

What is difficult about this approach is that Mr Tribe clearly intended to carry out an illegal act and he had done everything necessary to carry that illegal purpose through when he purported to transfer his shares to his son. It is a little like an assassin who takes aim and fires a bullet at her target only for a bus to kill the target half a second before the bullet would have struck. In both cases, an illegal act was intended and the actions necessary for that act were carried out; but good luck intervened so as to prevent those actions from having their intended effect. Ethically, it is suggested, Mr Tribe and the assassin would be in the same position because they intended their actions and willed their outcome; yet Mr Tribe has the assistance of equity in the form of a resulting trust in his favour.

Sham transactions

Thus far we have said that it is to the benefit of the rogue to argue that property is held on resulting trust. For example, Milligan and Tribe were able to retain rights in property by arguing for a resulting trust in their favour in spite of their illegal purposes. In the case of *Midland Bank v Wyatt* (1995), the finding of a resulting trust was to the detriment of the rogue. Mr Wyatt was entering into a risky business venture and wanted to put his home beyond the reach of any creditors in the event that the business went into insolvency. Therefore, Wyatt purported to transfer his half-share in the matrimonial home into an express trust in favour of his wife and daughters. However, Wyatt continued to use the house as security for business loans as if he continued to have an equitable interest in it. Also, when he and his wife divorced subsequently, neither his wife nor his wife's solicitors were aware of the express trust in her favour. In consequence, the court held that the express trust was a sham. Wyatt's business did collapse and Wyatt's personal creditors sought to argue that Wyatt retained rights in the house, which should therefore be sold and the proceeds divided amongst the creditors. Wyatt argued that the express trust had transferred title in the house to his wife and daughters. By demonstrating that the express trust was a sham (and by relying on the general powers to unpick transactions under s 423 of the Insolvency Act 1986) the court held that the house was held on resulting trust for Wyatt. In consequence, the house formed part of Wyatt's estate and therefore fell to be divided among his creditors. That was the very thing that Wyatt had wished to avoid. In this situation, good conscience was served by imposing a resulting trust and paying off Wyatt's creditors.

The death of the restitutionary resulting trust in *Westdeutsche Landesbank v Islington*

The law of restitution (of unjust enrichment)

So far, this book has presented resulting trusts as a subject untrammelled by dispute or controversy; unfortunately that is not the case. In 1966, Lord Goff and Professor Jones wrote a book called *The Law of Restitution*, which sought to show that there was a general principle of 'unjust enrichment' at work in English law.

It was said, broadly speaking, that a number of well-understood claims and remedies could be understood as operating on one common principle: the reversal of unjust enrichment. It was said that rescission of contracts, claims in tort and even the resulting trust operated so as to reverse unjust enrichment or to achieve restitution for some form of wrongdoing.

In 1992, Professor Birks contended that the principal means by which English law should develop was to recognise that the resulting trust should effect such restitution of unjust enrichment in all cases where the claimant sought to recover some particular property as part of her claim for restitution; claims merely for money would continue to be satisfied by personal claims for restitution. It was said that the resulting trust, was the perfect vehicle to effect restitution because under a resulting trust rights in property are held on trust by the common law owner of that property for the person who last had such rights in the property at issue. This resulting trust was said to arise in any situation in which the defendant had acquired rights in property belonging to the claimant as a result of some unjust factor. The term 'unjust factor' was in itself left undefined. Examples of unjust factors would include mistakes, misrepresentations and undue influence. Therefore, it was said that if the property rights passed from the claimant to the defendant as a result of a mistake, then the defendant ought to hold such rights on resulting trust for the claimant.

This suggested a huge expansion of the limited categories of resulting trust that had been recognised at English law before this time. In 1996, the House of Lords gave judgment in a case, *Westdeutsche Landesbank v Islington*, which put this new model resulting trust to the test.

The Westdeutsche Landesbank *litigation*

In *Westdeutsche Landesbank v Islington* (1996) a local authority had entered into a contract with a bank whereby the bank paid £2.5 million to the local authority, subject to an obligation on the local authority to repay that money over time. The terms of the contract are too complex to be worthy of discussion here. They related to a complex financial product known as an interest rate swap. The interested reader might wish to consult either Hudson (2013) or Hudson (1999a) for detailed examinations of these areas of finance law. The contract between the local authority and the bank was due to last for ten years but after five years another high-profile case informed the parties that their contract had been void *ab initio* (that is, the contract had never been validly made) because it was beyond the powers of the local authority to enter into it (*Hazell v Hammersmith & Fulham LBC* (1991)). By this time the local authority had spent the money transferred to it by the bank. The bank wished to recover its money and also to recover compound interest on that money. Compound interest is a higher effective rate of interest than simple interest because it would have entitled the bank to recover interest on the interest payments as well as on the capital payments owed to it by the local authority. However, it was held by the House of Lords that such compound interest would only have been available to the bank if the bank could have demonstrated that it had retained some proprietary right in the money that it had transferred to the local authority at the beginning of the contract.

If Professor Birks's analysis had been applied to this case, the House of Lords would have held that either the parties' mistake in thinking that their contract was valid, or alternatively the failure of consideration caused by the invalidity of their contract, constituted an unjust factor which should have meant that the local authority held the money for the bank on resulting trust – thus entitling the bank to compound interest, in effect, approximately an extra £1 million on their judgment. However, the majority of the House of Lords rejected Professor Birks's argument (referring to it expressly) by favouring an article written by another academic, Mr Swadling (1996), which recommended that the resulting trust be restricted to only two categories; as considered at the beginning of this chapter.

Lord Browne-Wilkinson gave the leading speech for the majority in the House of Lords. His Lordship held that the bank had transferred the money outright to the local authority and therefore had given up all title in that property. In consequence, it could not be said that any money was held on resulting trust for the bank by the local authority. Further, the local authority would not be bound by any principle of constructive trust (as considered in the following chapter) because at the time it received the money, the local authority honestly believed that the contract was valid and that it was therefore entitled to take that money; therefore, its conscience was not affected until after it had spent all of the money. Similarly, the bank was not entitled to trace its rights in the loan moneys into any of the local authority's bank accounts (as considered in Chapter 10) because all of the money had been spent. Furthermore, because the bank account into which the money had been paid had been run overdrawn, the local authority was held to have disposed of any last vestige of the original money loaned to it. In consequence, the bank acquired no proprietary rights at all in relation to the money and therefore was not entitled to compound interest.

Significantly, Professor Birks's theory was disposed of and the mooted massive expansion of the resulting trust was prevented. Lord Browne-Wilkinson held, as set out at the beginning of this chapter, that resulting trusts arise only in circumstances in which the equitable interest has not been fully disposed of or where the claimant has contributed to the purchase price of property. Importantly, the resulting trust will not operate in any other circumstances, it is said. Not even Lord Goff was prepared to go into bat for the restitution argument: his dissenting speech focused solely on the question of whether or not it was 'just' in general terms to allow compound interest in general terms without the need to demonstrate a proprietary interest in any property.

While this may seem in hindsight a minor point which caused a senior judge to reject one academic's argument, it did cause an extraordinary amount of ink to be spilled at the time – not least by this writer. The local authority swaps cases (as the 200 writs which were served on this and similar issues have become known collectively) raise a huge spectrum of questions as to the rights of local authorities to contract, the troubled interaction of equity and commerce, and the role of trusts and unjust enrichment. At present, equity has managed to stay the advances of restitution theory on this front. The trust was held to be based on conscience and on equitable principles. Thus everything remains safe, dependable and secure. For Professor Birks's own litany of his dead and wounded after the battle of *Westdeutsche*, the reader is referred to Birks (1996).

Moving on . . .

This chapter has given us a taste of one example of a trust implied by law. It has also suggested the ways in which theories about the desirability of expanding those doctrines in various ways have developed. This discussion has been necessarily brief. The reader is referred to my *Equity & Trusts* (Hudson, 2014), Chapter 11, for the full five courses and coffee on this topic.

The following chapter considers the broadest form of trust implied by law: the constructive trust.

Chapter 7

Constructive trusts

What is a constructive trust?

Constructive trusts arise by operation of law. That means that constructive trusts are imposed by the courts, and are not created expressly by the parties. Constructive trusts are the clearest example of how equity seeks to achieve fair results on a case-by-case basis. In *Westdeutsche Landesbank v Islington* (1996), Lord Browne-Wilkinson explained a constructive trust as arising in any circumstance in which the defendant deals with property in circumstances in which the defendant knows that she is acting in an unconscionable manner. For example, stealing property is an unconscionable act in relation to that property, and so the thief will be treated as constructive trustee of that property.

In this chapter we will consider the principal examples of unconscionability which give rise to constructive trusts. As will emerge in this chapter, there are two means of using constructive trusts: either to create an institutional, proprietary constructive trust over identified property, or as a means of imposing liability to account on a defendant who has participated in a breach of trust.

When considering the ways in which proprietary constructive trusts come into existence we can divide them between general constructive trusts, constructive trusts relating to interference with property, constructive trusts relating to voluntary agreements, and constructive trusts used to reinforce fiduciary responsibilities. These categories are considered in the discussion that follows in this chapter. Before coming to specifics, however, it is important to understand some of the key ideas underpinning this area of law and in particular the notion of 'good conscience'.

The idea of conscience

As considered in Chapter 2, the notion of good conscience is at the heart of the trust: it is said that a trust comes into operation to control the conscience of the common law owner of property. However, what is not clear is the precise ambit of this term 'conscience'. We may think it less than completely honest for me to lie to someone with a clipboard in the street wanting to do some market research that I have an urgent appointment and could not possibly stop, but we would not consider that to create any legal liability against me. Similarly, we would use the term 'white lie' if I told a friend who was wearing a grotesque nylon shirt that I thought they looked 'just fabulous', but we would not expect me to be legally liable to them in any way. I would suggest that we have a range of prima facie untruthful actions that we do not necessarily consider to be *unconscionable*, even though they involve some minor levels of deceit. So, in this chapter, we will identify more clearly where that boundary line is.

Conscience, knowledge and constructive trusts

Constructive trusts are imposed when a defendant had knowledge of some factor which should have affected her conscience in relation to property. To put it crudely:

Conscience + Knowledge = Constructive Trust

The question is to identify those situations in which a person's conscience will be deemed to have been affected. This chapter considers the principal categories of unconscionable activity but those categories are elastic and can develop in the future. It will be clear that someone who deliberately commits a fraud will be deemed to have acted unconscionably. The question is then as to the potential for expanding those categories further. Clearly, the decided cases constitute the best means of identifying the meaning of the term conscience in this context. A good example arose in *Bank of Ireland v Pexxnet Ltd* (2010), where the defendants presented forged documents to a bank so that the bank would credit their account with 2.4 million euro. This was held to constitute an unconscionable act which, further to *Westdeutsche Landesbank v Islington*, meant that that money was to be held on constructive trust by the fraudsters for the bank.

The tests of knowledge used in trusts law (particularly in Chapter 10 in relation to 'knowing receipt' of property in breach of trust) expressly not only incorporate standards of actual knowledge but also deem a defendant to have knowledge where that defendant wilfully shut her eyes to the obvious (i.e. pretended to ignore that something was obviously wrong) or failed to make the enquiries that an honest person would have made in their position (*Baden v Société Generale* (1993)). These adaptations to the standard of knowledge necessarily imply some objectivity: that is, the court will be using an objective standard of conscionable conduct to decide whether or not a given defendant had done what the court would have expected a person to do in that situation. That is very different from saying 'What did you actually know?' because, instead, it requires the court to ask merely 'What do I think someone acting in good conscience would have done in this situation?' This objective approach has been adopted by the courts in the creation of a test of *dishonesty*, considered later in this chapter and in Chapter 10 in relation to 'dishonest assistance', which focuses on what an honest person would have done in the defendant's situation, rather than on what the defendant can actually be proved to have known (*Royal Brunei Airlines v Tan* (1995)).

To frame this objective approach around a test of 'good conscience' feels uncomfortable precisely because a conscience seems at first blush to be such a personal thing. For a psychiatrist to unearth and explain the conscience of an individual would involve a necessarily subjective process of examining that person's childhood, their environment and so forth. However, the objective nature of this conscience was considered in Chapter 1 (at p 5): in psychological terms, the conscience contains a large amount of objectively constituted material and therefore is something which can be objectively assessed. What equity does is to identify an objective idea of what an honest person would have done in the circumstances and then ask whether or not the defendant behaved in that way. The concern is not with the subjective morality of the defendant.

It is suggested that the constructive trust is the clearest means by which this is done in relation to the use of property. The doctrine of constructive trust is criticised by Professor Birks (1989), among others, because it operates in such a broad number of contexts that to impose a constructive trust does not explain what the defendant has done wrong in the same clear way that the criminal offence of murder, for example, explains that the defendant has committed a murder. Nevertheless, it is suggested that the constructive trust operates generally as an ethical control of the manner in which a person may deal with another's property rights. That is a suitable project for equity to undertake.

The discussion to follow

In this chapter we will identify three key forms of unconscionable action that will merit the imposition of a proprietary constructive trust: first, actions seeking to breach a voluntary agreement or negotiations in relation to commercial contracts; second, actions abusing the rights of some other person; and third, actions performed by fiduciaries exploiting the trust. Noticeably, these categories will not consider whether to interfere or not with some person's human rights ought to give rise to a constructive trust. At present the categories are limited, it is suggested, to well-established claims involving fraud and the vindication of agreements, as considered below.

Fundamentals of constructive trusts

In English law a constructive trust arises by operation of law. That statement implies two things. First, that the constructive trust is imposed by a court in accordance with established principle and not purely at the court's own general discretion. This English constructive trust is dubbed an 'institutional' constructive trust, which means that the constructive trust arises automatically at the time when the defendant acted knowingly and unconscionably, with the result that the court at trial recognises that the constructive trust came into existence prior to trial and so gives effect to it retrospectively. This is important when the defendant goes into insolvency before the trial because the court will recognise that the constructive trust came into existence in the past at the date of the unconscionable act, which in the decided cases has tended to be before the date of the insolvency so that the claimant acquires the protection of that trust. (By contrast it is a 'remedial' constructive trust which is used in the USA prospectively from the date of the trial in whatever form is necessary to provide a remedy for the successful claimant. This distinction is considered further at the end of this chapter.)

Second, the constructive trust is imposed regardless of the intentions of the parties involved. This second statement should be treated with some caution because constructive trusts are often enforced in accordance with the intentions of one or other of the parties, but without the intention or formality necessary to create an express trust. The term 'constructive trust' itself is used because the court *construes* that the defendant is to be treated as a trustee of property.

The general approach of this book to the trust is that it is a creature of equity, which has developed principles of its own. The constructive trust is a form of trust most akin to those general principles of equity which prevent a person benefiting from fraud or some other unconscionable action. In what will follow there is a tension between those constructive trusts that are concerned to protect rights in property (*Westdeutsche Landesbank v Islington* (1996)), those so-called constructive trusts that provide the claimant with only a right in money (*Polly Peck International v Nadir* (1992)), and those constructive trusts that appear to be penalties for wrongs committed, which have proprietary consequences (*Attorney General for Hong Kong v Reid* (1994)). These subtly different approaches between categories make the area of constructive trusts both interesting and complex. Careful distinction between the categories is, it is suggested, the key.

The constructive trust grew rapidly in the latter part of the 20th century and is likely to continue to generate new forms of itself in the future. In *Paragon Finance plc v DB Thakerar and Co* (1999), Millett LJ did attempt a general definition of the doctrine of constructive trust:

> A constructive trust arises by operation of law whenever the circumstances are such that it would be unconscionable for the owner of property (usually but not necessarily the legal estate) to assert his own beneficial interest in the property and deny the beneficial interest of another.

This breadth of principle explains why the constructive trust is likely to continue to grow. As considered below in relation to the decision of the House of Lords in *Westdeutsche Landesbank v Islington* (1996), the constructive trust will arise in *any* situation in which the common law owner of property or some third party unconscionably denies or interferes with the rights of another; as such it is clearly a principle of broad application. However, it is suggested that even this definition will not capture the depth or variety of constructive trusts recognised in equity.

It is worth beginning with the words of Edmund-Davies LJ in *Carl Zeiss Stiftung v Herbert Smith and Co* (1969) that:

> English law provides no clear and all-embracing definition of a constructive trust. Its boundaries have been left perhaps deliberately vague so as not to restrict the court by technicalities in deciding what the justice of a particular case might demand.

This statement indicates the essential truth that the constructive trust is not a certain or rigid doctrine. Rather, its edges are blurred and the full scope of its core principles is difficult to define. Thus constructive trusts are useful because they achieve the core goal of equity in preventing a defendant from taking unconscionable advantage of another person or of a situation. It is easiest to think of constructive trusts as arising in particular situations, as set out in the remainder of this chapter. We shall begin with the general principle on which constructive trusts arise.

Constructive trusts are based on the knowledge and the conscience of the trustee

The most important recent statement of the core principles in the area of trusts implied by law was made by Lord Browne-Wilkinson in *Westdeutsche Landesbank v Islington*, where his Lordship went back to basics, identifying the root of any form of trust as being in policing the good conscience of the defendant. The first of his Lordship's 'Relevant Principles of Trust Law' was identified as being that:

> (i) Equity operates on the conscience of the owner of the legal interest. In the case of a trust, the conscience of the legal owner requires him to carry out the purposes for which the property was vested in him (express or implied trust) or which the law imposes on him by reason of his unconscionable conduct (constructive trust).

As considered in Chapter 2, this notion of the conscience of the legal owner is said to underpin all trusts. In relation to the constructive trust it arises as a result of the unconscionable conduct of the legal owner. His Lordship continued with his second principle:

> (ii) Since the equitable jurisdiction to enforce trusts depends upon the conscience of the holder of the legal interest being affected, he cannot be a trustee of the property if and so long as he is ignorant of the facts alleged to affect his conscience, i.e. until he is aware that he is intended to hold the property for the benefit of others in the case of an express or implied trust, or, in the case of a constructive trust, of the factors which are alleged to affect his conscience.

As a result of the requirement that the conscience of the holder of the legal interest is affected, 'he cannot be a trustee of the property if and so long as he is ignorant of the facts alleged to affect his conscience'. Therefore, the defendant must have knowledge of the factors that are suggested to give rise to the constructive trust.

Let us take a simple, everyday example. Suppose that Xavier is queuing to buy two cinema tickets. The price of those tickets is £7.50 each. He pays with a £20 note. Mistakenly, the person working on the till thinks that Xavier has bought only one ticket – despite giving him the two tickets he asked for – and so gives him £12.50 in change as though only one ticket had been bought with the £20 note. The question would be as to Xavier's obligations in relation to the £12.50 that he had received mistakenly from the till operator. There can be little doubt that in good conscience Xavier ought to have informed the till operator of her mistake and returned part of the change to her.

The important question for the law relating to constructive trusts is the time at which Xavier realises that he has been given £7.50 more than he is entitled to receive. If he realises at the moment when the till operator hands him the £12.50 that she has made a mistake and he runs to his friend laughing at their good luck, then he would be a constructive trustee of that excess £7.50 for the cinema as beneficiary from the moment of his receipt of that money. If he absent-mindedly received and pocketed the £12.50 (thus taking it into his possession) without realising the error and did not *ever* subsequently realise that he had £7.50 more than he should have had, then Xavier would never be a constructive trustee. If Xavier absent-mindedly pocketed the £7.50 without realising the mistake but was called back by the till operator once she realised the error, then from the moment he was informed by that till operator he would be a constructive trustee of the excess change – but not before. That is the importance of the statement in *Westdeutsche Landesbank* that there cannot be liability as a constructive trustee until the defendant has *knowledge* of the facts said to affect his conscience.

The *Westdeutsche Landesbank* case concerns a contract under which a bank paid £2.5 million to a local authority. The local authority spent the money, as it was prima facie entitled to do under the contract. Only after the money had been spent did the parties realise that the contract had been void from its very beginnings because it was not lawful for the local authority to have entered into it under the applicable legislation. The bank argued that the local authority ought to have held the money on constructive trust for the bank in good conscience because the money had been paid mistakenly. The House of Lords was unanimous (on this point at least) in holding that none of the amounts paid to the local authority by the bank were to be treated as having been held on constructive trust because at the time when the authority had dissipated the money the authority had had no knowledge that the contract was void. In consequence the authority had no knowledge of any factor that required it to hold the property as constructive trustee for the bank.

A further example cited by Lord Browne-Wilkinson in the *Westdeutsche* appeal was that of *Chase Manhattan v Israel-British Bank* (1980), in which a decision of

Goulding J to impose a constructive trust was reinterpreted by his Lordship. In the *Chase Manhattan* case, a payment was made by Chase to IB Bank and then that same payment was mistakenly made a second time. After receiving the second, mistaken payment, IB Bank went into bankruptcy. The question arose whether Chase was entitled to have that second payment held on constructive trust for it (thus making Chase a secured creditor) or whether Chase was merely an unsecured creditor owed a mere debt. Lord Browne-Wilkinson explained that this was an axiomatic constructive trust: where it could be shown that IB Bank had had knowledge of the mistake before its own insolvency then IB Bank would be bound in good conscience to hold that payment on constructive trust for Chase from the moment it had realised the mistake, not from the moment of receipt of the second payment. In this way we can see that the constructive trust is capable of arising in a range of general situations that are to do with the conscience of an individual defendant and not with any more refined principle. The remainder of this chapter will consider particular situations in which constructive trusts have arisen – although it is suggested that the following micro-categories are necessarily to be read in the light of the foregoing general principles.

Unconscionable dealings with land

Constructive trusts may arise in relation to land in three principal ways, all of which illustrate one function of constructive trusts highlighted earlier as a means of supporting voluntary agreements. First, by means of a common intention constructive trust where the parties either form some agreement by means of express discussions or demonstrate a common intention by their conduct in contributing jointly to the purchase price or mortgage over a property. This is an example of a constructive trust being applied in pursuance of a voluntary agreement: that is, the common intention formed as to the equitable interest in co-owned property.

Second, by entering into a contract for the transfer of rights in land there is an automatic transfer of the equitable interest in that land as soon as there is a binding contract in effect (*Lysaght v Edwards* (1876)). Again, the contract constitutes a voluntary agreement enforced by means of constructive trust.

Third, by entering into negotiations for a joint venture to exploit land and subsequently seeking to exploit that land alone when those negotiations had precluded the claimant from exploiting any interest in that land. So in *Banner Homes Group plc v Luff Development Ltd* (2000), two commercial parties entered into what was described as a 'joint venture' to exploit the development prospects of land in Berkshire. It was held that no binding contract had been formed between the parties when the defendant sought to exploit the site alone without the involvement of the claimant. Extensive negotiations were conducted between the claimant and the defendant and their respective lawyers with reference to documentation to create a joint venture partnership or company. The defendant continued the negotiations while privately nursing reservations about going into business with the claimant. The defendant decided, however, that it should 'keep [the claimant] on board' unless or until a better prospect emerged. It was held that the defendant could establish a constructive trust, even in the absence of a binding contract, to the effect that the claimant and defendant would exploit the land jointly, if the defendant had refrained from exploiting any personal interests in that land in reliance on the negotiations being conducted between the claimant and defendant.

The decision of the House of Lords in *Cobbe v Yeoman's Row* (2008) seemed to limit the *Banner Homes* principle significantly. In that case, the claimant and the defendant had negotiated the commercial development of land and the claimant had spent a large amount of money preparing for the development in anticipation of successful negotiations between them. However, the defendant reneged on their putative arrangements and sought to develop the property alone. The claimant contended that the property should be held on constructive trust or that proprietary estoppel should grant him rights in the property. It was held in a particularly forceful judgment by Lord Scott that the parties' negotiations had not reached the stage of being a contract, that the claimant was aware of this when he spent his money; therefore that the claimant should not receive rights in the property. In essence, commercial people were to be reminded of the need to reach a contractual agreement before spending their money, instead of relying on constructive trusts to save them. Similarly, the doctrine of proprietary estoppel would not be based on a general notion of unconscionability.

Lord Walker, who agreed in the outcome in *Cobbe*, sought in the later case of *Thorner v Major* (2009) to restrict the decision in *Cobbe* to requiring certainty in commercial dealings and not as erasing the doctrines of equitable estoppel or constructive trust in this area. Indeed, later cases yet have focused on the *Banner Homes* principle and not on the purported limitations set out in *Cobbe* (as in *Baynes Clarke v Corless* (2009)). The Court of Appeal, in *Crossco No 4 Unlimited v Jolan Ltd* (2011), accepted that *Banner Homes* remains good law but, on the facts of that case, refused to find a constructive trust in relation to the development of a retail building because there was insufficient certainty as to the terms of the parties' putative agreement.

Unconscionable interference with another's rights in property

It has been accepted by Millett LJ in *Paragon Finance plc v Thakerar and Co* (1999) that 'well-known examples' of constructive trusts that are 'coloured from the first by the trust and confidence' include the doctrine in *Rochefoucauld v Boustead* (1897), which holds that a person may not rely on a statutory provision to perpetrate a fraud. For example, in *Lyus v Prowsa* (1982), a mortgagor sought to deal with property in contravention of the mortgage on the basis that the mortgagee had failed to register the mortgage. It was held that the mortgagor held the property on constructive trust for the mortgagee nevertheless, because the mortgagor had undertaken in the mortgage contract to respect the rights of the mortgagee. Therefore, as an example of a constructive trust that prevents unconscionable use of another's property, if the common law owner of property attempts to deny the rights of some other person in property, that common law owner will be required to hold that property on constructive trust for the person intended to take that benefit.

Another situation in which a constructive trust has been found was in the case of *Re Rose* (1952), which was considered in Chapter 3. In that case, Mr Rose had intended to make a gift of shares to his wife. He had performed all of the acts required of him to effect that transfer but, at the material time, the board of directors had not approved the transfer. It was held, in effect, that it would have been unconscionable for Mr Rose to have denied the transfer to his wife and therefore it was said that the equitable interest in the property ought to have been deemed to have been transferred to Mrs Rose. Thus, it is said that a constructive trust arises in such a situation that a person in Mr Rose's position ought to be considered to be a constructive trustee of the property for the person intended to receive that gift. Therefore, this doctrine illustrates that the constructive trustee is prevented from dealing unconscionably with property intended to be transferred to the beneficiary of that trust, once the trustee has done everything required of her to transfer title in the property.

Unlawful interference with property rights by means of theft

A clear example of a constructive trust imposed to prevent interference with property rights would include those rules of the law of property imposed to prevent criminal or generally unlawful behaviour benefiting the perpetrator of that act. The simplest example exists in relation to theft. A thief is considered by the law of trusts to be a constructive trustee of the stolen property from the moment that the theft is committed (*Westdeutsche Landesbank v Islington* (1996)). This rule operates as an extension of the jurisdiction of the criminal law to punish the thief: the property rule entitles the beneficiary of the constructive trust (that is, the victim of the theft) to recover her property.

There is a logical weakness with this approach. By declaring a constructive trust in this situation, the law of trusts succeeds in categorising the actions of the thief as being unconscionable, but it is suggested that a better approach would be for the court to order that no property rights in the stolen goods ever left the victim of crime. This second approach would vindicate the victim's property rights by means of the court simply ordering that no rights ever left the victim precisely because the victim did not voluntarily surrender those rights to the thief. By definition the thief appropriated the property without the permission of its owner. By suggesting that the thief is a trustee of the property, the court is accepting that the thief acquires common law title in the goods. It is suggested that that is an unfortunate rationale.

One difficult ramification of accepting that the thief acquires common law title is that if the thief purported to sell the stolen property to a bona fide purchaser for value without notice of the victim's rights then equity would accept that the purchaser would take good title over those stolen goods (*Westdeutsche Landesbank v Islington* (1996)). In short, the purchaser acquires the goods and the victim of crime is left with a mere claim against the thief for the value of the property stolen rather than for the property itself. This assumes that the thief will have sufficient money to pay such compensation: an unlikely contingency given the thief's occupation. The purchaser is known as 'equity's darling' precisely because equity will always protect a purchaser acting in good faith. The reason for this approach is straightforwardly commercial: English law and equity as practised in the courts wish to encourage trade. To do so the courts have long since taken the view that purchasers must know with confidence that if they give valuable consideration for property they will acquire good title in that property. The ramification of this principle is that victims of crime lose title in their property quite easily in practice.

For our purposes, it is interesting to note that equity prioritises purchasers over victims of crime, and commerce over ethics.

Constructive trusts wherever a fiduciary exploits a trust

The central principle: constructive trusts over a fiduciary's unauthorised profits

A fiduciary is not entitled to take an unauthorised profit from a trust. Any profit taken by a fiduciary without authorisation will be held on constructive trust by that fiduciary, with the result that any profits flowing from that profit will also be held on that constructive trust. To protect the rights of beneficiaries to all their worldly possessions under marriage and family settlements, the courts of equity have always prevented even the semblance of a possibility that a fiduciary could take an unauthorised profit. Fiduciaries must avoid conflicts of interest in general, and not simply the taking of unauthorised profits. Lord Herschell suggested in *Bray v Ford* (1895) that this rule was observed because, human nature being what it is, trustees would otherwise be tempted to interfere with their trusts. So, in the old case of *Keech v Sandford* (1726), a trustee held a lease on trust for an infant. The lease expired and the infant, being merely an infant, was not entitled to renew that lease. Therefore, the trustee purported to renew the lease in his own name. The court held that, even though there was no suggestion that the trustee was acting wrongly, the trustee must hold the new lease on constructive trust for the infant so that there was no possibility of that trustee having taken a benefit from his fiduciary office.

Similarly, in the leading case of *Boardman v Phipps* (1967), a solicitor advised a family trust to such an extent that he effectively assumed control of the trust's activities and thus made himself a fiduciary in relation to that trust. While analysing the financial information of a private company on trust business (information that he would not have been permitted to read if he had not been acting for the trust) he learned of some confidential information that indicated to him that if the trust took over the company and changed its business plan, that company would become very profitable. Therefore, the solicitor used his own money to acquire sufficient shares in the company so that acting together with the trust's shareholding he was able to control the company and to make the company very profitable. The House of Lords held that the solicitor had made an unauthorised profit from his fiduciary office and therefore was required to hold all of the profits he had made from this transaction – even those profits generated by the use of his own money – on constructive trust for the trust that he advised.

One interesting feature of this case is that two judges in the House of Lords justified their imposition of the constructive trust by finding that the solicitor had misused trust property to generate these personal profits when he exploited the confidential information acquired on trust business. For those judges it was important that the trust's property had been misused before the solicitor's actions could be considered sufficiently unconscionable to impose a constructive trust. The other judges were silent on the matter, the majority being prepared to uphold the *Keech v Sandford* principle.

Significantly, though, in exercise of its general equitable powers the House of Lords took pity on the solicitor for all of the hard work he had done to benefit the trust and therefore held that he was entitled to some equitable accounting from the trust, effectively, in the form of a deduction from the amount he had to pay to the trust so as to compensate him for his hard work. That this is a discretionary part of the court's jurisdiction was illustrated in *Guinness v Saunders* (1990), where a director who had been convicted of fraud in the carrying out of his fiduciary duties was held not to be entitled to any equitable accounting because his criminal acts were found to have made him undeserving of equity's help, illustrating again that *He who comes to equity must come with clean hands*.

Therefore, a trustee or other form of fiduciary will be a constructive trustee of any personal profits made from that office, even where she has acted in good faith. The rule is a strict rule that no profit can be made by a trustee or fiduciary which is not authorised by the terms of the trust. A fiduciary who profits from that office will be required to account for those profits. There is no defence of good faith in favour of the trustee.

Acquiring authorisation for profits

In effect, the only defence for a fiduciary in these sorts of cases is to acquire authorisation for the profit which she has taken. The bulk of the decided cases have related to directors taking unauthorised profits in relation to the companies to which they owe their duties. One case in which the fiduciary was able to show sufficient authorisation when taking personal profits was in *Queensland Mines v Hudson* (1977). In that case a managing director of a company had tried to encourage a company to exploit opportunities to mine specific land but the board of directors in full meeting had decided not to do so. Therefore, the managing director left the company and exploited those mining opportunities on his own account, making large profits. It was held that the managing director did not hold those profits on constructive trust for the company because the company had effectively authorised his independent actions when the board of directors agreed not to become involved. In that situation the beneficiaries of the fiduciary duty (in the person of the company) were taken to have impliedly authorised the transactions. However, the cases of *Industrial Development Consultants Ltd v Cooley* (1972) and *Regal v Gulliver* (1942) both concerned directors purportedly exploiting commercial opportunities on their own account with the agreement of their boards of directors: in both cases the court decided that the fiduciary duties must be strictly observed and that the fiduciaries were not entitled to benefit personally from their office. It was felt that in *Regal* in particular the entire board of four directors had simply sought to give themselves permission to make profits for themselves outside the company and thus defraud the shareholders. *Queensland Mines v Hudson* therefore appears to be an anomalous case in a sea of countervailing authority.

In *Equiticorp Industries Group Ltd v The Crown* (1998), it was held that it was the shareholders of a company who were competent to authorise a fiduciary making such profits on a personal basis; similarly it would appear that only all of the beneficiaries making an informed decision could authorise a trustee to do the same. In *Boardman v Phipps*, the solicitor had not given any information to the beneficiaries and only dealt with one of the trustees. Therefore, there could be no suggestion that he had been adequately authorised by the beneficiaries to make the personal profits that he did make.

Recent cases in company law

There has been a trend in the company law scholarship which has identified the following principle in relation specifically to directors: a director will only be liable for taking unauthorised profits where she has diverted a business opportunity away from the company towards herself. Thus *Hudson* did not divert an opportunity which the company wanted to pursue, whereas in *Cooley* the director had not made the company aware of the opportunity.

In a short line of cases it has been suggested that if the director had been excluded from the management of the company, before then exploiting an opportunity on her own account, then that would not constitute a breach of the principle (*In Plus Ltd v Pyke* (2002) and *Foster v Bryant* (2007)). However, in subsequent cases, the traditional principle in *Regal v Gulliver* (1942) and *Boardman v Phipps* has been restored. So in *Berryland Books Ltd v BK Books Ltd* (2009), the defendant director was required to hold on constructive trust the profits which he had earned by using the company's staff, facilities and marketing to set up a business in competition with that company. (See also *Re Allied Business and Financial Consultants Ltd* (2009).) The Court of Appeal in *Towers v Premier Waste Ltd* (2011) held that even just using machinery hired from a customer of the company was itself a conflict of interest and consequently the profits made by using that equipment in developing land would be held on constructive trust. These recent cases suggest that the strict principle remains in good health.

The Companies Act 2006 and directors' duties

The Companies Act 2006 created a statutory code of directors' duties for the first time so that company directors could know their obligations more easily than attempting to assimilate obligations contained in centuries of case law. The statutory code explicitly retains the case law principles set out above. Directors are required by s 175 of the Companies Act 2006 to avoid a situation in which they have, or can have, a conflict of interest. The obligation is incumbent on each individual director separately. Significantly, s 175(4) provides for two contexts in which there will be authorisation for the profit: where the situation could not 'reasonably be regarded as likely to give rise to a conflict of interest'; or where the directors have 'authorised' the particular transaction. In relation to a private company, the articles of association may prevent an authorisation being granted by the directors. If there is no such prevention of authorisation being granted in the private company's constitution, then the directors may authorise something which might otherwise be a conflict of interest. By contrast, in relation to public companies the company's constitution must contain a power for directors to authorise what would otherwise be a conflict of interest.

Profits from other unlawful acts: killing and bribery

Profits from bribery

The law relating to bribery has pitched and yawed over the years between finding that when a bribe is received by a fiduciary then that bribe should be treated as a debt owed by its recipient to their beneficiaries, and finding that when a bribe is received by a fiduciary then that bribe should be treated as being held on constructive trust by its recipient. Authority for the former approach is found in *Lister v Stubbs* and in *Sinclair Investments v Versailles Trading*; whereas the latter approach has been found in several cases, including *Attorney General for Hong Kong v Reid*.

So, in *Attorney General for Hong Kong v Reid* (1994), it was held that a fiduciary receiving a bribe holds that bribe on constructive trust from the moment of receiving it. In *Reid*, the former Director of Public Prosecutions for Hong Kong had accepted bribes not to prosecute certain individuals accused of having committed crimes within his jurisdiction. The bribes that he had received had been profitably invested. In the old case of *Lister v Stubbs* (1890), it had previously been held that the fiduciary merely owed the claimant a cash sum equal to the amount of the bribe. In that case, however, the fiduciary had invested the bribe very profitably and would therefore have been able to keep the profitable investments while only having to account for the comparatively small value of the bribe actually received. The judgment of Lord Templeman in *Reid* operated on two principal bases. First, it was concerned to punish those who received bribes in breach of their fiduciary duties and therefore pronounced that, because in good conscience the Director of Public Prosecutions ought to have given up the bribe when it was received, a constructive trust should be deemed to have come into existence automatically. Second, because equity looks upon 'as done that which ought to have been done', the bribe would be deemed to have belonged to the claimant from the moment it was received, therefore anything bought with that bribe would be considered to be the property of the claimant. The device for effecting this transfer of ownership to the claimant was by means of a constructive trust. His Lordship held that this constructive trust arose in general terms on the basis of the unconscionability of receiving a bribe, something which Lord Templeman described as being 'an evil practice'. This decision had the support of several earlier authorities and a large number of subsequent cases in the English High Court. Therefore, the investments made with the bribes in *Reid* were held on constructive trust and *Lister v Stubbs* was displaced.

Interestingly, Lord Templeman went one step further and held that, if the bribes had been invested unsuccessfully so that they had lost money, the constructive trustee would be liable not only to hold those investments on constructive trust but also to make good the loss suffered on those investments out of her own pocket. Thus, Lord Templeman succeeded in adding that element of punishment to the claim: that is, the defendant would effectively be fined if the investments had fallen in value.

The decision of the Court of Appeal in *Sinclair Investments (UK) Ltd v Versailles Trading Ltd* (2011) has cast doubt on the *Reid* principle. Versailles operated a fraudulent investment scheme, taking money from investors but failing to make any investments with that money; as part of that the controlling mind of Versailles, Cushnie, used some of the money to buy a valuable house in Kensington. Versailles went into insolvency. The claimant investors sought to recover the house by relying in part on the principle in *Reid* to the effect that the house should be deemed to be held on constructive trust for them. Because of the insolvency, Lord Neuberger did not wish to permit the valuable house to be held on constructive trust for the claimants because that would have meant that it was not available to be divided up among the other unsecured creditors of Versailles. Therefore, Lord Neuberger followed *Lister v Stubbs* in holding that this money taken by Cushnie should be treated as being a debt owed to the company, and therefore the house bought with that money was not held on constructive trust. The complicating fact in this case was the insolvency (which was not the case in *Reid*).

The principle which Lord Neuberger advocated was that there would be a difference between a misuse of trust property (which would lead to a constructive trust) and a misuse of a fiduciary office without misuse of property (which would lead only to a debt claim, as in *Lister v Stubbs*). Therefore, in the former situation, receipt of a bribe would require only a debt claim because ordinarily that would only involve misuse of a fiduciary office. However, if the recipient of the bribe allowed trust property to be misused, then that would result in a constructive trust. The principal reason for making this distinction was to permit insolvencies to be conducted differently so that valuable assets like the house in *Sinclair* would be made available to all of the unsecured creditors equally, as opposed to being hived off for one group of creditors who would benefit from the constructive trust.

The unhappy outcome of *Sinclair Investments* in a case involving a solvent defendant would be that the defendant would only be required to pay an amount equal to the bribe (or other unconscionable payment received) but would be able to keep any profits earned with that money. Thus the shyster who receives a bribe will be able to keep her profits. It would be better to apply *Reid* generally and to develop another rule specifically in relation to insolvency situations.

An article written by Professor Goode (2011) has asserted that the *Sinclair* decision is to be preferred because it will promote the fair administration of insolvencies by preventing valuable assets (such as the house bought in *Sinclair*) from being separated off from the insolvent person's other assets by being held on trust. However, this does not deal with the situation in which there is no insolvency. Hayton J has argued in an article (2012) that the distinction between an abuse of fiduciary office and an abuse of trust property may be difficult to identify in many circumstances. Lord Millett has suggested (2012) that the moral basis of equity requires that a bribe be held on constructive trust – otherwise, the false fiduciary will be able to keep the profits of their wrongdoing. Moreover, the Federal Court of Australia in *Grimaldi v Chameleon Mining NL (No 2)* (2012) has argued that it is anomalous for English law to treat the unconscionable receipt of bribes differently from all other unconscionable acts by denying a constructive trust.

Profits from killing

Similarly, where a person makes some personal gain out of an unlawful killing – for example, where the killer is named as the sole beneficiary in the dead person's will, in the best traditions of detective stories – then that person will hold any benefit received on constructive trust for the deceased's estate so that it is passed to some other person. In the case of *In the Estate of Crippen* (1911), the infamous Dr Crippen had murdered his wife Cora Crippen. Crippen had intended to flee the country with his mistress but was, equally famously, captured on the boat while in flight. The *Crippen* appeal itself considered the question whether or not property which would ordinarily have passed to Crippen as his wife's next of kin ought to pass to his mistress as Crippen's legatee. It was held that, given the context of the murder, no rights would transfer to the mistress because Crippen was deemed to hold them on constructive trust for his wife's estate and therefore could not pass them to his mistress beneficially.

The murderer becomes constructive trustee of all rights and interests in property which would have vested in him under the deceased's will or even as next of kin in relation to a deceased who did not leave a will. The killer does not acquire any rights under any life assurance policy that has been taken out over the life of the deceased.

Exceptionally, in the case of *Re K (Deceased)* (1985), a wife, who had been the victim of domestic violence, had snatched up a shotgun during an attack by her husband with the result that the shotgun went off accidentally, killing her husband. Under the Forfeiture Act 1982 the court exercised its discretion to make an order not to oblige the wife to hold property received as a result of her husband's death on constructive trust, given her provocation and the accidental nature of the killing.

Secret trusts and mutual wills

There are situations in which people will choose to use trusts to deal with their property after their deaths – as though their hands were still on their chequebooks from the grave. The law of trusts will ensure that their wishes are observed, even after their deaths, by preventing anyone from acting unconscionably so as to take a personal benefit from that property that the deceased person had never intended them to take. A mutual wills arrangement takes effect by means of a constructive trust in that the arrangement between the two testators by reference to which neither of them alters their will operates on the conscience of the surviving testator once that arrangement has been made, as the Court of Appeal has confirmed in *Olins v Walters* (2009).

In Chapter 4 the secret trust was discussed in which a testator would seek to create a trust arrangement outwith the scope of his will. This would be achieved by means of leaving a bequest to a named person with the intention that that person would hold that property on the terms of a trust known only to the testator and the named legatee. Such arrangements are invalid on the terms of the Wills Act 1837, but are nevertheless effected by the equitable doctrine of secret trust. It has been suggested that either these trusts operate simply as a one-off exception to the Wills Act 1837, or they constitute a form of constructive trust which operates to prevent the named legatee from claiming to be absolutely entitled to the property left to her under the will in the knowledge that the property was intended to be held in accordance with the terms of the secret trust arrangement.

Similarly, the doctrine of mutual wills operates beyond the precise terms of the Wills Act 1837 in situations in which two people reach an arrangement that they will create wills to leave property to specific people after the last of them dies. The intention of the doctrine is to prevent the last person living under the arrangement from reneging on it and leaving the property to some other person (*Dufour v Pereira* (1769)). The essence of the doctrine is therefore the prevention of a fraud being committed by the survivor in failing to comply with the terms of the mutual will arrangement. Unusually, in *Olins v Walters* (2009), the surviving spouse in a mutual wills arrangement denied the existence of the arrangement but it was held that on the balance of probabilities there had been a mutual wills agreement between them, not least because other family members who were solicitors remembered the discussions and the terms which the couple had agreed.

Intermeddlers as constructive trustees

A further means of preventing unconscionable interference with another's property arises when third parties – those who are neither beneficiaries nor trustees – interfere with trust property to the detriment of the beneficiaries. In such situations, those third party intermeddlers fall to be treated as trustees either proprietarily – that is, by holding any profits they generate or any property they take on trust for the beneficiaries – or personally – that is, by being held to account to the beneficiaries for the amount of the loss suffered by the trust as a result of their interference.

Making oneself a trustee by intermeddling

Therefore, at the first level someone who interferes with the running of a trust sufficiently when not a trustee will be deemed to have made themselves a constructive trustee and will therefore bear all the obligations and liabilities of a trustee. Smith LJ framed the nature of this form of constructive trust in the case of *Mara v Browne* (1896) in the following way:

> [I]f one, not being a trustee and not having authority from a trustee, takes upon himself to intermeddle with trust matters or to do acts characteristic of the office of trustee, he may therefore make himself what is called in law trustee of his own wrong – i.e. a trustee *de son tort*, or, as it is also termed, a constructive trustee.

Therefore, a trustee *de son tort* is a trustee who intermeddles with trust business. So, in *Blyth v Fladgate* (1891), Exchequer bills had been held on trust by a sole trustee. That trustee had deposited the bills in the name of a firm of solicitors, thus putting the bills within the control of the solicitors. The trustee died and, before substitute trustees had been appointed, the solicitors sold the bills and invested the proceeds in a mortgage. In the event the security provided under the mortgage was insufficient and accordingly the trust suffered a loss. It was held that the firm of solicitors had become a constructive trustee by dint of its having dealt with the trust property then within its control. As such it was liable to account to the beneficiaries for the loss occasioned to the trust.

Similarly, where a manager of land continued to collect rents in respect of that land after the death of the landlord, without informing the tenants of their landlord's death, that manager was held to be a constructive trustee of those profits that had been held in a bank account (*Lyell v Kennedy* (1889)). The aim of the constructive trust here is to preserve the sanctity of the beneficiaries' proprietary rights.

Personal liability to account

Two alternative forms of liability arise when there has been a breach of trust, as considered in Chapter 10 in some detail. The aim of the court is to make people other than the trustee liable, so that the beneficiaries will be able to recover their loss from third parties who were in some way involved with the breach of trust either by receiving trust property or by assisting that breach of trust. By creating such wide-reaching remedies, the courts effectively secure that even if the trust property cannot be recovered, the beneficiaries will be able to obtain the cash equivalent of their loss. So, where a person receives trust property in the know-ledge that that property has been passed in breach of trust, the recipient will be personally liable to account to the trust for the value of the property passed away (*Re Montagu* (1987)), provided that the defendant has also acted unconscionably (*BCCI v Akindele* (2001)).

Under a different head of claim, where a person dishonestly assists another in a breach of trust, that dishonest assistant will be personally liable to account to the trust for the value lost to the trust (*Royal Brunei Airlines v Tan* (1995)).

'Dishonesty' in this context requires that there be some element of fraud, lack of probity or reckless risk-taking. It is not necessary that any trustee of the trust is dishonest; simply that the dishonest assistant is dishonest.

Both of these claims are considered in detail in Chapter 10. The remedies for both claims are the same: a personal liability to account for the whole of the loss suffered by the beneficiaries. What is important to understand is that no property is in the hands of defendants to these actions. No property is held on trust. Rather, their involvement with the breach of trust in itself makes them personally liable for the whole of the loss. In effect, this is a form of equitable wrong, imposing liability on the defendants, and not a part of the law of property at all.

Remedial constructive trusts: the future?

The *Westdeutsche Landesbank* appeal raised one further question for the House of Lords to those questions already considered in Chapter 6 and above: Should the constructive trust operate on an institutional basis or on a remedial basis? Perhaps it would be as well to reprise the difference between those two terms. An institutional trust is a trust that arises automatically – that is, without the court exercising any discretion of its own. This is the form of trust that exists under English law. The judge identifies a situation in which the defendant has acted unconscionably and it is from the point in time when the defendant knows of that unconscionable act that the constructive trust is said to come automatically into existence. Therefore, an institutional constructive trust operates retrospectively back to the time of the defendant's knowledge. In cases of insolvency, this means that if the constructive trust came into existence before the time of the insolvency, then the beneficiary of such a trust takes proprietary rights ahead of the unsecured creditors.

Of course, there is still some scope for judicial discretion in relation to whether or not the defendant is found to have acted unconscionably – but that is not mentioned by their Lordships. The courts are keen to downplay their own room for manoeuvre. In effect, by downplaying the possibility for their own discretion they are also masking the power that they possess.

A remedial constructive trust, on the other hand, takes effect prospectively from the date of the court order. Therefore, it would not be advantageous, for example, in the event of an insolvency, because the constructive trust does not come into existence until the date of the court order – which will usually only be made once the defendant has gone into insolvency. That is the downside of the remedial constructive trust. However, its advantages are written into its flexibility. The next chapter considers the doctrine of equitable estoppel and will be at pains to point out that that doctrine allows the court to impose any order that it thinks appropriate – whether personal or proprietary. There is no reason why, in theory, one could not have a remedial constructive trust that operated retrospectively.

As the French philosopher Foucault has told us, social phenomena such as law are simply made up of things that are said; those laws could as simply be unmade by different things being said. Therefore, why are remedial constructive trusts said not to be retrospective? The principal argument returns us to the question of insolvency: it is said that to allow the courts to award constructive trusts in whatever shape the court wishes would mean that the certainty achieved by cases like *Re Goldcorp* (1995) in the allocation of title to property would be lost. What *Goldcorp* achieves in cases of insolvency is a restriction on the ability of claimants to acquire the status of secured creditors without specifically identifiable property having been settled validly on trust for them.

This was the argument similarly deployed to refuse validation to Professor Birks's mooted extension of the resulting trust to reverse unjust enrichment in *Westdeutsche Landesbank v Islington*. But perhaps it is time to recognise that cases of insolvency could simply have their own rules while the rest of the law of property is freed up sufficiently to deploy remedial constructive trusts (in the manner used in relation to equitable estoppel) to achieve that core equitable goal of doing justice in individual cases.

Moving on . . .

The institutional trusts implied by law fall to be contrasted with the freewheeling scope of equitable estoppel in Chapter 8 and also the more flexible uses of constructive trusts which have been deployed in relation to rights in the home in Chapter 9. Bound up in these debates is that central tension between the desire for certainty in rule-making and the need for equity to be flexible and responsive to circumstance. These issues are therefore considered in the next two chapters.

Equitable estoppel

Introduction

To call this chapter 'equitable estoppel' raises the question whether such a category even exists. In truth, there are a range of estoppels available both at common law and in equity. The most significant form of estoppel available in equity is proprietary estoppel and that doctrine will be the principal focus of this chapter. There are a range of other forms which will be considered in outline too. The purposes of proprietary estoppel divide between preventing claimants from suffering detriment, creating rights in property and circumventing statutory formalities to achieve fairness.

The earliest forms of estoppel related to situations in which a defendant had told the claimant that x was the case, when it turned out in fact that y was true. The doctrine evolved so as to prevent the defendant from reneging on having the claimant believe that x was the case. In its modern form, estoppel in equity typically bites on an assurance given to the claimant in circumstances in which the claimant then acts to her detriment in reliance on the statement made to her.

What is difficult about estoppel, and in particular proprietary estoppel, is in deciding whether the doctrine grants new rights to the claimant, or whether the doctrine is concerned to compensate a claimant for some detriment that she has suffered, or whether it is concerned more generally to stop a defendant from unconscionably reneging on the effect of her assurance.

An example may make this point clearer. Suppose that Dorrit is promised by her wicked stepfather that if she works for no wages on his farm, he will give her a young racehorse called Lightning. Dorrit knows that if she were able to train Lightning properly she would be able to win a large number of valuable horse races. Dorrit works for her stepfather for a period of time during which she would ordinarily have been paid £1,000 if it were not for their arrangement. Her stepfather does not leave her the horse Lightning. Furthermore, Lightning wins £10,000 in prize money over the next year, which the stepfather keeps. Now, if Dorrit were able to make out a claim for estoppel (on the basis that in reliance on an assurance her stepfather had made to her that if she acted to her detriment (that is, worked for no wages) she would receive the horse) the problem arises as to the value of the remedy to which she should be entitled.

If the remedy is concerned to compensate her for her detriment, then Dorrit would be entitled (prima facie) to the £1,000 she should otherwise have been paid in wages. If the remedy is concerned to enforce the promise, then Dorrit should receive a transfer of the horse Lightning to her and also any prize money that the horse had won. If the remedy was concerned with avoiding unconscionable behaviour in general terms then it may require the stepfather to transfer any prize money won by Lightning with, perhaps, some accounting to the stepfather for the cost of training Lightning in the meantime – that is, a measurement of the extent to which he has actually acted in bad conscience. Therefore, the underlying purpose of the doctrine may have different results in different factual situations. It may therefore be surprising to the reader to learn that it is not always obvious on which basis the various doctrines of estoppel do act.

In short, estoppel appears to fulfil a number of these objectives at different times in different contexts depending on the merits of the individual case, which makes it appear to be a particularly *equitable* doctrine, in the sense given to that term in Chapter 1, because the judge is free to select the best remedy on any particular set of facts. First we shall consider that form of estoppel that is of most importance in the context of equity: proprietary estoppel.

Proprietary estoppel – the operation of the doctrine

The doctrine of proprietary estoppel will grant an equitable interest to a person who has been induced to suffer detriment in reliance on a representation (or some assurance) that they would acquire some rights in the property as a result. Whereas rights based on constructive trust and resulting trust are 'institutional' trusts, taking retrospective effect, proprietary estoppel may give a different kind of right.

The test underlying the doctrine of proprietary estoppel

The common understanding of the doctrine of proprietary estoppel in modern cases was set out by Edward Nugee QC in *Re Basham* (1986). That case supported the three-stage requirement of representation, reliance and detriment. In short, proprietary estoppel will arise where the claimant has performed some act (argu-ably, which must be done in relation to the property) to her detriment in reliance upon a representation made to her by the cohabitee from whom the claimant would thereby seek to acquire an equitable interest in the property.

It is clear from the cases that the representation made by the defendant need only amount to an assurance and it can be implied, rather than needing to be made expressly (*Crabb v Arun DC* (1976)). Therefore, it is sufficient that the defendant allowed the claimant to believe that her actions would acquire her property rights; it is not necessary that there be any express, single promise. The reliance is generally assumed (on an evidential basis) where a representation has been made. The question of what will constitute 'detriment' is considered below.

The nature of the representation

It is important that the assurances of the representor have been intended by their maker to lead the claimant to believe that she would acquire rights in property. So, for example, it would not be sufficient that the representor was merely teasing the claimant without either of them forming a belief that the claimant would in fact acquire any rights in property. As Robert Walker LJ put it in *Jennings v Rice* (2002), 'it is notorious that some elderly persons of means derive enjoyment from the possession of testamentary power, and from dropping hints as to their intentions, without any question of any estoppel arising'. Therefore, the court will consider the general context and consider whether or not it would be reasonable for the claimant to rely on the things that were said, or whether it would be unconscionable for the defendant to deny them.

It is clear that in general terms it will be sufficient if the defendant makes an express representation to the claimant, but it would also be sufficient to establish an estoppel if some implied assurance were made in circumstances in which the defendant knew that the claimant was relying on the impression she had formed. This breadth of the concept of a representation in proprietary estoppel was illustrated by the decision of the Court of Appeal in *Gillett v Holt* (2000). That case concerned a friendship between a farmer, Holt, and a young boy of 12, Gillett, which lasted for 40 years, during which time the boy worked for the farmer. Gillett left his real parents and moved in with Holt when aged 15. There was even a suggestion that the farmer would adopt the boy at one stage. On numerous occasions the claimant, Gillett, was assured by Holt that he would inherit the farm. The claimant's wife and family were described as being a form of surrogate family for the farmer. In time, a third person, Wood, turned Holt against Gillett, which led to Gillett being removed from Holt's will.

Robert Walker LJ held that there was sufficient detriment by Gillett in the course of their relationship over 40 years, evidenced by the following factors: working for Holt and not accepting other job offers, performing actions beyond what would ordinarily have been expected of an employee, taking no substantial steps to secure his future by means of pension or otherwise, and spending money on a farmhouse (which he expected to inherit) that had been almost uninhabitable at the outset. The combination of these factors over such a long period of time was considered by the Court of Appeal to constitute ample evidence of representations and detriment sufficient to found a proprietary estoppel.

Another important illustration of the concept of a representation arose in *Thorner v Major* (2009) between two farmers who were found at first instance to be so taciturn such that they rarely spoke to one another. It was considered to be a trait of farmers in Somerset. The younger man worked on the older man's farm for up to sixteen hours per day, and at times for seven days per week. The work was hard and gruelling. While there was no specific discussion about the rights which the younger man could expect to receive in the farm when the older man died, it was found that the younger man had formed a reasonable expectation that the farm would be left to him in the older man's will, and that the fact that documents relating to the farm were left on a table so that the younger man would see them was considered in itself to be a confirmation of this situation. It was held that this was sufficient to constitute a representation between the two men. Remarkably this means that a representation or assurance can be made without any words being spoken between the people involved, provided that the representor is aware of the expectation which is being formed in the mind of the claimant.

This does not mean that representations will be found to exist in all circumstances. A good example is *Lissimore v Downing* (2003), in which a wealthy heavy metal musician who lived in a large stately home in the English Midlands met a married woman in a pub and began a casual sexual relationship with her. She claimed that on one evening, when he had taken her to the edge of his estate and, looking back over his land, had asked her something to the effect of 'How would you like to be lady of a manor like this?' that he had effectively made her a representation that she would acquire rights in the property. Their relationship had been entirely casual and had not involved many meetings. Mann J held (after a lot of consideration) that this did not constitute a meaningful representation and consequently that she should not be entitled to claim proprietary rights in his property.

Examples of the test for proprietary estoppel in operation

A typical situation in which proprietary estoppel claims arise is where promises are made by the absolute owner of land to another person that the other person will acquire an interest in the land if they perform acts that would otherwise be detrimental to them (e.g. *Gillett v Holt* (2000)). Typically, then, the person making the promise dies without transferring any right in the property to that other person. For example, in *Re Basham* the plaintiff was 15 years old when her mother married the deceased. Over a number of years she worked unpaid in the deceased's business, cared for the deceased through his illness, sorted out a boundary dispute for the deceased, and refrained from moving away when her husband was offered employment with tied accommodation elsewhere.

All of these acts were performed on the understanding that she would acquire an interest in property on the deceased's death. The deceased died intestate. It was held that the plaintiff had acquired an equitable interest in the home on proprietary estoppel principles. It was found that proprietary estoppel arises, in the words of Judge Nugee QC:

> [where] A has acted to his detriment on the faith of a belief which was known to and encouraged by B, that he either has or will receive a right over B's property, B cannot insist on strict legal rights so as to conflict with A's belief.

This can be contrasted with *Layton v Martin* (1986), in which a man had promised to provide for his mistress in his will. He died without leaving any of the promised bequests in his will and therefore the mistress sued his estate claiming rights on constructive trust. Her claim was rejected on the basis that she had not contributed in any way to the maintenance of his assets. At one level it is a decision based on the absence of detriment. This can be compared with the decision in *Re Basham*, in which the claimant was found to have made sufficient contributions to the defendant's assets. Similarly, where a wife contributes to her husband's business activities generally it may be found that she has suffered detriment that will ground a right in property (*Heseltine v Heseltine* (1971)), particularly if this evidences a common intention at some level which may be undocumented (*Re Densham* (1975)). Other relatives will be entitled to rely on their contributions to the acquisition or maintenance of property where there have been assurances made to them that they would be able to occupy that property as their home (*Re Sharpe* (1980)). In such situations it is essential that the expenditure is made in reliance on a representation that it will accrue the contributor some right in the property and cannot simply be general expenditure without any focus on acquiring rights in property.

Another classic example of proprietary estoppel arose in the decision of Lord Denning in *Greasley v Cooke* (1980). There, a woman, Doris Cooke, had been led to believe that she could occupy property for the rest of her life. She had been the family's maid, but then had formed an emotional relationship with one of the family and become his partner. In reliance on this understanding she looked after the Greasley family, acting as a housekeeper, instead of getting herself a job and providing for her own future. The issue arose of whether or not she had acquired any equitable interest in the property.

It was held by Lord Denning that she had suffered detriment in looking after the family and not getting a job in reliance on the representation made to her. Therefore, it was held that she had acquired a beneficial interest in the property under proprietary estoppel principles because she had acted to her detriment in continuing to work for the Greasleys in reliance on their assurance to her that she would acquire some proprietary rights as a result. The form of rights that Lord Denning granted was an irrevocable licence to occupy the property for the rest of her life. (What is particularly satisfying about this case is that, had Charles Dickens sought to incorporate these events into a novel such as *Nicholas Nickleby*, he could have found no better name for the exploitative family than 'the Greasleys'.) That such a particular remedy was awarded brings us to the more general question: what form of remedy can be awarded under proprietary estoppel principles?

Proprietary estoppel – a breadth of remedies

What is most significant is that the court will have complete freedom to frame its remedy once it has found that an estoppel is both available and appropriate (*Lord*

Cawdor v Lewis (1835)). Thus, a two-stage process develops: first, find whether or not there is an estoppel and, second, decide on the most appropriate remedy in the context, in the light of both the assurance made and the most effective method of compensating the claimant's detriment. The remedies available can range from the award of the entire interest in the property at issue to a mere entitlement to equitable compensation. They may be enforceable, not only against the person who made the assurance, but also against third parties, thus underlining the proprietary nature of such remedies in circumstances where the court considers such a remedy appropriate (*Hopgood v Brown* (1955)). This indicates the nature of estoppel as a pure form of equity: the court is entirely at liberty to grant personal or proprietary awards that operate only against the defendant or also against third parties (as proprietary rights ought to).

It may not even be clear whether the remedy will be proprietary or merely personal. The cases have provided different types of remedies in different contexts. The following two cases are best thought of as being at two ends of the spectrum of possible remedies, where one is proprietary and the other entirely personal. In the case of *Pascoe v Turner* (1979), the court awarded the freehold over land to a woman absolutely in circumstances in which she had paid for small amounts of decorating to a house in which she had been promised she would be able to live for the rest of her life. Despite the smallness of her contribution, the court found that there was no way to secure her occupation of the property throughout her lifetime unless she was granted the entire freehold. That should be compared with *Baker v Baker* (1993), in which an elderly father gave up a secure tenancy and used the money to which he was entitled under statute to acquire a home with his children. When their relationship broke down, the court could have ordered (it appears) that the old man should have had some proprietary right in the home; instead the court ordered that he should be entitled to a sum of money from his children which would acquire him sheltered accommodation for the rest of his life. These two cases demonstrate the breadth of remedy that is open to the court.

There have been a large number of cases in-between these two which have used hybrid forms of remedy. A good illustration is the decision of the Court of Appeal in *Jennings v Rice* (2002). Mr Jennings began working for Mrs Royle, a widow, as a gardener (for 30 pence an hour) in 1970 on Saturdays and for three evenings per week in summer. Over time Mr Jennings' duties expanded so that he carried out maintenance work, took Mrs Royle shopping and starting running errands for her. By the late 1980s, Mrs Royle had stopped paying Mr Jennings, but he continued with the work. In 1993, Mrs Royle was burgled and Mr Jennings took to sleeping every night at Mrs Royle's house on a sofa in the living room so that she would not be alone in the house, something she feared after the burglary. From the 1970s onwards, the amount of time that Mr Jennings spent at Mrs Royle's house had caused problems with his wife. Before Mrs Royle's death in 1997, Mrs Jennings had begun to help care for the old woman with her husband. There was no evidence that Mrs Royle had ever made a clear representation to

Mr Jennings that he would acquire a right in her house, although it was suggested that there were occasions when she said words to the effect that 'this will all be yours one day'.

It was found that the pattern of the parties' relationship was such that Mrs Royle would be deemed to have made sufficient representation to Mr Jennings over time to found a right under proprietary estoppel. The court was concerned to avoid unconscionability. In so doing the court held that Mr Jennings was entitled to a payment of £200,000 as the minimum equity necessary in the circumstances. This sum of money did not represent any particular right in property, but rather sought to prevent unconscionable treatment of Mr Jennings by compensating him.

The demonstration that proprietary estoppel is a remedial doctrine

The cases considered in the previous subsection demonstrate that proprietary estoppel is a remedial doctrine in that the remedy that the claimant may receive does not necessarily constitute a pre-existing property right. Rather, the court has the power to award merely an amount of money instead of a right to identified property. This is a powerful range of discretion for the courts of equity. So, in *Jennings v Rice* the claimant received an amount of money considered appropriate to ensure that 30 years of unskilled labour would not have been taken advantage of unconscionably. At the other end of the spectrum, in *Pascoe v Turner*, the claimant received absolute title in the property in question. Somewhere in-between the claimant in *Gillett v Holt* received a package of money and property to prevent unconscionable detriment being suffered without compensation. Proprietary estoppel is truly an example of equity at its purest, in that the court can do almost anything it wishes to prevent an unconscionable benefit being taken by the defendant or uncompensated detriment being suffered by the claimant.

Consequently, proprietary estoppel is a remedial institution unlike the constructive trust (which was described in Chapter 7 as being 'institutional' in that it operates so as to recognise retrospectively the presence of pre-existing equitable property rights), precisely because the court does not simply recognise that some person has rights but rather the court examines the circumstances before it and awards whatever rights it considers appropriate. It is suggested that that is a remedial discretion in the court and not an institutional response like a trust. Perhaps the most remarkable illustration of the breadth of this doctrine came in *Porntip Stallion v Albert Stallion Holdings Ltd* (2009), to the effect that where a former wife of the deceased had been promised that she could occupy their former home for the rest of her life, then she would be entitled to occupy that property in common with the deceased's widow. That the two women had managed to co-exist within the same property previously does not detract both from the breadth of remedy which this illustrates and also the unusualness of the court's response.

Avoiding detriment

Proprietary estoppel is very different, in a number of ways, from the institutional resulting and constructive trusts considered in Chapters 6 and 7. The principal aim of proprietary estoppel is generally said to be to avoid detriment rather than to enforce the promise. Whereas the common intention constructive trust appears to be quasi-contractual (in that it enforces an express or implied agreement), estoppel is directed at preventing detriment being caused by a broken promise. In *Walton Stores v Maher* (1988), Brennan J held that:

> The object of the equity is not to compel the party bound to fulfil the assumption or expectation: it is to avoid the detriment which, if the assumption or expectation goes unfulfilled, will be suffered by the party who has been induced to act or to abstain from acting thereon.

Similarly, Lord Browne-Wilkinson has held in *Lim v Ang* (1992), that the purpose of proprietary estoppel is to provide a response where 'it is unconscionable for the representor to go back on the assumption that he permitted the representee to make'; that is, to avoid the detriment caused from retreating from that representation. This approach is important because the court's intention is not merely to recognise that an institutional constructive trust exists between the parties, but rather to provide a remedy that prevents the claimant from suffering detriment.

The determination of the courts to prevent detriment therefore requires the court both to identify the nature of the property rights that were the subject of the representation and to mould a remedy to prevent detriment resulting from the breach of promise. Typically, this requires the demonstration of a link between the detriment and an understanding that property rights were to have been acquired. Thus, in *Wayling v Jones* (1995), two gay men, A and B, lived together as a couple. A owned a hotel in which B worked for lower wages than he would otherwise have received in an arm's length arrangement. A promised to leave the hotel to B in his will. The hotel was sold and another acquired without any change in A's will having been made to reflect that assurance. B sought an interest in the proceeds of sale of the hotel. The issue turned on B's evidence as to whether or not he would have continued to work for low wages had A not made the representation as to the interest in the hotel. Initially, B's evidence suggested that it was as a result of his affection for A that B had accepted low wages. This would not have acquired him rights in the property because it was a purely personal detriment and not directed at the acquisition of rights in the property. However, before the Court of Appeal, B's evidence suggested that he accepted low wages from A in reliance on the assurance that B would acquire property rights in the hotel. Consequently, the Court of Appeal held that B was entitled to acquire proprietary rights under proprietary estoppel because his detrimental acts were directed at the acquisition of rights in property and were not merely the sentimental ephemera of their relationship.

Circumventing unfair applications of statute: a vitiating doctrine

Proprietary estoppel underlines one of the key tenets of equity: that it can do justice between the parties where the ordinary rules of the common law or of statute would have been unfair or unconscionable. While some commentators seek to restrict proprietary estoppel to cases involving land, its remit is in truth much broader. Proprietary estoppel will operate over any form of property in relation to which the defendant has made assurances to the claimant that the claimant will acquire interests in that property and in reliance on which the claimant acts to her detriment. This may even operate so as to displace statutory provisions.

An example of this broader sweep of proprietary estoppel is provided by *Yaxley v Gotts* (2000), in which a joint venture was formed for the acquisition of land. The joint venture did not comply with the requirement in s 2 of the Law of Property (Miscellaneous Provisions) Act 1989 that the terms of any purported contract for the transfer of any interest in land be in writing. The defendant therefore contended that the claimant could have acquired no right in contract to the land because there was no writing in accordance with the formal requirements of the statute. However, the court was prepared to uphold that between the parties there had been a representation that there would be a joint venture between the parties in reliance on which the claimant had acted to its detriment. It was held by the Court of Appeal that a constructive trust had arisen between the parties on the basis of their common intention – and that this constructive trust was indistinguishable in this form from a proprietary estoppel.

The general issue arose as to whether or not the general public policy underpinning the statutory formalities ought to be rigidly adhered to, so as to preclude the activation of any estoppel on the basis that it was a principle of fundamentally important social policy. It was held that in deciding whether or not a parliamentary purpose was being frustrated, one should 'look at the circumstances in each case and decide in what way the equity can be satisfied' (*Plimmer v Mayor of Wellington* (1884)). The court is able to apply the doctrine of proprietary estoppel where it is necessary to do the minimum equity necessary between the parties. In effect this opens the way for the return of the part-performance doctrine in the guise of proprietary estoppel and constructive trust. While the doctrine of the creation of equitable mortgages by deposit of title deeds was deemed to have been removed by the 1989 Act, the equitable doctrine of proprietary estoppel remained intact, even where it would appear to offend the principle that an ineffective contract ought not to be effected by means of equitable doctrine (*King v Jackson* (1998)).

The approach taken by Lord Scott in *Cobbe v Yeoman's Row* (2008), has been described as being the end of proprietary estoppel. In that case, the claimant had spent a large amount of money in reliance on what he claimed was a representation made by the defendant that they would develop land together. The representation was said to be the result of negotiations between the parties which had not matured sufficiently to constitute a binding contract but which suggested that the parties would exploit this opportunity together. Lord Scott and the House of Lords held that the claimant could not make out a claim in proprietary estoppel because the representation was too indistinct and, in general terms, because in commercial situations it was incumbent on the participants to complete a contract before taking the risk of investing money in a future opportunity. However, in the later decision in *Thorner v Major* (2009), Lord Walker and the House of Lords held that the decision in *Cobbe* should be understood only as requiring that commercial people act with sufficient certainty and not so as to eviscerate the doctrine of proprietary estoppel. The position of *Yaxley v Gotts* is difficult to conceptualise because in *Cobbe v Yeoman's Row* Lord Scott sought to overrule *Yaxley v Gotts* but it is not clear that the other members of the House of Lords nor the court in *Thorner v Major* intended to overrule that case. Indeed, the judgment of Lord Scott was eccentric – relying on a model of estoppel which pre-dated *Re Basham* and the other cases considered above – and which was very much against the current trend in the law. It is suggested that the decision of Lord Scott in *Cobbe v Yeoman's Row* should be ignored, and the later approach taken in *Thorner v Major* (which was in line with the authorities considered above) should be followed instead.

Other forms of estoppel

Estoppel licences: from contract to property rights

The doctrine of proprietary estoppel has been used in many situations to attempt to elevate purely personal claims into proprietary claims. One clear example of this tendency relates to estoppel licences. Lord Denning held in a number of cases that a contract that granted a licence to the licensee constituted a representation that the licensee would acquire rights effectively equivalent to a leasehold interest for the duration of the licence (*Errington v Errington* (1952)). The general application of this rule – seeking to enlarge licences to the status of leases – was roundly rejected by the Court of Appeal in *Ashburn Anstalt v Arnold* (1988) in favour of a more traditional test that asserted that the licensee might be able to acquire rights by virtue of proprietary estoppel or constructive trust.

In short, the contention was that a licensee may acquire estoppel rights against property where a rightholder in that property has made some assurance to that licensee that she would acquire some rights in the property, whether by way of a lease or otherwise. The remedy available to a claimant is as broad as that for proprietary estoppel, considered above. This may lead to the acquisition of limited rights of secure occupation. Where a licensee had spent £700 on improvements to the bungalow in reliance on representations made to them that they would be able to remain in occupation, the court held that they could remain in secure occupation until their expenditure had been reimbursed (*Burrows and Burrows v Sharpe* (1991)), or generally 'for as long as they wish to occupy the property' (*Inwards v Baker* (1965)). Thus, whereas Lord Denning sought originally to raise personal rights in contract to the status of rights in property, the possibilities for contractual licences to constitute rights in property now rest on ordinary principles of proprietary estoppel.

Promissory estoppel

The principle of promissory estoppel establishes that a party to a contract will be estopped from reneging on a clear promise where it would be inequitable to renege on that promise and where the other party has altered its position in reliance on the promise. This is illustrated by the leading case of *Central London Property Trust Ltd v High Trees House Ltd* (1947), in which Lord Denning held that an agreement not to renegotiate the level of rental payments under a lease for the duration of the 1939–45 war estopped the landlord from seeking to rely on a term in the lease, which he could rely on at a higher level of rent during that period, after a rent review.

The promise is required to be clear, but it can be implied from the conduct or words used by the parties (*Scandinavian Trading Tanker Co AB v Flota Petrolera Ecuatoriana* (1983)). In terms of the inequity of the action, it is within the court's discretion to decide whether it would be conscionable for the defendant to insist on her strict contractual rights (*D & C Builders v Rees* (1966)). The alteration of position is broadly equivalent to the detriment required in proprietary estoppel and would include a party waiving its strict legal rights in reliance on a promise by another person that they would similarly waive their own rights.

What promissory estoppel will not do is to replace the doctrine of consideration and lead to the creation of contracts without such consideration (*Combe v Combe* (1951)). The concern would be that, even though there was no valid consideration, Xena could claim that Yasmin had made a promise to Xena in reliance on which Xena had altered her position, thus entitling her to rely on promissory estoppel.

Promissory estoppel will not be used as a sword: that is, it will not create new rights, but rather it will only protect the claimant's existing rights. This, in itself, constitutes a significant difference from proprietary estoppel, which does appear to grant rights to the claimant, which that claimant had not previously owned: for example, the freehold awarded in *Pascoe v Turner* (1979).

Foundations of the estoppel(s)

There is no single doctrine of estoppels, nor would it be possible to create one out of the existing categories. There is no single explanation for the manner in which all estoppels operate – both those forms considered in this short chapter and the others that are beyond the scope of this book. Estoppel in all its forms is based on a variety of underlying conceptions, varying from 'honesty' to 'common sense' to 'common fairness'. What emerges from this list is that common principles underpinning all estoppel can only be identified at the most rarefied levels – those of fairness, justice and so forth. Some academics argue that estoppel arises on the basis of 'unconscionability' (Cooke, 1995), but nevertheless have to acknowledge that there is a distinction between those forms of proprietary estoppel that arise variously on the basis of avoidance of detriment (*Lim v Ang* (1992)), enforcement of promise (*Pascoe v Turner* (1979)), or on grounds of mistake (*Wilmot v Barber* (1880)).

What is remarkable, and little discussed, is that even if estoppels arise on the basis of unconscionability there is only a narrow class of acts that we might ordinarily recognise as unconscionable behaviour, which is legally actionable. For example, if you promise to drive me home in return for me paying for your meal, but you know when you make the promise that you have neither a driving licence nor a car, we might consider that action to have been unconscionable (in that your lying to me is not the act of a completely honest person) but it is unlikely that we would consider it to be legally actionable, even if I then have to wait for the bus in the rain. Here there is a disjunction between our notion of 'good conscience' and our notion of 'good conscience which is legally actionable'. The fundamental weakness of purporting to base these doctrines on abstract notions of 'justice' or 'fairness' is that none of the jurists actually intend to capture all unconscionable behaviour; only unconscionable behaviour that falls into established legal and equitable categories.

In common among the various forms of estoppel is the notion of detrimental reliance: that is, some reliance by the claimant on some act, representation or similar behaviour of the defendant. The requirement for reliance is weaker in promissory estoppel than in proprietary estoppel. In both of these doctrines there is some requirement that the defendant must have acted unconscionably in some way. The principal difference between the doctrines is that of the form of belief required of the claimant. In promissory estoppels the claimant must have been led to believe by the defendant that the defendant's rights will not be enforced. Proprietary estoppel requires that the claimant believes that she will acquire some right in property. Third, there is a distinction between those estoppels that operate only in relation to the past and those that make actionable some representation about the future. Promissory and proprietary estoppel will reflect on future conduct, whereas estoppel by deed and others will relate only to past conduct.

In conclusion

This discretionary power that we have observed in proprietary estoppel above has in common with the fundamental tenets of equity that it should do justice between the parties in individual cases. In that sense, equitable estoppel is in line with the doctrine in *Rochefoucauld v Boustead* (1897), and doctrines such as secret trusts. It accords with the ancient Greek attitude to 'equity' that it achieves a better result than formalistic 'justice' in cases where it is applied between the parties, in spite of the decision in *Cobbe v Yeoman's Row*, which it is suggested is wrong in principle. As with many equitable doctrines its shortcoming is that it sees the actionable detriment as being focused primarily on expenditure of money and less often on 'detrimental' acts that have no pecuniary effect.

Having considered the doctrines of resulting trust, constructive trust and estoppel, it is time to apply them to one of the most complex and interesting areas of equity and trusts: that is, the manner in which people acquire proprietary rights in their homes.

Chapter 9

Trusts of land and of the home

Introduction

Law has a social aspect. It is important that the impact of legal rules and court decisions is never forgotten. The subject matter of this chapter is of particular social significance because it concerns the manner in which individuals acquire rights in the family home. The law in this area is self-contradictory and driven by the variety of political impulses which inform all discussions about policy concerning the family. The reader is encouraged to follow the layout of principles considered in this chapter and simply to accept that they are not possible to reconcile. What the reader should seek to do instead is to understand why differently constituted courts have come to different conclusions. (You are referred to Part 5 of Hudson (2014) for a more detailed analysis of the issues in this chapter: in particular Chapter 15.)

The layout of the discussion on trusts of homes

The law on trusts of homes has been reformulated by the decision of the Supreme Court in *Jones v Kernott* (2011), which in turn re-interpreted the decision of the House of Lords in *Stack v Dowden* (2007), in particular with Lady Hale and Lord Walker explaining what they had meant originally in *Stack v Dowden*.

Two things should be recognised about this area of the law. First, it relates to unmarried couples (with or without children, in long-term or short-term relationships), homesharers who are not romantically linked, and other people who come to co-own their home in some way. Therefore, these are not groups of people who have bought into the clarity of a marriage, in which there is a legal relationship created on one magical wedding day. Consequently, the circumstances in which these cases arise will tend to be slightly random. Second, the history of the law in this area has been that every time in which the highest court has attempted to clarify the law (i.e. *Pettitt v Pettitt* (1970), *Gissing v Gissing* (1971), *Lloyds Bank v Rosset* (1990), *Stack v Dowden* (2007), and even *Thorner v Major* (2009)), their judgments have led only to confusion, or the lower courts have either focused unexpectedly on one minor detail in those judgments or they have chosen to follow the principles set out in other decisions in other lower courts.

There is no reason to suppose that *Jones v Kernott* will make the law any clearer, not least because the Supreme Court has allowed those lower courts to do what they consider to be 'fair' in certain circumstances or to 'infer objectively' a common intention from the parties' conduct; both of these principles are inadequately explained in the judgments and in any event leave the lower courts with an enormous amount of leeway in reaching their own decisions. The result will be the emergence in the years to come of a number of contrary trends in the case law applying these principles.

Consequently, the approach taken in this chapter is as follows. First, to explain the principles which emerge from *Jones v Kernott* (as it re-interprets *Stack v Dowden*) and, second, to examine the different approaches taken in the previous decisions because they will continue to be important in future cases.

The issues raised in this area are among the most fascinating in equity. Those issues are also easy to understand because they arise out of ordinary domestic circumstances, without any of the complexities of other areas of trusts law. Because there are so many contradictory currents in the case law it would be easy to think of it as a confusing mess; but you should not be downhearted. The secret to understanding this area of the law is to recognise that the different judges simply have different opinions about the way in which people should be allowed to acquire rights in their homes. If you simply think of the judgments as being different views (e.g. some people want to focus only on who paid for the property, others think that raising children is in itself enough to raise a right in the home, and so forth) then those differences of opinion are not only easier to understand but they are also to be expected among any group of thoughtful people.

Express trusts of homes

When attempting to decide which of a number of co-owners is to acquire equitable rights in the home, the most straightforward factual situation is where there has been an express declaration of trust allocating the whole of the equitable interest in the land at issue. Such a trust may arise under the terms of the conveyance of the property to the co-owners, or as a result of an express declaration of trust between the parties, or in a situation in which the property is provided for the co-owners under a pre-existing settlement.

In short, there is no need to consider any surrounding circumstances in the context in which the equitable interest in the property has been allocated between the parties on express trust. It should be remembered that, in order for there to be a valid declaration of trust over land, the declaration must comply with s 53(1)(b) of the Law of Property Act 1925:

> . . . a declaration of trust respecting any land or any interest therein must be manifested and proved by some writing signed by some person who is able to declare such trust or by his will.

Failure to comply with that formality requirement will lead to a failure to create a valid express trust over land. It should also be remembered that under s 53(2) there is no formality requirement in relation to constructive, resulting or implied trusts. The following sections will consider the creation of constructive and resulting trusts, which is when the issues become more interesting.

The principles in *Jones v Kernott* and *Stack v Dowden*

The joint judgment delivered by Lady Hale and Lord Walker in the Supreme Court in *Jones v Kernott* (2011) contained a summary of the principles they wished to establish in this area. Both of those judges also gave judgment in agreement in the House of Lords in *Stack v Dowden* (2007). Unfortunately, the decision in *Stack v Dowden* failed to clarify the law; and therefore the decision in *Jones v Kernott* was primarily aimed at clarifying the position in the light of *Stack v Dowden*. It must be assumed that the principles set out by Lady Hale and Lord Walker (and the very similar summary set out by Lord Kerr) will come to establish the leading principles in this area for the immediate future. We will only know for sure when future cases are decided by the county courts, the High Court and the Court of Appeal. Those principles do nevertheless contain a lot of flexibility within them.

Those principles in the wake of the decision of the Supreme Court in *Jones v Kernott* should be understood as follows.

(1) If there is a clear express trust or a provision to that effect of the parties' rights in the conveyance of the property, then that will be decisive of the matter. If there is no such clear trust, then the court must follow through the other principles.

(2) Distinguish between cases in which there is only one person entered on the legal title in the home on the Land Register, and cases in which both parties are entered in the legal title. If only one person was entered on the legal title, then the presumption is that that person is intended to take the entire equitable interest. If both parties were entered on the legal title, then the presumption is that they are intended to take the equitable interest between them.

(3) Either of those presumptions can be rebutted by evidence to the contrary. That contrary evidence will be based on the 'common intention' of the parties. The concept of common intention is that set out in the cases before *Stack v Dowden*. So, the presumption can be rebutted by evidence that the parties had a different common intention at the time of acquiring the property, or that at a later date the parties formed a common intention that their shares would change.

(4) On the basis of the earlier case law, there are a number of possible approaches to what constitutes a common intention. The court should seek out a common intention between the parties, by undertaking a survey of their entire course of dealing, and by inferring objectively from their conduct what that common

intention was. The awkward idea of an 'objective inference' means that the court cannot simply impute a common intention (although Lord Wilson was keen on the idea that the court should impose, or impute, such an intention) but rather the court must try and infer from the evidence what the parties' intention must have been.

(5) If the evidence as to the parties' common intention is inconclusive, then the court may do what it considers to be 'fair' in the circumstances. (This concept, which had been excluded in *Stack v Dowden*, is not explained at all.)

It was held in *Jones v Kernott* that financial contributions made by the parties in relation to the property will be considered but that they will not be decisive of the equitable interest in the property. The older case law was based on ideas like the resulting trust, which had been focused almost entirely on financial contributions to the property. The Supreme Court in *Jones v Kernott* preferred to bring other considerations into play. Ironically, however, neither *Stack v Dowden* nor *Jones v Kernott* ultimately found equitable interests for either of the parties which were different from their financial contributions to the acquisition of the property. However, there are some interesting sociological changes from the early cases in this field which were decided in the 1970s. For example, in the recent cases it has been the women who have made the majority of the financial contributions instead of the men; this was not the case in cases such as *Gissing v Gissing* and *Pettitt v Pettitt* in the House of Lords in the 1970s.

In *Jones v Kernott* itself, Ms Jones had contributed about 90 per cent of the cash towards the property, including a period of over 14 years in which Mr Kernott had left Ms Jones and their two children without making any contribution to the property nor any regular contribution to the maintenance of the children. Ms Jones was held to receive 90 per cent of the equitable interest in the parties' former home. Similarly, in *Stack v Dowden*, Ms Dowden made approximately 65 per cent of financial contributions to the parties' home. It was held that she would acquire 65 per cent of the equitable interest in the property. The same outcome resulted in *Oxley v Hiscock*. Therefore, even though the courts have signalled an intention to take a different approach in the future, they have nevertheless tended to come to conclusions which are broadly in accordance with the parties' financial contribution to the property in any event.

The principal issue which concerned the Supreme Court was whether the parties' common intention must be *inferred* from the evidence, or whether the court can *impute* the parties' common intention: that is, a distinction between the parties forming their own common intention so that the court merely unearths it from the evidence, and the court telling the parties what their common intention should have been. The majority preferred to infer the parties' common intention after examining the evidence. Thus it is said that the parties' common intention will be inferred objectively from the circumstances. This will be difficult in practice because, when the litigation begins, the parties tend to remember the circumstances differently and in partisan terms, each preferring their own rights. Consequently, establishing the objective truth is difficult. This is why, in practice, it may often be the case that the court will resort to deciding what they consider to be 'fair' in the circumstances.

Resulting trusts – contribution to purchase price

As considered in Chapter 6, where a person contributes to the purchase price of the home, an amount of the total equitable interest proportionate to the size of the contribution will be held on resulting trust for that person. Alternatively, this might be expressed as a constructive trust based on the mutual conduct of the parties evidenced by their contribution to the purchase price or the mortgage repayments, as discussed in the next section.

Therefore, the simplest rule in situations where there is no express trust over land is that any person who contributes to the acquisition of property will obtain an equitable interest in that property proportionate to the total interest in the property. The only exceptions to such a finding would occur in situations in which the contribution to the purchase price was made by way of a gift of money to purchasers, or by way of a loan to the purchasers, thus negating an intention to take an equitable interest in the property (*Grant v Edwards* (1986)). If that were not the case, banks lending money under mortgage agreements would acquire equitable interests in property beyond their statutory right to repossession. Similarly, a gift of money involves an outright transfer to the donee but does not entitle the donor to any rights in property acquired with the money (*Westdeutsche Landesbank v Islington* (1996)). Therefore, it is important to ascertain the underlying purpose of applying the money in that way.

Nevertheless, in *Jones v Kernott* and in *Stack v Dowden* it was held that resulting trusts should not decide question as to the equitable ownership of the home. This means that financial contributions to the purchase price are not the only factors that should be considered. Indeed, only Lord Neuberger, in his dissenting judgment in *Stack*, sought to rely on the resulting trust. Nevertheless, as outlined above, the decisions in *Kernott* and in *Stack* both came to conclusions which closely mimicked the parties' cash contributions to their properties.

The principal weakness identified with the doctrine of resulting trusts by feminist theorists is that in many situations it will be the male breadwinner who will have contributed the most financially to a relationship whereas women who do not work or who interrupt careers because they care for the children, for example, will typically be disadvantaged by a rule that is based entirely on contributions in the form of money. Relationships are about more than mere money and yet it is financial contributions that are valued most highly by the law of trusts.

The shape of the discussion to follow

The principles in *Jones v Kernott* enable the courts to infer a common intention and to decide what is fair. This means that all of the other case law concepts established before that case, which were not overruled either in *Jones v Kernott* or in *Stack v Dowden*, will be important in deciding how those principles are to be effected. The discussion to follow will trace a variety of approaches to these questions which were present in the earlier case law: common intention constructive trusts, the balance sheet approach, the family assets approach, the unconscionability approach, and the proprietary estoppel approach. The purpose of these comparative discussions is to identify different trends in the law of trusts when deciding how different claimants might establish rights in the home by means of a common intention. In particular, it will identify those approaches that are predicated entirely on the acquisition of rights through money and those predicated on the acquisition of rights through other forms of participation in a relationship. The principal benefit of this chronological and thematic discussion is that it will illustrate the key principles which arise in this area and it will explain the problems which gave rise to the judgments in *Kernott*.

Common intention constructive trusts

Foundations of the common intention constructive trust

The decision of the House of Lords in *Gissing v Gissing* (1971) created the possibility of looking behind the formal arrangements between the parties to uncover their informal, common intention rather than considering other aspects of their relationship, such issues being typically relied upon by family lawyers (such as the need to consider the welfare of children). It was held that this common intention ought to be the element that is decisive of the division of equitable interests between them.

The case law following the decision in *Gissing* offered a scattered reading of the nature of the constructive trust. The decisions in cases such as *Cowcher v Cowcher* (1972), *Grant v Edwards* (1986) and *Coombes v Smith* (1986) proffered readings of this concept ranging from divisions in the meaning of consensus, common intention coupled with detriment, and proprietary estoppel, respectively. In the light of this welter of contradictory and difficult authority, there was some momentum for rationalisation of the law. Just such a rationalisation of the operation of the constructive trust in this area was set out in the leading speech of Lord Bridge in the House of Lords in *Lloyds Bank v Rosset* (1990). Lord Bridge set out the terms on which a claimant may acquire an equitable interest in the home on grounds of 'constructive trust or proprietary estoppel'.

The facts of *Rosset* were as follows. A semi-derelict farmhouse was put in H's name. The house was to be the family home and renovated as a joint venture. H's wife, W, oversaw all of the building work. W had understood that the property was to be acquired without a mortgage; however, H acquired the property with a mortgage registered in his sole name. The bank sought repossession in lieu of money owed by H under the mortgage. W sought to resist sale (*inter alia*) because of her equitable interest in the property, which she claimed, grounded an overriding interest in her favour on grounds of actual occupation under s 70(1)(g) of the Land Registration Act 1925. It was held that W had acquired no equitable interest in the property. Lord Bridge delivered the only speech in the House of Lords. In that judgment, Lord Bridge sought to redraw the basis on which a common intention constructive trust would be formed.

In short, there are two forms of constructive trusts identified by the leading House of Lords case of *Lloyds Bank v Rosset*. What is remarkable about this test is that it seeks to impose a very rigid framework on arguably the most complex area of our society (the family) and that it has been ignored by most courts subsequently as a consequence of its rigidity. The two forms of 'common intention constructive trust' it creates can be set out in the following way.

First, where there is no express declaration of trust, the equitable interest in the home will be allocated according to the common intention of the parties by means of constructive trust ('common intention constructive trust by agreement') based on an express agreement between the parties. Two points are worthy of note. First, the discussions are expected to have been carried out in advance of the purchase. Subsequent discussions between the parties are not important, or less important. This approach does not seem to recognise the reality of relationships in which intentions alter over the years with the birth of children, the death of family members, the advent of unemployment and the thousand other shocks that flesh is heir to. Similarly, the agreement is related to each property individually (subject to what is said below about deposits and the use of sale proceeds of previous properties). It is not the case that the parties are deemed to acquire personal rights between one another; rather, they are related solely to each individual property.

Furthermore, the assumption is that there are express discussions, rather than an emerging but unspoken intention between the parties. For example, where one party ceases to work to bring up children, thus interrupting the ability to earn money to be applied to the mortgage instalments, the intention of the parties is altered. It is unlikely that there will be an express discussion as to rights in the property each is intended to receive, although it is likely that the parties will adjust their lifestyle to accommodate the need to meet their household expenses and so forth. The second limb of the test is the only one that permits this type of flexibility.

Second, where a person contributes to the purchase price of the home this might be expressed as a constructive trust based on the mutual conduct of the parties evidenced by their contribution to the purchase price or the mortgage repayments ('common intention constructive trust by mutual conduct'). The type of conduct envisaged by Lord Bridge is, however, very limited. He has in mind 'direct contributions to the purchase price' only. In recognition of the reality of those families who finance the purchase of the property by mortgage, rather than by cash purchase, it is sufficient for the contributions to be made either 'initially [that is, by cash purchase or cash deposit] or by payment of mortgage instalments'. The limitation of these means of contribution is underlined when Lord Bridge explicitly holds that 'it is at least extremely doubtful whether anything less will do'.

The need for detriment in common intention constructive trust

It was held in *Rosset* that it is also necessary for the claimant to demonstrate that she has suffered detriment before being able to demonstrate a common intention constructive trust. The core principles of the common intention constructive trust were set out in *Grant v Edwards* (1986), in which Browne-Wilkinson VC sought to re-establish the core principles as found by Lord Diplock in *Gissing v Gissing*. In his Lordship's opinion there were three important principles to be analysed: (1) the nature of the substantive right, in that there must be a common intention that the claimant is to have a beneficial interest *and* that the claimant has acted to her detriment; (2) proof of the common intention, requiring direct evidence or inferred common intention; (3) the quantification of the size of that right. The requirement for detriment in the context was mirrored in *Midland Bank v Dobson* (1985), where it was held insufficient that there be a common intention, unless there was also some detriment suffered by the claimant.

In *Grant v Edwards* it was held that there must be an agreement or conduct on the part of the non-property-owning party which can only be explained as being directed at acquiring rights in property. While the plaintiff had not made a financial contribution to the purchase of the property, the defendant had made excuses to her for not putting her on the legal title, which indicated an intention that she would otherwise have been such an owner. In short, he had sought to keep her off the title through deceit, indicating that otherwise she would probably have had formal rights. Further, it was found that her contributions to family expenses were more than would otherwise have been expected in the circumstances and thereby enabled the defendant to make the mortgage payments. It was found that this behaviour could not have been expected unless she understood that she would acquire an interest in the property. The roots of the modern approach are discernible in this focus on both any agreement made between the parties and also on an analysis of the parties' conduct in respect of the purchase of the property and on the mortgage repayments. The somewhat heretical conclusion reached in this case was that it is possible that purely personal acts will be evidence of an intention that a proprietary interest is to be acquired by the claimant.

However *Coombes v Smith* (1986), took the view that for the plaintiff to leave her partner to have children with the defendant would not lead to the acquisition of a right in property because that was purely personal detriment, not the sort necessary to acquire rights in property. As considered below, it is generally the case that detriment that is suffered merely as a part of a plaintiff's personal life (e.g. where that person leaves her current partner on the promise that the defendant will give her a right in property) will not be sufficient to grant a right in property.

In line with *Gissing*, the Court of Appeal in *Burns v Burns* (1984), held that mere contribution to household expenses would not be sufficient to acquire an interest in property. This approach has been applied in a number of cases, including *Rosset* and *Nixon v Nixon* (1969). Therefore, there is a need for some substantive (typically financial) contribution to the property beyond mere work within the normal context of the family, such as housework.

The difficulties with the strict Rosset test

The aim of this section is to consider, in broad terms, the commentary specific to the *Rosset* decision. Much of this thinking is then taken up in the final section of this chapter. Any test that is rigid necessarily creates the possibility for unfairness at the margins. That would appear to be the case in respect of the test for common intention constructive trust in *Rosset*.

Suppose the following situation. A and B are an unmarried couple without children. A buys a trendy flat in Central London entirely by means of a mortgage. It is agreed that A will be the sole mortgagor and entirely responsible for the repayments. Suppose that they like to live the high life from their trendy apartment and that B pays for all of their entertainment expenses, for their car, and for their regular holidays in Aspen, Cannes, St Lucia and the Seychelles. So lavish is their lifestyle that B's expenditure is exactly the same as A's expenditure: both of them spending 100 per cent of their incomes on these items.

A strict application of the *Rosset* test would deny B any interest in the property on the basis that B had not contributed directly to the purchase price nor to the mortgage repayments, even though she had spent exactly the same amount of money as A; all this despite the necessity of B's contribution to their shared expenses to make it possible for A to discharge all of the mortgage expenses. B would clearly wish to argue that her expenditure made the mortgage payments possible and therefore ought to lead to the acquisition of some equitable rights. The 'family assets' approach considered below may offer greater hope to B of acquiring rights in the property by acknowledging that the *Rosset* test will not always be appropriate in cases of family breakdown. These equivocal factual situations must form the background to much of the ensuing discussion in this chapter.

The balance sheet approach

Introduction

The doctrine of precedent appears to have been thrown to the four winds in the area of trusts of homes. There were House of Lords' decisions in *Gissing* and in *Pettitt*, which redressed the balance of the rights of spouses to acquire rights in the family home. Subsequently, the House of Lords' decision in *Rosset* has set out a very strict test based on the common intention constructive trust – as set out above. Whatever one might think of the merits of that test, one thing is evident: it is very clear. And yet the Court of Appeal moved in a number of different directions in the 1990s, effectively sidestepping the didactic test in *Rosset* in favour of a range of flexible, case-by-case judgments. This section considers the first of the Court of Appeal's approaches; the following section, at p 150, considers a second trend in the Court of Appeal, which leans towards an equal division of the equitable interest for couples who have terminated a long relationship.

The essence of the 'balance sheet approach' is that the court draws up a list of financial contributions made by each party towards the property, akin to an accountant preparing a balance sheet, and calculates each party's proportionate equitable interest in the home according to that calculation.

Calculating the size of the equitable interest

The trend towards balance sheet calculation began in the decision of the Court of Appeal in *Bernard v Josephs* (1982) with a decision entitling the courts to consider the mathematical equity contributed by each party across the range of transactions contributing to the acquisition of a property.

As considered above, direct contribution will give rise to a resulting trust. The second possibility, where it can be proved that the cohabitee contributed to the price of the property after the acquisition, will give rise to an equitable interest in the cohabitee's favour on resulting or constructive trust. The size of the interest in such circumstances will be proportionate to the contribution to the total purchase price (*Huntingford v Hobbs* (1993)). The Court of Appeal in *Huntingford v Hobbs* was prepared to look behind the documentation signed by the parties, which suggested that they held the equitable interest in the property in equal shares. However, it was held that there must be cogent evidence that any documentation signed by the parties was not intended to constitute the extent of their beneficial interests. Therefore, where a house costs £100,000 and X provides £40,000, where Y procures a mortgage for £60,000, Y is taken to have contributed 60 per cent of the purchase price (*Huntingford v Hobbs*). There is also the possibility of equitable accounting to take into account periods of rent-free occupation, and so forth, by one or other of the parties (*Bernard v Josephs* (1982)).

What can be taken into account?

What is clear from the preceding discussion is that direct cash contributions to the purchase price, or to the mortgage repayments, will be taken into account in calculating an equitable interest (*Lloyds Bank v Rosset*). What is less clear is the extent to which non-cash provisions of value can be taken into account similarly, particularly given that *Rosset* would not include them in any calculations of an equitable interest. An interesting question arose in *Springette v Defoe* (1992) as to whether or not a person who procures a discount on the purchase price of property is entitled to bring that discount (or a reduction) on the price of the property into the calculation of her equitable interest in the property. The argument runs that getting a discount on the property constitutes an indirect contribution to the purchase price, being reliant on the use of some other right that person has.

On the facts of *Springette v Defoe*, Miss Springette had been a tenant of the London Borough of Ealing for more than 11 years. She began to cohabit with Mr Defoe and they decided to purchase a house in 1982. Neither party was able to raise the necessary mortgage because their incomes, jointly or severally, were not large enough. However, Miss Springette was entitled to a discount of 41 per cent, under the applicable right-to-buy legislation, on the purchase price of her home from the council because she had been an Ealing council tenant for more than 11 years. The purchase price was therefore £14,445 with the discount. The parties took out a mortgage for £12,000. There was an agreement between the parties that they would meet the mortgage repayments half each. Mr Defoe provided £180 in cash. Miss Springette provided the balance of £2,526 in cash. Their relationship broke down in 1985. The issue arose as to the proportionate beneficial interest which each should have in the house.

The Court of Appeal held that there should be a resulting trust imposed unless there was found to be sufficient specific evidence of a common intention to found a constructive trust. Such a common intention must be communicated between the parties and made manifest between them at the time of the transaction. On the facts of *Springette* there was no evidence to support the contention that the parties had had any sort of discussion as to their respective interests (within Lord Bridge's test in *Rosset*) nor that they had reached any such agreement. Therefore, the presumption of resulting trust could not be displaced. The court performed a calculation exercise in the following terms, calculating the amount of value that each party had contributed to the purchase price.

Springette		Defoe	
£10,045	(discount on property price)	£6,000	(half of mortgage payments)
£6,000	(half of mortgage payments)	£180	(cash)
£2,526	(cash contribution)		
£18,571		£6,180	

Therefore, Springette was taken to have contributed 75 per cent of the equity and Defoe 25 per cent (after rounding).

Effect of merely contributing 'value', not cash

Importantly, the court looked at the *value* contributed and not at the *amount of cash paid*. It is interesting to see how this compares to Lord Bridge's insistence in *Rosset* that it is at least extremely doubtful whether anything less than a direct contribution to the mortgage or to the purchase price will do. If it is accepted that procuring a reduction in the purchase price is a sufficient contribution, why should it be impossible to argue that if A pays for the household costs, the car and the children's clothes, thus enabling B to defray the mortgage, that A is not making it possible for B to pay off the mortgage and thus making a financial contribution to the purchase? After all, once you accept that the contribution need not be made in cash, at what point is the line to be drawn under the range of non-cash contributions which are possible?

The nature of the acceptable contribution is complicated even on the facts of *Rosset*. It is accepted that the courts should allow the parties to include contingent or future liabilities, such as the mortgage obligations, as part of the calculation of their respective contributions. Rather than a straightforward application of the principle in *Dyer v Dyer* (1788) that such a contribution denotes an interest under resulting trust, the parties are being permitted to include in the calculations amounts that they will have to pay in the future, but which they have not paid yet under the mortgage contract. This issue is considered further below.

Unpaid mortgage capital and other issues

Judgment in *Springette* was delivered by the same Court of Appeal and on the same day as *Huntingford v Hobbs* (1993), discussed briefly above. *Huntingford* pursued the issue of the means by which contributions to the acquisition of the property should be calculated and reflected in the equitable interests which were ultimately awarded to the parties. The plaintiff and the defendant lived together, but did not marry. The plaintiff was living on social security benefits; the defendant had been recently divorced and was living in her former matrimonial home. The plaintiff moved in but was uncomfortable living in his partner's matrimonial home and therefore they decided to sell up. The plaintiff wanted to move to Woking, where he felt he had a better chance to make money as a music teacher. The parties also wanted to be able to provide a home for the defendant's 21-year-old daughter.

The plaintiff and the defendant bought a property, in which they lived, for £63,250 in 1986. The defendant sold her previous property and put £38,860 towards the purchase of the new property. The remaining £25,000 was provided by way of an endowment mortgage. The mortgage liability was undertaken in the names of both plaintiff and defendant. It was agreed between the plaintiff and the defendant that the plaintiff would make the mortgage repayments. In 1988, the plaintiff left the defendant. The plaintiff had paid £5,316.30 in mortgage interest and £1,480.25 in premium payments. The plaintiff spent £2,000 on the construction of a conservatory – this did not increase the value of the property although it did make it more saleable. The defendant did not have any real income – the plaintiff paid for most income expenses and household bills. The property was valued at £95,000 at the time of the hearing and there remained £25,000 in capital outstanding on the mortgage.

The plaintiff contended that the property was to be held in equity under a joint tenancy on the basis of the terms of the conveyance into the names of both plaintiff and defendant. Therefore, he sought an order that the property should be sold and the sale proceeds divided in equal shares between the parties. The Court of Appeal held that the property should be sold but that the sale should be postponed to give the defendant a chance to buy out the plaintiff. Further, it was found that the plaintiff must have been intended to have some equitable interest in the property. In terms of establishing the parties' respective balance sheets, the defendant should be deemed to have contributed the cash proceeds of the sale of her previous home, whereas the plaintiff should be deemed to have contributed the whole amount of the mortgage because he was to have made the mortgage repayments, and the plaintiff should receive some credit for the cost of the conservatory. The issue then arose: what about the remaining, unpaid capital left on the mortgage? The Court of Appeal held that the plaintiff should have deducted from his interest an amount in recognition of the fact that he had not yet paid off the capital of the mortgage and that it was the defendant who had agreed to meet that cost in the future.

Therefore, the Court of Appeal calculated that:

- the plaintiff should receive £2,000 (conservatory);
- the defendant should receive £25,000 (capital of the mortgage);
- the plaintiff should receive 39 per cent (proportion contributed by mortgage); and
- the defendant should receive 61 per cent (proportion of cash contribution).

Once the defendant bought the plaintiff out, the 39 per cent would be transferred to her.

Deposits and sale proceeds from previous properties

One of the common shortcomings of English property law is that the rules focus on specific items of property rather than taking into account the range of dealings between individuals which might impact on the property but which were perhaps not related to it. In this way, sales of properties generate capital to acquire further properties, typically after discharge of the mortgage. It is important therefore that focus on the particular land in issue does not ignore interests held previously in other properties. So if A and B acquired 55 Mercer Road with equal cash contributions on the basis of a tenancy in common, that 50–50 division in equitable interest ought to be carried forward when 55 Mercer Road is sold and the proceeds are used to buy 1 Acacia Avenue.

Similarly, it will typically be the case that individuals buying a home will generate most of the capital to acquire the property by means of mortgage. Those individuals may be required to pay a deposit from their own funds by the mortgagee, or may choose to do so, thereby reducing the size of their debt. Where these deposits are the only cash contributions made by the parties (otherwise than by way of mortgage), their proportionate size may be decisive of their respective equitable interests, or may contribute to their part of the balance sheet, as seen above in relation to *Springette* and *Huntingford*, and below in relation to *Midland Bank v Cooke* (1995) and *McHardy v Warren* (1994).

In *Midland Bank v Cooke* it was held that a common intention constructive trust can arise where H and W equally provide a deposit on a house purchased in the name of one or both of them. (The facts of this case are considered in greater detail below.) W had contributed nothing to the purchase price, but contributed the deposit for the purchase of the property equally with H. The question arose whether or not she had any beneficial interest in the property in any event. Waite LJ held that the judge must survey the whole course of dealing of the parties. Further, the court is not required to confine its survey to the limited range of acts of direct contribution of the sort that are needed to found a beneficial interest in the first place. If that survey is inconclusive, the court should fall back on the maxim 'equality is equity'. Part of the judgment of Waite LJ was that equal contribution to the original deposit was an indication that the parties intended to split the equitable interest in their home equally between them. However, as considered above, it is difficult to reconcile this focus on equality with the other cases in this area (e.g. *Rosset*) or the balance sheet cases (e.g. *Huntingford*), which would consider such an equal division to be inequitable.

On the issue of deposits and subsequently purchased homes, in *McHardy v Warren*, H's parents had paid the whole of the deposit on the matrimonial home acquired by H and his wife, W. The legal title in the property was registered in H's sole name. The remainder of the purchase price of the property was provided entirely by means of a mortgage. The mortgage was taken out in H's name only. Two subsequent homes were bought out of the sale proceeds of the first home. The mortgagee sought to recover their security by ordering a sale of the house. W sought to resist their claim on the basis that she had an equitable interest in the property too, grounded on the argument that the deposit provided by her father-in-law constituted a gift to them both and therefore that she acquired an equitable interest at that stage. Therefore, she claimed that she had 50 per cent of the equitable interest in the original property, which translated into 50 per cent of all subsequent acquisitions.

It was contended on behalf of the mortgagee that W had only a right equal to the cash value of W's half of the deposit in proportion to the total purchase price of the house; that is, a right to half of the original £650 deposit (that is, £325) out of the total value of the property. The central principle was held to be that the parties must have intended that there be equal title in the property to sustain W's argument. On the facts, the court felt that the only plausible conclusion to be drawn was that the intention of the father in putting up the deposit was to benefit H and W equally and that their intention must be that the property be held equally in equity. Therefore, the court held that W was entitled to an equal share of the house with H because W put up the deposit equally with H.

The family assets approach

Alternative Court of Appeal decisions have developed a family assets approach which suggests that property should be deemed to be held equally between couples. This approach created many of the principles on which the Supreme Court relied in *Jones v Kernott* (and in *Stack v Dowden*).

Where equality is equity

In most cases involving long relationships and children, there will be a complicated list of items of property and communal undertakings. Picking between real and personal property, and including voluntary work in a partner's business, will all confuse the issue whether or not there have been any rights in property acquired. One of this writer's favourite cases explores this point. *Hammond v Mitchell* (1991) was a decision of Waite J in which the question arose as to rights in real property, business ventures and chattels. Hammond was a second-hand-car salesman who had recently left his wife, then aged 40. He picked up Mitchell when she had flagged his car down to ask directions in Epping Forest. She was then a Bunny Girl at the Playboy Club in Mayfair, aged 21. Very soon after that first meeting they were living together. It was said that '[t]hey both shared a zest for the good life'. The relationship lasted 11 years and spawned two children. The issue arose whether or not Mitchell had acquired any interest in any property which, predominantly, was held in his name.

The history of the equitable interest in property followed a familiar pattern in that '[t]hey were too much in love at this time either to count the pennies or pay attention to who was providing them'. He had told her that they would marry when he was divorced. He also told her not to worry about herself and the children because 'everything is half yours'. In time they bought a house in Essex in which they continued to live until the break-up of the relationship. They lived hand-to-mouth, trading in cash and filling their house with movable goods. She worked in his business ventures with him. There were no formal accounts and no formal agreements as to rights in any form of property. They both acquired interests in restaurant ventures in Valencia. She decided to leave him and so stuffed the Mercedes he had bought her with lots of movables and left him when he was abroad. They were briefly reconciled before she left him again with a large amount of personal property crammed into a Jaguar XJS.

Waite J was clear that he considered the question of finding a common intention 'detailed, time-consuming and laborious'. The first question for the court to address was whether there was any agreement. Here there had been discussions as to the house. Echoing the words of Lord Pearson in *Pettitt v Pettitt* (1970), Waite J held that '[t]his is not an area where the maxim "equality is equity" falls to be applied unthinkingly'. However, in the light of all the facts, it was suggested that the process of establishing her share of the house should begin from a base of assuming her to have one half of the total interest, on the basis that it appeared that the couple had intended to muck in together and thereby share everything equally.

The second question was whether or not there is any imputed intention that should be applied to the parties. It was found that, while he contributed personally to the business which she had set up in Valencia, this did not justify any re-allocation of any proprietary rights without more. His cash investment had not, it was found, been made with an intention to acquire any further property rights in that Spanish property. With reference to the household chattels it was held that 'the parties must expect the courts to adopt a robust allegiance to the maxim "equality is equity"'. Therefore, everything was divided down the middle.

The confusion which remains at the doctrinal level in these cases is well illustrated by the decision of the Court of Appeal in *Midland Bank v Cooke*. In 1971 a husband and wife purchased a house for £8,500. The house was registered in the husband's sole name. The purchase was funded as follows.

£6,450	(by way of mortgage loan)
£1,100	(wedding gift from H's parents to the couple)
£950	(H's cash contribution)
£8,500	(total purchase price)

In 1978 the mortgage was replaced by a more general mortgage in favour of H, which secured the repayment of his company's business overdraft. In 1979 W signed a consent form to subordinate any interest she may have to the bank's mortgage. Subsequently, the bank sought forfeiture of the mortgage and possession of the house in default of payment. W claimed undue influence (pre-*Barclays Bank v O'Brien* (1993)) and an equitable interest in the house to override the bank's claim.

The Court of Appeal, in the sole judgment of Waite LJ, went back to *Gissing* without considering the detail of *Rosset* (although accepting that the test in *Rosset* was ordinarily the test to be applied). Waite LJ had trouble with the different approaches adopted in *Springette* and *McHardy*. The former calculated the interests of the parties on a strictly mathematical, resulting trust basis. The latter looked to the intentions of all the parties as to whether or not the deposit should be considered to be a proportionate part of the total purchase price or as establishing a half share in the equity in the property. He claimed to find the difference in approach 'mystifying'.

Waite LJ returned to the speech of Lord Diplock in *Gissing* and to the decision of Browne-Wilkinson VC in *Grant v Edwards*, before holding the following:

> [T]he duty of the judge is to undertake a survey of the whole course of dealing between the parties relevant to their ownership and occupation of the property and their sharing of its burdens and advantages. That scrutiny will not confine itself to the limited range of acts of direct contribution of the sort that are needed to found a beneficial interest in the first place. It will take into consideration all conduct which throws light on the question what shares were intended. Only if that search proves inconclusive does the court fall back on the maxim that 'equality is equity'.

This concept that the court should 'undertake a survey of the whole course of dealing between the parties' (as opposed simply to looking to see who paid for the purchase price of the property) was a significant influence on the Supreme Court in *Jones v Kernott*. On the facts In *Cooke*, the matter could not be decided simply by reference to the cash contributions of the parties. The court accepted that the parties constituted a clear example of a situation in which a couple 'had agreed to share everything equally'. Facts indicating this shared attitude to all aspects of their relationship included evidence of the fact that Mrs Cooke had brought up the children, worked part-time and full-time to pay household bills, and had become a co-signatory to the second mortgage.

What is not clear is how this decision is to be reconciled with the findings in *Burns v Burns* and *Nixon v Nixon* that activities revolving only around domestic chores could not constitute the acquisition of rights in property. Further, it is not obvious how the decision can be reconciled with the *dicta* of Lord Bridge in *Rosset* that a common intention formed on the basis of conduct must be directed at the mortgage payments and that it 'is difficult to see how anything less will do'. Returning to *Gissing*, as Lord Pearson held: 'I think . . . that the decision of cases of this kind has been made more difficult by excessive application of the maxim "equality is equity".' Therefore, Waite LJ's approach in *Hammond* and in *Cooke* is fundamentally different from that.

Proprietary estoppel

Introduction

The doctrine of proprietary estoppel was considered in detail in Chapter 8. This discussion is necessarily much shorter and is focused specifically on the acquisition of rights in the home. Proprietary estoppel is a two-step process: first, the claimant must demonstrate that the estoppel arises, then there is a second question as to the appropriate remedy. Each element is taken in turn.

The basis of proprietary estoppel

Proprietary estoppel will arise in circumstances in which a representation or assurance is made to the claimant, such that the claimant relies on that representation to her detriment (*Re Basham* (1986)). So, in *Basham*, a woman cared for a relative on the understanding, which was known to that relative, that the woman would inherit her relative's house after his death. She also solved a boundary dispute in relation to the property and her husband turned down an offer of accommodation from his employer in the expectation the she would inherit the house. When the relative died without leaving her the house in his will, it was held that a representation had been made to her in reliance on which she had performed all of those acts.

A representation can be made in a single moment or it can be in the nature of an impression which the defendant allows the claimant to form over time. So, in *Thorner v Major* (2009), it was held that there could be a representation in circumstances in which two taciturn farmers from Somerset hardly spoke a word to one another but in which the claimant had been allowed to form the impression that the other farmer would leave the farm to him by will. Importantly, then, it is possible to make a representation without even speaking. Which is unusual.

It had been held by the Court of Appeal in *Gillett v Holt* (2000) that a representation did not need to be in the form of a single statement made on a single date, but rather it could be the aggregate of many things said within a family over many years. So, a farmer befriended a young man and had the young man work on his farm and turn down his academic future. The young man renovated a disused cottage on the land and sorted out problems in a particular field, as well as working generally on the farm. The young man moved in his girlfriend in time. On a number of occasions, including birthdays and other celebrations, it was suggested that the farm would pass to the young man in the future. It was found that this was sufficient to constitute a representation, and that all the acts performed by the young man constituted sufficient detriment for him to be entitled to the cottage, the field and an amount of money.

The available remedies in outline

The range of remedies in relation to proprietary estoppel is very broad indeed. Given that the court appears to be able to award proprietary or non-proprietary remedies, or some combination of the two, then proprietary estoppel is clearly a remedial doctrine (as distinct from institutional constructive trusts). So, in *Pascoe v Turner* (1979), the entire freehold interest in property was awarded so as to enforce the promise that the claimant could occupy property for life. At the other end of the spectrum, however, in *Jennings v Rice* (2002), it was held that the claimant would be entitled only to money of an amount sufficient to prevent unconscionability being suffered by the claimant. In cases like *Gillett v Holt* (2000), it has been held that the appropriate remedy is a combination of money and the entire freehold in identified property: so the claimant in that case received the freehold in the disused cottage which he had renovated and the field on which he had done a lot of work, together with a sum of money appropriate to the context. More eccentrically, in *Porntip Stallion v Albert Stallion Holdings Ltd* (2009), it was held that where a former wife of the deceased had been promised that she could occupy the former matrimonial home for life, then the appropriate remedy would be a right to occupy that property in common with the deceased's widow (on the basis that the two had managed to co-exist in that property acceptably previously).

The extent and nature of the interest awarded under proprietary estoppel

What the preceding overview demonstrated was that the nature of the remedy connected to proprietary estoppel is at the discretion of the court. The decision of the Court of Appeal in *Pascoe v Turner* (1979) is illustrative of the breadth of the remedy potentially available under a proprietary estoppel claim. The plaintiff and the defendant cohabited in a property that was registered in the name of the plaintiff alone. The plaintiff often told the defendant that the property and its contents were hers – however, the property was never conveyed to her. In reliance on these representations, the defendant spent money on redecoration and repairs to the property. While the amounts were not large, they constituted a large proportion of the defendant's savings. The defendant sought to assert rights under proprietary estoppel when the plaintiff sought an order to remove the defendant from the property.

The decision of the Court of Appeal in *Pascoe v Turner* was that the size of interest applicable would be that required to do the 'minimum equity necessary' between the parties. Therefore, it was decided to award the transfer of the freehold to the defendant, to fulfil the promise that a home would be available to her for the rest of her life, rather than (apparently) merely to avoid the detriment that had actually been suffered in reliance on the representation. It is impossible to grant a larger interest in land than an outright assignment of the freehold. Therefore, the court apparently has within its power the ability to award any remedy that will prevent the detriment that would otherwise be suffered by the claimant.

However, it is not the case that proprietary estoppel will always lead to an award of property rights. For example, in *Baker v Baker* (1993), the plaintiff was deemed entitled only to compensation in respect of the cost of giving up secure accommodation. The plaintiff was a 75-year-old man with a secure tenancy over a house in Finchley. The defendants were his son and daughter, who rented accommodation in Bath. It was agreed that the plaintiff should vacate his flat and that the parties should buy a house together in Torquay. The plaintiff contributed £33,950 in return for which he was entitled to occupy the property rent-free. The defendants acquired the remainder of the purchase price by way of mortgage. The parties decided to terminate the relationship and the plaintiff was rehoused as a secure tenant with housing benefit.

It was not held that there was a resulting trust in favour of the plaintiff (a matter accepted by the court, and presumably the parties, although the reason is not clear from the judgment). Therefore, the plaintiff sought to establish rights on the basis of proprietary estoppel. It was held that the appropriate equitable response was to provide compensation rather than an interest in the Torquay house. The amount of compensation was valued in accordance with the annual cost of the accommodation he enjoyed, capitalised for the remainder of his life. The amount of the award would then be discounted as an award of a capital sum. Some account was also taken of the costs of moving and so forth. The application of equitable compensation, while a matter of some complexity (considered in Chapter 10), does not convey proprietary rights in the land at issue, but only a right to receive something akin to common law damages, namely equitable compensation, to remedy the detriment suffered as a result of the failure of the representation.

The unconscionability approach

The courts have begun to develop an approach that is concerned to prevent the claimant from suffering unconscionability at the hands of another person claiming an equitable interest in the home. Interestingly, the concept of unconscionability was generally absent from the leading judgments in *Stack v Dowden* and *Jones v Kernott*, even though it was significant in cases on which those judgments relied. This approach was described in *Oxley v Hiscock* (2004) in the following manner by Chadwick LJ:

> ... what the court is doing, in cases of this nature, is to supply or impute a common intention as to the parties' respective shares (in circumstances in which there was in fact no common intention) on the basis of that which, in the light of all the material circumstances (including the acts and conduct of the parties after the acquisition) is shown to be fair ... and it may be more satisfactory to accept that there is no difference in cases of this nature between constructive trust and proprietary estoppel.

It is suggested that the 'unconscionability' element of this approach is encapsulated in the notion that the court is looking for an understanding of the parties' common intention which would be 'fair', to quote Chadwick LJ. This finding of unconscionability usually begins with a consideration of whether or not the parties have in fact reached an agreement, but even then the often vague finding of an agreement is usually tempered by a consideration of the entire course of dealing between the parties. The court is thus concerned with establishing a fair result, as opposed to giving effect to the pre-existing rights of the parties. This is, it seems to me, a very significant point: the court is prepared to 'supply' the parties' common intention, not simply to find it on the facts. That means the court is prepared to make up what the court thinks their common intention would have been, not simply to try to find out what it actually was. This is, therefore, a fiction of sorts. The court is doing what the court thinks is 'fair', not necessarily what the parties agreed to do. Furthermore, this may yet lead to a fusing of the principles of constructive trust and of proprietary estoppel in this context.

The idea of the court looking for what is considered to be fair is accepted in *Jones v Kernott*, where the evidence is not conclusive as to the parties' common intention. Interestingly, however, Baroness Hale had seemed to exclude the idea of looking for what is fair in *Stack v Dowden*, only to accept it in *Jones v Kernott*.

Problems with the *Jones v Kernott* concepts

The principal difficulty with the English law in this area is the idea of a 'common intention'. It is very rare in life for people to form a 'common intention' whereby they agree to the same course of action or to the same state of affairs, unless they sit down and create a formal contract or settlement. Therefore, it is difficult to know how or when a common intention has been formed between two people who do not sit down and create such a formal agreement as to the ownership of their home. What would a common intention be required to cover? People will ordinarily agree who will pay for what and what their role will be in relation to the children, the cooking, the cleaning and so forth, but not necessarily what their respective property rights will be.

The courts tend to assume that a common intention will be formed at the date of acquisition, but what about a situation in which one party moves into the other party's existing home? What about the couple changing their minds after a few years of living together: what sort of change of mind would be sufficient to change their property rights, and how formal must that change of mind be? What if they never discuss any of these things out loud because they are too embarrassed, or it does not occur to them, or their relationship is one in which they do not discuss things much? What if, unexpectedly, one of them becomes ill or loses their job, so that the burden of their responsibilities changes? Should the court decide in the absence of a formal change in their common intention that their intention should be deemed to be something else?

The very idea of a common intention that the court either has to infer from the evidence or, even worse, which the court imputes to the parties (i.e. which the court imposes on them) is the opposite of a common intention which the parties had for themselves. Courts elsewhere in the Commonwealth have referred to this as 'the phantom common intention' precisely because it is so meaningless. If the parties do not have a common intention, and if the court therefore has to assemble what the court thinks that intention would have been, then it is simply not *the parties'* common intention at all. Instead it is the court deciding what it thinks is appropriate between the parties in those circumstances. And if that is what the judges are going to do, then it would be infinitely better if they just admitted it and explained what they were doing instead. In truth, English judges are nervous about appearing to hand out property rights without the pretence of finding that it is the parties' own intention that they are enforcing.

Of course when relationships begin and people move in together, they usually do not take the time calmly to allocate their rights in the property (although hopefully you, dear reader, will do exactly that when the time comes). At the start of a relationship, the people involved are too excited to think about those sorts of niceties. They focus far more of their energies on bouncing around together and looking into one another's eyes than they do on the ramifications of *Jones v Kernott* on their lives when the inevitable happens and they split up or the mortgagee seeks to sell their home. The whole idea of a common intention suggests a calm rationality which most people do not possess in their personal lives. Even the two barristers who were the parties in *Cox v Jones* did not sort this out between them, so why should we expect that other people will? In most relationships, the couple will cede responsibility for all sorts of issues to one another: who chooses the curtains, who books the holiday, who chooses the takeaway meal on Friday night, who argues with the neighbours, who takes the kids to school, who has possession of the television remote control, and so on. It is rare for a couple to agree about all of these things – they are more likely to have prickly arguments about them once in a while, but not a formal negotiation. Otherwise any sensible couple will just lapse into a way of living which forms a silent compromise between what each of them would ideally do if they lived alone, and doing what the other person wants so as to stave off the horrible loneliness of actually living alone. As Mark Corrigan put it in *Peep Show*, being in a relationship and doing things that you do not really want to do is the cost of not being lonely. So, is the idea of a common intention within a relationship even a feasible or useful one? What does it even mean?

If the court is *inferring* the existence of such a common intention from the evidence, then what that really means is that the court is deciding what the court thinks the couple would have been likely to decide if they had talked about it properly. This inference will be mixed with a tiny element of what the court thinks is fair because, after all, the parties may have agreed to something entirely unfair in practice because one of them had all the money, or because one of them was in charge in most aspects of their relationship in practice, or because one of them was human enough to feel scared of losing the other person or of upsetting them by broadcasting the subject. At this level, for the court to do what is 'fair' is no bad thing, but only if the courts start to discuss what sorts of issues might be relevant in deciding what is 'fair' in any given circumstances. Otherwise, the whole thing will become a lottery for litigants depending on the judge involved. Perhaps this area of law needs to become self-consciously more like family law or child law with its use of high-level principles and a flexible approach to precedent which give general guidance to all involved as a result.

The operation of the Trusts of Land and Appointment of Trustees Act 1996

Context

The introduction of the Trusts of Land and Appointment of Trustees Act (TOLATA) 1996 sought the conversion of all strict settlements under the Settled Land Act 1925 and all trusts for sale under the Law of Property Act 1925 into a composite trust known as a 'trust of land'. However, within that recomposition of the property law understanding of rights in the home were some larger objectives concerned with the rights of beneficiaries under trusts of land to occupy the home and an extension of the categories of person whose rights should be taken into account when reaching decisions on questions such as the sale of the home.

As part of this technical aim to reform the manner in which land was treated by the 1925 legislation, s 3 of TOLATA 1996 sets out the abolition of the doctrine of conversion. Significantly, this change altered the automatic assumption that the rights of any beneficiary under the old trust for sale were vested not in the property itself, but rather in the proceeds of sale. This notion of conversion of rights flowed from the understanding of trusts for sale as being trusts whose purpose was the sale of the trust fund and its conversion into cash. Clearly, this ran contrary to the intention of most people acquiring land for their own occupation, in which it was not supposed for a moment that their sole intention was to dispose of the property as though a mere investment. Therefore, the common law developed the notion of a 'collateral purpose' under which the court would resist the obligation to sell the property in place of an implied ulterior objective for families (for example) to retain the property as their home.

The specific notion of trusteeship

One of the underlying aims of the changes introduced by TOLATA 1996 was to grant beneficiaries under trusts of land the right to occupy land: for the first time by statute rather than by express trust provision. The contexts in which that right of occupation was permitted will, in some circumstances, limit the rights of some beneficiaries to occupy the land at the expense of others. The obligations of trusteeship under TOLATA 1996 include duties to consult with the beneficiaries before taking any action under the statute (s 11). Further, under s 12 the right of occupation is provided in the following way:

> A beneficiary who is beneficially entitled to an interest in possession in land subject to a trust of land is entitled by reason of his interest to occupy the land at any time if at that time –
>
> (a)   the purposes of the trust include making the land available for his occupation (or for the occupation of beneficiaries of a class of which he is a member or of beneficiaries in general), or
> (b)   the land is held by the trustees so as to be so available.

Therefore, the Act provides for a right of occupation to any beneficiary whose interest is in possession at the material time. It is necessary that the interest must entitle the beneficiary to occupation. That is, within the purposes of the trust there must not be a provision that limits the beneficiary's rights to receipt of income only or that restricts those who can occupy the land to a restricted class of persons. The right of occupation can be exercised at any time and therefore need not be permanent nor continuous.

The further caveats are then in the alternative. The first is that the purposes of the trust include making the land available for a beneficiary such as the applicant. Again, this serves merely to reinforce the purposes of the trust of land – excluding from occupation those beneficiaries who were never intended to occupy and permitting occupation by those beneficiaries who were intended to be entitled to occupy the property. The second means of enforcing a right to occupy is that the trustees 'hold' the land to make it available for the beneficiary's occupation. The problem is what is meant by the term 'held' in these circumstances. There are two possibilities: either the trustees must have made a formal decision that the property is to be held in a particular manner, or more generally that it must be merely practicable that the land is made available for the beneficiary's occupation given the nature and condition of the land.

The more contentious part of the legislation is that in s 13(1), whereby the trustees have the right to exclude beneficiaries:

> Where two or more beneficiaries are entitled under s 12 to occupy land, the trustees of land may exclude or restrict the entitlement of any one or more (but not all) of them.

The limits placed on this power by the legislation are set out in s 13(2):

> Trustees may not under subsection (1) –
>
> (a) unreasonably exclude any beneficiary's entitlement to occupy land, or
> (b) restrict any such entitlement to an unreasonable extent.

Expressly the trustees are required, beyond these requirements to act reasonably, to take into account 'the intentions of the person or persons . . . who created the trust' (s 13(4)(a)), 'the purposes for which the land is held' (s 13(4)(b)) and 'the circumstances and wishes of each of the beneficiaries' (s 13(4)(c)). Therefore, all that the s 13 power to exclude achieves is the application of the purposes of the trust. It is submitted that these intentions could be expressed in a document creating the trust or be divined in the same manner as a common intention is located in a constructive trust over a home.

The argument has been made that the 1996 Act does violence to the concept of unity of possession, reawakening the spectre of *Bull v Bull* (1955), whereby a trustee who is also a beneficiary under a trust of land could abuse her powers as trustee to exclude other persons who were also beneficiaries, but not trustees under the trust of land. As to the merits of that argument, it seems that s 12 operates only where it is the underlying purpose of the trust that the claimant–beneficiary be entitled to occupy that property (s 12(1)(a)) or that the property is otherwise held so as to make that possible (s 12(1)(b)). Consequently, the exclusion of beneficiaries under s 13 will only apply where it is in accordance with the purpose of the trust.

Furthermore, an unconscionable breach of the trustees' duty to act fairly as between beneficiaries would lead to the court ordering a conscionable exercise of the power. In any event there is a power to make an order in relation to the trustees' functions under s 14 to preclude the trustee from acting in flagrant breach of trust or in a manner that was abusive of her fiduciary powers in permitting a personal interest and fiduciary power to come into conflict.

Of course, the other way to look at TOLATA 1996 is as a permissive provision in s 12, granting a qualified right of occupation in relation to which it is necessary to protect the trustees from an action for breach of the duty of fairness by means of s 13 if some beneficiaries are protected rather than others.

None of this would be of importance in relation to 'de facto unions' (marriages and so forth) because the purpose would clearly be to allow all parties to occupy. Therefore, it is only in relation to the odd cases where land is acquired with a purpose that only some of them might occupy that the *Bull* problem is of any great concern. It seems that TOLATA 1996 intends to move away from interests in possession as the decisive factor, rather than replacing the pre-1925 law.

In the wake of *Bernard v Josephs* (1982), *Huntingford v Hobbs* (1993), and the other cases considered earlier in this chapter, the courts are more likely to allocate interests between beneficiaries and decide on the parties' respective merits, rather than step back to the idea of interests in possession (beyond the necessary inclusion in the legislation requiring that the rights must be in possession at the time of the claim). Therefore, the approach of the courts appears to be more likely to support the underlying purpose of the legislation in granting rights of occupation to beneficiaries under trusts of land.

Orders for sale of land

The more difficult area on the cases has been the question of whether or not to order a sale of land where one or more beneficiaries wishes it, but where others do not. Formerly personified in s 30 of the Law of Property Act 1925, s 14 of TOLATA 1996 provides a power for the court to order sale of the property, in effect, on terms. The terms are set out in s 14(2):

> . . . the court may make any such order . . .
>
> (a) relating to the exercise by the trustees of their functions . . ., or
> (b) declaring the nature or extent of a person's interest in property subject to the trust . . .

Therefore, the court is empowered to make any order as to the performance of any of the trustees' duties under the trust of land – including whether or not to sell and whether or not to permit a beneficiary to occupy the land. As to the *locus standi* of persons to apply (s 14(1)):

> Any person who is a trustee of land or has an interest in property subject to a trust of land may make an application to the court for an order . . .

Therefore, occupants of property cannot apply unless they can demonstrate that they have an 'interest in property' relating to the land in question. This would include mortgagees and other secured creditors, but not children of a relationship, subject to what is said in relation to s 15 below, whereas children are entitled to have their interests taken into account, but not to apply to the court in relation to the trustees' treatment of the land.

Section 15 sets out those matters that are to be taken into account by the court in making an order in relation to s 14. There are four categories of issues to be considered in relation to an exercise of a power under s 14:

(a)   the intentions of the person or persons (if any) who created the trust;
(b)   the purposes for which the property subject to the trust is held;
(c)   the welfare of any minor who occupies or might reasonably be expected to occupy any land subject to the trust as his home; and
(d)   the interests of any secured creditor of any beneficiary.

Therefore, the underlying purpose of the trust is to be applied by the court in reaching any decision. However, that purpose may be flexible in that (b) refers to the purposes for which the property is being held at any time (which might then be different to the underlying purposes set out in (a)). Importantly, the rights of children in relation to their homes are to be taken into account. At the time of writing it is impossible to gauge how the courts will apply this provision but, it is submitted, that ought to lead to the importation of elements of child law and the Children Act 1989 to this area, whereby the welfare of the child is made paramount. The final category (d) refers to any creditor of any beneficiary, not requiring that the beneficiary be bankrupt at the time. Therefore, mortgagees will be entitled to have their interests taken expressly into account. The courts have indicated that mortgagees ought to be protected with the same enthusiasm as bankruptcy creditors in these contexts (*Lloyds Bank v Byrne* (1991)).

In the case of an application made by a trustee in bankruptcy, different criteria apply, as set out in s 335A of the Insolvency Act 1986 (further to s 15(4) of TOLATA 1996). In line with the principle set out in *Re Citro* (1991), the court will order sale automatically in a situation relating to bankruptcy. The only situation in which no sale has been ordered was that in *Re Holliday* (1981), in which the debt was so small in comparison to the sale value of the house that there was thought to be no hardship to the creditors in waiting for the bankrupt's children to reach school-leaving age before ordering a sale. However, that hardship will be caused to the children or to the family in general as a result of a sale in favour of a trustee in bankruptcy is considered to be merely one of the melancholy incidents of life. What this demonstrates is the obsessive concern of the English judiciary to protect the creditors in a bankruptcy at the expense of any other third person who might be affected along the way.

Therefore, what is clear from TOLATA 1996 is that the case law growing from *Jones v Challenger* (1961) is likely to continue in operation, looking to the underlying purpose of trusts of land arrangements and making decisions about the treatment of the property on that basis. The decision in *Mortgage Corporation v Shaire*

(2001), for example, makes it less likely that the courts will always order a sale in favour of creditors now that s 15 of TOLATA has required that the position of children be taken into account. Similarly, the case law relating to the protection of creditors before the interests of occupants of homes appears likely to continue. The most interesting development is the potential for the introduction of child law concepts to this area.

Understanding the law's manifold treatment of the family home

There is no single attitude to the home in the common law nor in equity, in spite of developments in the legislation since the housing statutes of 1977, the Children Act 1989 and the variety of family law, housing and property legislation passed in 1996 and the well-established divisions between trusts law, family law, child law, public law and housing law. Rather, each area of law appears to advance its own understanding of the manner in which such rights should be allocated, resulting in an inability to understand the changing nature of the family or to account for it in the current jurisprudence. The result is a hotchpotch of rules and regulations coming at the same problem from different directions. A comprehensive legislative code dealing with title to the home, the rights of occupants, the rights of children and the rights of creditors is necessary to reduce the cost and stress of litigation, and to ensure that this problem is given the political consideration that it deserves. The Law Commission has proposed a legislative model based on the length of the parties' relationship and similar factors.

Moving on . . .

This chapter has attempted to outline the complex range of case law and statute dealing with the acquisition of rights in the home. Of further interest are the different approaches taken in the various Commonwealth jurisdictions, as discussed in Chapter 15 of Hudson (2014). The next chapter turns to a very different issue: namely, the ways in which the beneficiaries can make good their losses in the event that there has been some breach of trust.

Chapter 10

Breach of trust, strangers and tracing

Introduction

The various claims considered in this chapter in outline

This chapter considers the liability of trustees for *breach of trust*; the personal liability of third party '*strangers*' for their involvement in a breach of trust, whether because they assisted that breach of trust dishonestly or because they received property from a breach of trust unconscionably; and the possibilities for *tracing* property which was originally held on trust or which was a substitute for that trust property. It is easiest to think of these three different types of action as being the alternatives which are open to beneficiaries if there is some breach of trust (or a breach of some other fiduciary duty). The beneficiaries are effectively able to recover their loss from the trustees, or from strangers, or from any person who holds the traceable proceeds of the trust property. It is quite an arsenal of equitable doctrines available to the beneficiaries.

The theme running through this chapter is that the law of trusts will always try to come to the aid of the beneficiary: in effect, wrapping the beneficiary in cotton wool. In this chapter what we will see is a relic from the past of the law of trusts as the main means by which many members of the landed classes would have their incomes protected and their homes provided for them in family settlements. To have permitted either trustees or third parties to take benefit from those people would have been to strip them of their possessions; therefore, the courts of equity took the approach of enforcing the rights of beneficiaries as strictly as possible.

The distinction between personal claims and proprietary claims

It is important to distinguish between proprietary claims and personal obligations in this chapter. A proprietary claim is a claim that specific property must be held on trust or subject to a charge or held on some other basis, whether because that property was the original trust property or because it is a substitute which has been acquired with the original trust property. By contrast, a personal claim is a claim seeking compensation from a specified individual which grants no rights in property. The defendant to a personal claim must therefore find the cash compensation from their own personal resources. A proprietary claim will provide protection against the defendant's insolvency, but a personal claim will not. Therefore, a personal claim gives the beneficiary no effective remedy if the defendant does not have sufficient wealth to make good that loss or if the defendant is bankrupt. Of the doctrines considered in this chapter, tracing is directed at providing proprietary remedies; whereas the claims against strangers for dishonest assistance or unconscionable receipt are purely personal claims against those strangers to account for the beneficiaries' loss. The claim for breach of trust against a trustee provides for one proprietary remedy or two alternative, personal remedies, as discussed below. The beneficiary will frequently seek to bring a number of claims at once until she finds a person with sufficient wealth to compensate her for her loss.

The hypothetical example on which this chapter is based

An example may help to introduce the material considered in this chapter. Suppose that Charlie Croker was the beneficiary of a trust on which Tommy holds all three of the original Mini Cooper cars used in the getaway sequence in the seminal 1960s film *The Italian Job*. These cars are uniquely valuable: let us suppose that together they are worth £1 million. Tommy then transferred these cars away in breach of trust by giving possession of them to a car dealer, Freddie. Tommy was advised to do this by Bridger, a corrupt lawyer who also claimed to be an expert in movie memorabilia – although Bridger did not take possession of the cars at any time. Let us suppose that both Freddie and Bridger knew that Tommy was acting in breach of trust. The question is: what remedies are available to Charlie Croker? Let us take them in reverse order.

Clearly, Charlie Croker would want to recover the cars if they are uniquely valuable and particularly if they are likely to increase in value. Therefore, as part of the discussion of *tracing*, Charlie Croker will attempt to bring what is known as a 'following' claim to recover the three original cars. This is clearly a proprietary claim to recover the original property, and not to recover a substitute for that property. If the cars had been sold, however, to a purchaser acting in good faith then Charlie Croker would not have been able to recover the very cars that were taken from him. Instead, he would have to bring a 'tracing' claim to recover the sale proceeds of the cars, or any property that has been acquired with those sale proceeds. The sale proceeds are a substitute for the original cars which are held in the defendant's hands. These issues are considered at the end of this chapter in the *tracing* section.

Alternatively, Charlie Croker could bring a claim for breach of trust against Tommy as trustee to recover the cash value of the trust property. These issues are considered immediately below. Similarly, Charlie Croker would be able to bring a claim for *unconscionable receipt* against Freddie for receiving the cars in the knowledge that they were transferred to him in breach of trust and on the basis that he acted unconscionably in so doing. The claim would be for 'receipt' on the basis that Freddie took possession of the cars. Charlie Croker could also claim against Bridger for *dishonest assistance* in that breach of trust, on the basis that he facilitated the breach of trust even though he did not come into possession of the property. The principal issue would be in proving that he acted dishonestly in so doing. Freddie and Bridger would both face a form of personal liability as constructive trustees to account to Charlie Croker for the total loss to the trust. Clearly, there is a complex web of claims at play here: this chapter will attempt to separate out the various principles.

Breach of trust

The key principles

The main principles governing liability for breach of trust are as follows. The trustees will be liable for any loss which is caused by a breach of trust. If there is a breach of any term of a trust instrument or any breach of any of the duties of trustees described in Chapter 5, then there will be a breach of trust. The trustees face any of three remedies. First, an obligation to restore any property transferred away in breach of trust to the trust ('specific restitution'). Second, if the original trust property cannot be recovered, then the trustee bears a personal obligation to restore the trust fund in cash terms. That means that the trustee must pay the beneficiaries an amount of money (or other property) equal to the amount of the reduction in the trust fund. Third, the trustees bear a general obligation to compensate the beneficiaries for any other loss which results to the trust. These core principles are expanded on in the discussion to follow.

The decision in Target Holdings v Redferns

The leading decision in relation to breach of trust is that of the House of Lords in *Target Holdings Ltd v Redferns* (1995). Target was seeking a mortgage over land. To achieve this it required a valuation of the property and the legal services of Redferns, a firm of solicitors, to ensure that it acquired a valid legal charge over it. To facilitate this underlying purpose, the valuer provided a fraudulently high valuation of the property's free market value. The valuers were crooks and part of a larger conspiracy to defraud Target; we can forget about the crooks because they were untraceable in this litigation. Redferns was entirely innocent of the fraud. Redferns was to hold the loan moneys on trust for Target solely for the purpose of the transaction. In fact, Redferns misused the moneys; thus, there was a technical breach of trust at this time. Later, Redferns replaced the money and the transaction went ahead as planned. Subsequently, the crooks disappeared with Target's money, leaving Target with only a mortgage over property worth much less than it expected.

Therefore, in its desperate search for someone to sue, Target brought a claim against Redferns for breach of trust. The House of Lords held that Redferns would not be liable because there was no causal connection between the loss suffered by Target and the breach committed by Redferns. In short, the loss was caused by the fraudulent over-valuation of the land and not by Redferns' short-term misuse of the money, even though that was technically a breach of trust by Redferns. Under older authorities the trustees would have been liable for their beneficiaries' loss, even though their breach of trust had not directly caused that loss. Consequently, the rule emerges: the loss must be caused by the breach of trust, and not by something else.

The nature of the remedies for breach of trust against a trustee

The liability that a trustee faces, as set out by *Target Holdings v Redferns*, is three-fold. First, a liability to recover the specific property that had previously been held on trust and which was misapplied in breach of trust. Second, a liability to account to the beneficiaries for the cash equivalent of the loss caused to the trust fund: in short, to write a cheque for that amount. Third, by extension to the second remedy, a right to equitable compensation for any further loss caused by the breach of trust. Each is considered in turn in this section. It should be noted that the common law standards of foreseeability of harm, proximity, causation and so forth do not apply in equity to breach of trust claims (*Target Holdings v Redferns*).

Specific restitution

The first form of remedy is to require the trustee to recover any property that was transferred away in breach of trust. This is a proprietary remedy and involves recovery of the very property that was formerly held on trust, as opposed to any substitute property. Where it is a particularly valuable or important item of property that is lost to the trust fund, then this remedy will be particularly important to the beneficiaries. The trustee will be required to deliver up that specific property if it is in her possession or under her control. (The law on *tracing*, as considered later in the chapter, deals with the problem of recovering the trust property if it has been passed to someone else.)

In *Target Holdings v Redferns*, Lord Browne-Wilkinson expressed liability for breach of trust to be in the form of an action against the trustee personally to recover the trust property in the first place. However, where the original trust property has passed out of the trustee's control or possession, the action against the trustee for breach of trust converts to a mere action in money to recover from the trustee personally the equivalent cash value of the specific assets misapplied in breach of trust, as considered in the next section.

Restoration of the value of the trust fund and equitable compensation

The second cause of action is then for restoration of the value of the trust fund by means of an amount of money or other property equal to the value of the property lost to the trust fund by the breach of trust. The amount of compensation to be paid will be an amount to return the trust to the position it had occupied before the breach of trust. This covers two different heads of liability (it is suggested): first, compensation for the value of any property lost from the fund, which cannot be recovered by specific restitution, and, second, equitable compensation for any other loss caused to the trust. This remedy will apply if specific restitution is not possible because the original trust property cannot be located.

Lord Browne-Wilkinson explained the method for valuing the loss to the trust in the following way. The amount of compensation required is that required to 'put [the trust fund] back to what it would have been had the breach not been committed'. In other words, the aim of the second remedy is to calculate the amount of money that is necessary to restore the value of the trust fund. It is important to note that there is a difference between personal compensation for loss suffered as a breach of trust, and compensation equivalent to the value of property lost to the trust (*Swindle v Harrison* (1997), *Bristol & West BS v Mothew* (1996)).

It is possible that this could take a number of forms other than straightforwardly paying cash. For example, it might permit the acquisition of an annuity, which would generate similar levels of income to any trust capital misapplied in breach of trust. The level of compensation, as a matter of evidence, must equate to the loss that the beneficiary can demonstrate was caused by the breach of trust such that the trust fund is placed back in the position it would have occupied, but for the breach. This might include any loss that the trust would have suffered subsequently as a result of the nature of the trust property – for example, accounting for a large fall of the value of such property subsequently.

Defences to breach of trust

There are a number of defences to an action for breach of trust that are considered in Chapter 18 of Hudson, *Equity & Trusts* (2014). Among the most significant defences are the following. In *Nestlé v National Westminster Bank plc* (1994), it was held that a trustee would have a good defence to a claim for breach of trust, which was based on a contention that the trustee had failed to generate sufficient profit from trust investments, that the trustee had done what other trustees in the same position had done in the financial market. It is also a good defence if the beneficiaries have consented to the trustees' actions or have agreed to release the trustees from liability for breach of trust.

Trustees will have a good defence to liability for breach of trust if there is a clause in the trust instrument that excludes or limits their liability for the breach complained of by the beneficiaries (*Armitage v Nurse* (1998)). The trustees will not be permitted to exclude their liability for dishonest activity, but they will be able to exclude their liability in this way for gross negligence (*Armitage v Nurse*).

Further to s 61 of the Trustee Act 1925 the trustee may be excused from liability by the court if the court considers that she has 'acted honestly and reasonably, and ought fairly to be excused for the breach of trust'. Thus, it would be a reasonable excuse that the trustee had searched for a beneficiary from whom nothing had been heard for 30 years and whom everyone thought to be dead (*Re Evans* (1999)).

The personal liability of strangers to account as constructive trustees

Introduction

The status of the trustee and the fiduciary is easily comprehensible. The rule that a fiduciary cannot profit from that office is well established in equity. The further question is: in what circumstances will a person who is not a trustee be held liable in respect of any breach of that trust? Such a person is referred to in the case law and in the following sections as a 'stranger' to the trust, having no official position as trustee connected to it. Equity has always sought to impose fiduciary duties on those who misuse trust property, whether holding an office under that trust or not. This has extended to the imposition of the duties of a trustee on people who meddle with the trust fund. One of the practical reasons for pursuing this remedy is that the intermeddler is frequently an advisor or professional who is solvent and therefore capable of making good the money lost to the trust if the property itself is lost and the trustees have no money.

In short, the applicable principles can be stated in the following terms. First, a stranger will be personally liable to account to the trust for any loss suffered in a situation in which she dishonestly assists in a breach of trust, without receiving any proprietary right in that trust property herself (*Royal Brunei Airlines v Tan* (1995)). The test for 'dishonesty' in this context extends beyond straightforward deceit and fraud into reckless risk-taking with trust property and other unconscionable behaviour demonstrating a 'lack of probity'. Second, a stranger will be personally liable to account to the trust for any loss suffered in a situation in which she receives trust property with knowledge that the property has been passed to her in breach of trust (*Re Montagu's ST* (1987)) and provided that she can be shown to have acted unconscionably. 'Knowledge' in this context includes actual knowledge, wilfully closing one's eyes to the breach of trust, or failing to make the inquiries that a reasonable person would have made.

These claims are best understood as part of the web of claims that may be brought by beneficiaries in the event of a breach of trust. To return to the original example of Charlie's cars at the beginning of this chapter, personal liability to account would concern the claims against Freddie and against Bridger as knowing recipients and as dishonest assistants of the trust property, respectively. These claims would impose on Bridger and Freddie, respectively, personal liability to account to the beneficiaries for the value of the property passed. However, it should not be forgotten that in many cases these claims will form part of a much larger web of actions commenced by beneficiaries. The beneficiaries may also seek a proprietary claim to recover the cars, or the proceeds from their sale, by way of tracing, which is discussed later.

Unconscionable receipt

The core principles

The first category of personal liability to account concerns strangers who receive some trust property when it has been paid away in breach of trust. This doctrine has been known as 'knowing receipt', although the current formulation of the test suggests that it should now be known as 'unconscionable receipt'. The main principles relating to unconscionable receipt are as follows. A stranger to the trust (i.e. someone who is not a trustee) will be personally liable to account to the beneficiaries for any loss caused by a breach of trust as a constructive trustee if that stranger both received property in the knowledge that there had been a breach of trust and had done so as a result of unconscionable behaviour. The concept of knowledge is satisfied if the stranger has actual knowledge of the breach of trust, or if the stranger wilfully shut their eyes to the obvious, or if the stranger wilfully and recklessly failed to make the inquiries which an honest and reasonable person would have made in the circumstances. These core principles are expanded on in the discussion to follow.

This form of liability has been described as a receipt-based claim analogous to equitable compensation (*El Ajou v Dollar Land Holdings* (1993)). Where a person knowingly receives trust property that has been transferred away from the trust or otherwise misapplied, that person will incur personal liability to account. The details of this claim will be considered in detail below: first, in relation to what constitutes 'receipt', then the concept of knowledge, and finally the concept of unconscionability.

The nature of 'receipt'

The first question is: what actions will constitute 'receipt' under this category? In *El Ajou v Dollar Land Holdings* (1993) Hoffmann LJ held that the defendant must have taken beneficial ownership in the property. By contrast, in the decision of Millett J in *Agip v Jackson* (1990), his Lordship held that:

> there is receipt of trust property when a company's funds are misapplied by any person whose fiduciary position gave him control of them or enabled him to misapply them.

Therefore, anyone who has control of trust property is taken to have received that property. Seemingly, it is enough that the property passes through the stranger's hands, even if the stranger never had the rights of an equitable or common law owner of the property. For example, a bank through which payments are made appears to be capable of being accountable for knowing receipt of money paid in breach of trust (*Polly Peck International v Nadir No 2* (1992)); and in general terms a bank becomes the absolute owner of any money deposited with it (*Foley v Hill* (1848)).

The nature of 'knowledge'

It is important to note that the test is this area is one of 'knowledge' and not 'notice'. Rather than depend on the imputed notice as used in conveyancing law, the courts have focused instead on whether or not the defendant has knowledge of material factors. If the defendant is to be fixed with personal liability to account, then it is thought that the defendant must be demonstrated to *know* those factors that will attach liability to her. The further question, however, is what a person can be taken to 'know'. The test for knowledge was whittled down to the following three types of knowledge in relation to liability for knowing receipt in *Re Montagu*:

(1)   actual knowledge;
(2)   wilfully shutting one's eyes to the obvious; and
(3)   wilfully and recklessly failing to make inquiries that an honest person would have made.

The common factor between these categories is that they include a necessary element of wilful or deliberate behaviour on the part of the defendant who cannot be proved to have actually known of the facts that were alleged. As Scott LJ held in *Polly Peck*, these categories are not to be taken as rigid rules and 'one category may merge imperceptibly into another'.

Suppose that Eric was handed £1,000 in cash by Stan as he ran around the corner of the street. 'Don't ask me any questions, just hide this for me,' yelled Stan as he thrust the money into Eric's hands and ran away. Meanwhile, Eric could hear Kyle shouting, 'Where is the trust's money?' from the neighbouring street. Let us assume that Stan had taken the money from his fellow trustee Kyle and sprinted away with it. Clearly, Eric does not have actual knowledge of what has happened because he has not had a full explanation of the facts, nor can he see Kyle. However, Eric would be shutting his eyes to the obvious if he turned around, walked away from Kyle's voice in the neighbouring street and folded the money into his trouser pocket because it must be obvious to any reasonable person that there has been a theft of some sort here. Given the context and the noise of Kyle shouting, this would be a wilful failure. The idea that Eric should 'hide' the money clearly suggests that something is amiss. Equally, if Eric purported to follow Stan's instructions later that evening to invest the money in a particular account without asking any questions, then we would say that Eric had failed to make the inquiries an honest person would have made (such as asking Stan what had happened earlier in the day and where the money had come from) and it is also suggested that this would be wilful and reckless of Eric in such clear circumstances. Therefore, the second and third forms of knowledge would have been made out here.

The acid test – 'Should you have been suspicious?'

The third category of knowledge is more difficult to define, dealing with situations in which the defendant could have been expected to have asked more questions or investigated further. This constructive knowledge is best explained by Scott LJ in *Polly Peck International v Nadir No 2* (1992), where he held that the acid test was whether or not the defendant 'ought to have been suspicious' that trust property was being misapplied (*Eagle Trust v SBC (No 2)* (1996)).

Similarly, in *Macmillan v Bishopsgate* (1996) money had been passed through a series of bank accounts by shysters who had looted money from a pension trust fund in breach of trust. The issue arose whether the bank through which the money had passed should be treated as a knowing recipient of that money after the breach of trust. It was held that account officers were not detectives and therefore were not to be fixed with knowledge that they could only possibly have had if they had carried out extensive investigations in a situation in which they had no reason to believe that there had been any impropriety. It was held that they were 'entitled to believe that they were dealing with honest men' unless they had some suspicion raised in their minds to the contrary. In *El Ajou v Dollar Land Holdings*, Millett J held that liability for knowing receipt would attach 'in a situation in which any honest and reasonable man would have made inquiry'. In short, the issue is whether or not the circumstances would necessitate a person to be suspicious, such that her conscience would encourage her to make inquiries.

Two illustrations

The case of *Polly Peck International v Nadir No 2* is a useful illustration of the principle in action. The facts related to the actions of Asil Nadir in respect of the insolvency of the Polly Peck group of companies. This particular litigation referred to a claim brought by the administrators of the plaintiff company against a bank controlled by Nadir – IBK – and the Central Bank of Northern Cyprus. It was alleged that Nadir had been responsible for the misapplication of substantial funds in sterling, which were the assets of the plaintiff company, which were passed through IBK into Northern Cyprus. Then IBK sought to change the sterling amounts into Turkish lire. It was claimed that the Central Bank had exchanged the sterling amounts for Turkish lire either with actual knowledge of fraud on the plaintiff company or in circumstances in which the Central Bank ought to have put in an inquiry as to the source of those funds. The plaintiff claimed that the Central Bank should be personally liable to account as knowing recipient of the sterling amounts that had been exchanged for lire.

The Central Bank contended that it had no such knowledge, actual or constructive, of the source of the funds. It argued that large amounts of money passed through its systems as a Central Bank on a regular basis and that, as such, it should not be on notice as to title to every large amount.

The Court of Appeal held that it was enough to demonstrate that the recipient had the requisite knowledge both that the funds were trust funds and that they were being misapplied. On the facts of this case it was held that the simple fact that the plaintiff company was exchanging amounts of money between sterling and lire via IBK was not enough to have put it on suspicion that there had been a breach of trust. In deciding whether or not the Central Bank ought to have been suspicious, Scott LJ preferred to approach the matter from the point of view of the 'honest and reasonable banker'. It does appear, therefore, that the reasonableness of the recipient's belief falls to be judged from the perspective of the recipient itself. On the facts it was held that there was no reason for suspicion because large amounts of money passed through the Central Bank's accounts regularly and there was nothing at the time of this transaction to cause the bank to be suspicious of this particular transaction.

The case of *Polly Peck* can be compared with the earlier decision of Megarry J in *Re Montagu* (1987), in which the 10th Duke of Manchester was a beneficiary under a settlement created by the 9th Duke, subject to the trustees appointing chattels to other persons. In breach of trust, the 10th Duke and the trustees lapsed into the habit of treating all of the valuable chattels held on trust as belonging absolutely beneficially to the 10th Duke. The 10th Duke made a number of disposals of these valuable chattels during his lifetime, including auctioning off valuable historical treasures such as Catherine of Aragon's travelling trunk. The issue arose whether or not the 10th Duke's estate should have been held liable for knowing receipt of these chattels in breach of trust. There was no doubt that as a matter of fact the property had been received in breach of trust.

His Lordship took the view that there had been 'an honest muddle' in this case. Further, although the 10th Duke had undoubtedly had actual knowledge of the terms of the trust at one stage, it was held that one does not have the requisite knowledge on which to base a claim for knowing receipt where the defendant has genuinely forgotten the relevant factors. Megarry J went further, in support of the idea that one should only be liable for knowing receipt if one had knowledge of the relevant factor, in finding that the knowledge of a trustee-solicitor or other agent should not be imputed to the defendant. That is, you do not 'know' something simply because your agent knows it. Thus, the distinction is drawn with the doctrine of notice under which notice can be imputed from agent to principal. Thus, while the Duke had forgotten the terms of the trust, he was not to be imputed with his lawyers' knowledge that for him to treat the property as his own personal property would have been in breach of trust. Megarry J thus narrowed the scope of the knowledge test to acts that the defendant conducted wilfully or deliberately, or to facts of which he had actual knowledge. Consequently, no liability for knowing receipt attached to the 10th Duke or his estate.

The requirement for unconscionability

Significantly, the recent case law has required that the defendant is also shown to have acted unconscionably and not simply to have had knowledge of the breach of trust in the manner discussed above. This requirement of 'unconscionability' has been advanced in the Court of Appeal decisions in *Bank of Credit and Commerce International v Akindele* (2001), *Criterion Properties v Stratford Properties* (2002), and *Charter plc v City Index* (2006), in which it was held that for a defendant to be liable in knowing receipt the defendant must be shown to have acted unconscionably. So, in *Akindele* it was held that the defendant had received more money than he was entitled to receive from his bank as a result of a breach of fiduciary duty by his bankers, but it was held that he had not acted unconscionably himself in so doing and therefore that he would not be liable to account for the loss caused by that breach of fiduciary duty.

This new test requires that the defendant be demonstrated to have had knowledge, on the basis outlined above, and also that they acted unconscionably in more general terms. In essence, this second element means that a defendant will not be held to be liable unless there was something unconscionable about their actions over and above the attribution of knowledge to them.

Dishonest assistance

The key principles

The key principles relating to dishonest assistance are as follows. A stranger to the trust (i.e. someone who is not a trustee) will be personally liable to account as a constructive trustee to the beneficiaries for any loss caused by a breach of trust if that stranger had dishonestly assisted that breach of trust. The test for 'dishonesty' has been the subject of many decisions. In *Royal Brunei Airlines v Tan* (1995) and *Barlow Clowes v Eurotrust* (2005), two different Privy Councils held that the test should be an objective test as to what an honest person would have done in the circumstances. In *Twinsectra v Yardley* (2002), the House of Lords held that there should also be a requirement that the defendant must have realised that honest people would have considered their behaviour to have been dishonest, thus adding an element of subjectivity which narrowed the test markedly. The objective test has purportedly been followed, although hints of subjectivity have crept in as a result of later cases. These core principles are expanded on in the discussion to follow.

Where a stranger dishonestly assists a trustee in a breach of trust, that dishonest assistant will be personally liable to account to the trust for the value lost to the trust. 'Dishonesty' in this context does require that there be some element of fraud, lack of probity or reckless risk-taking. It is not necessary that any trustee of the trust is dishonest; it is sufficient that the dishonest assistant is dishonest. The distinction from knowing receipt is that there is no requirement for the imposition of liability that the stranger has had possession or control of the property at any time. Therefore, some commentators have doubted whether or not this form of liability should really be described as a 'constructive trust' in any event because no property is held on trust by the stranger. However, the term 'constructive trusteeship' is correct because the defendant is being *construed* to be liable to compensate the trust for its loss as though she was a trustee.

The nature of dishonest assistance

The leading case for the test of dishonest assistance is *Royal Brunei Airlines v Tan* (1995). In that case, the appellant airline contracted an agency agreement with a travel agency, BLT. Under that agreement BLT was to sell tickets for the appellant. BLT held money received for the sale of these tickets on express trust for the appellant in a current bank account. The current account was used to defray some of BLT's expenses, such as salaries, and to reduce its overdraft. BLT was required to account to the appellant for these moneys within 30 days. The respondent, Tan, was the managing director and principal shareholder of BLT. From time to time amounts were paid out of the current account into deposit accounts controlled by Tan.

BLT held the proceeds of the sale of tickets as trustee for the appellant. In time, BLT went into insolvency. Therefore, the appellant sought to proceed against Tan for assisting in a breach of trust. The issue between the parties was whether 'the breach of trust which is a prerequisite to accessory liability must itself be a dishonest and fraudulent breach of trust by the trustee'. It was held that Tan would be liable because he had acted dishonestly in assisting the breach of trust.

In describing the nature of the test Lord Nicholls held the following:

> . . . acting dishonestly, or with a lack of probity, which is synonymous, means simply not acting as an honest person would in the circumstance. This is an objective standard.

This *Tan* test is therefore based on an objective understanding of 'dishonesty', whereas knowing receipt, in the judgment of Scott LJ in *Polly Peck* (1992), sets out a subjective test of whether or not the recipient ought to have been suspicious and thereby have constructive notice of the breach of trust. One can therefore be dishonest if one *fails to act honestly*: significantly, you do not have to be actively deceitful. Therefore, if I were to find a £10 note on the floor of a train carriage next to the foot of another passenger when there is only one other passenger, an honest person would ask that other passenger if the note was theirs. If I were to pocket the note, Lord Nicholls would find me dishonest for failing to do what an honest person would have done. He would not ask whether I *actually knew* the note belonged to that other person, and so forth.

Nevertheless, as considered below, Lord Nicholls's judgment has been adapted and remoulded by later cases. We shall begin our discussion with an analysis of the misjudged foray by Lord Hutton in the House of Lords into turning the test into a partially subjective test, its reversal by the Privy Council, and then the remodelling of the objective test by the lower courts more recently.

Whether dishonesty is subjective or objective in this context

There have been two subsequent House of Lords decisions on the meaning of 'dishonesty' in this context since *Royal Brunei Airlines v Tan*. In the first, *Twinsectra v Yardley* (2002), a solicitor was appointed to manage a client's affairs in place of the former solicitor. The client had borrowed money by way of a loan. The terms of the loan had limited the purposes for which the loan moneys could be used. The replacement solicitor was nevertheless directed by the client to use the loan moneys for purposes other than those set out in the loan contract, in breach of the solicitor's own obligations under that agreement. The money was dissipated. The lender sued the replacement solicitor to recover the dissipated loan moneys, contending that the solicitor had been a dishonest assistant in the client's breach of his fiduciary obligations (in the form of a *Quistclose* trust, as discussed in Chapter 11). The solicitor contended that he had not known of the nature of his client's duties to the lender and in consequence that he had not acted dishonestly.

The House of Lords was therefore faced with a dilemma. If the test for dishonesty were objective, as Lord Nicholls had suggested in *Royal Brunei Airlines v Tan* (1995), then it would not matter that the solicitor had not known that he was acting dishonestly because his liability would be assessed objectively. Lord Hutton in *Twinsectra v Yardley* therefore held that the test for dishonesty should be made up of two components: first, it must be shown that an honest person would not have acted as the solicitor had acted, and, second, it must also be shown that the solicitor had himself known that his action would have been considered to be dishonest by such an honest person. This second limb is subjective. Consequently, the solicitor was found not to be liable for dishonest assistance. (It was unclear whether or not the majority agreed with Lord Hutton's view of this test.)

This conclusion seems to me to be somewhat remarkable. It is remarkable in the first place that a solicitor should be entitled to demonstrate his lack of dishonesty by contending that he did not understand the nature of his own client's legal obligations. Second, it is a remarkable conclusion because it transforms the nature of liability for dishonesty in this context into a semi-subjective test. In *Walker v Stones* (2001), it had been held by the Court of Appeal that a person would not be absolved from liability for dishonesty simply by suggesting that he or she did not consider his or her actions to have been dishonest. Instead, it was enough for the court to impose such liability if it could be shown objectively that an honest person would not have acted in the manner that the defendant had acted. This notion of subjective and objective liability is taken up again in Chapter 14. In short, it is argued there that a doctrine predicated on conscience (such as the law of trusts) ought to operate on an objective basis, in the manner envisaged as long ago as 1615 by Lord Ellesmere in the *Earl of Oxford's Case*, to inquire into the defendant's actions and to judge whether or not the defendant had acted properly in the court's eyes. That is, the test ought properly to be an objective test.

In the second House of Lords' decision in *Dubai Aluminium v Salaam* (2003), a partner in a firm of lawyers was alleged to have been a dishonest assistant in his client's breach of trust. The focus of the appeal was on the liability of the remaining partners in that law firm to share out their partner's potential liability. Lord Nicholls re-asserted the test as being one of objective dishonesty without reference to Lord Hutton in *Twinsectra v Yardley*. The basis of the liability for dishonesty was again explained as being that of a person construed to be liable as though an express trustee to account to the beneficiaries for any loss that they may have suffered as a result of a breach of trust.

The weakness in Lord Hutton's test in *Twinsectra v Yardley* was illustrated in *Barlow Clowes v Eurotrust* (2005), before the Privy Council. Lord Hutton's test permits a defendant to say, in effect, 'my personal morality does not consider that to be dishonest and I did not think anyone else would consider that to be dishonest' such that the defendant can escape liability. In *Barlow Clowes v Eurotrust* the defendant controlled a financial institution through which very large amounts of money were paid by fraudsters who were taking money in breach of fiduciary duty from a number of investment funds under their control. The defendant, perhaps blinded partly by the prospect of going into partnership with these well-heeled fraudsters in the future, did not ask where these large sums of money were coming from and so did not actually discover the underlying breach of trust. It was argued that the defendant had dishonestly assisted these breaches of trust by acting as a conduit for the misappropriated money. The defendant argued that his personal morality required that he did whatever his clients asked of him without question, and therefore that under Lord Hutton's test he had not been dishonest because he had not appreciated that other people would consider him to have been dishonest. The Privy Council upheld the finding of the court at first instance that the defendant had been dishonest on these facts. The Privy Council reiterated the principle that the appropriate test in this context is an objective test; that means it is not open to a defendant to claim to have a personal moral code that absolves her from liability for dishonesty. This objective approach has purportedly been followed by the Court of Appeal in *Abou-Rahmah v Abacha* (2006).

The remodelling of the objective test in recent cases

The Court of Appeal (*Abou-Rahmah v Abacha* (2006) and *Starglade v Nash* (2010)) and the High Court (*AG Zambia v Meer Care & Desai & Others* (2007)) have focused latterly on a couple of sentences in the judgment of Lord Nicholls in *Royal Brunei Airlines v Tan* (which otherwise focused solely on objectivity) which suggested that the court should consider the defendant's knowledge and experience, and the circumstances in which she was acting, as opposed to looking solely at the likely attitude of an honest person without considering anything else. The more of the defendant's personal characteristics that are considered, the more likely it is that any given individual defendant will escape liability by referring to their own stupidity, lack of experience or naivety. This approach was taken in the

Court of Appeal in *Starglade v Nash*, where the court considered the defendant's lack of education and lack of understanding of legal concepts as being important, even though an objectively honest person might have found the defendant to have been dishonest in the context without considering those factors. What emerges from this discussion is that Lord Nicholls's judgment in *Royal Brunei Airlines v Tan* has been warped slightly out of shape by the lower courts choosing to focus on a few sentences in a judgment otherwise concerned only with objectivity.

Risk as dishonesty

Lord Nicholls expanded his discussion of 'dishonesty' to consider the taking of risk. Risk therefore is expressly encompassed within the new test. Lord Nicholls held:

> All investment involves risk. Imprudence is not dishonesty, although impru-dence may be carried recklessly to lengths which call into question the honesty of the person making the decision. This is especially so if the transac-tion serves another purpose in which that person has an interest of his own.

Therefore, an investment advisor who is employed by the trust could be liable for 'dishonesty' if she advises the trust to take a risk that is considered by the court to have been a reckless risk. The thinking is that, if X advises the trustees to take a risk that is objectively too great, then X could be considered to have been dishonest in giving that advice. The basis of liability is that a third party 'takes a risk that a clearly unauthorised transaction will not cause loss . . . If the risk materialises and causes loss, those who knowingly took the risk will be accountable accordingly'. For these purposes it is said that 'fraud includes taking a risk to the prejudice of another's rights, which risk is known to be one which there is no right to take'. Therefore, there is enormous potential liability in respect of advisors who advise trustees in any matter to do with investment or the treatment of their property.

The nature of the remedy of personal liability to account

As mentioned above, the form of relief awarded in this type of claim is the impo-sition of a personal liability to account on the stranger who is found to be liable as a constructive trustee. In *Selangor v Craddock (No 3)* (1968), it was held by Ungoed-Thomas J that this form of relief is 'nothing more than a formula for equitable relief. The court of equity says that the defendant shall be liable in equity, as though he were a trustee'.

In short, this is not a trust as ordinarily understood. There is no specific prop-erty that is held on trust by the stranger. The cases on dishonest assistance are excluded by Lord Browne-Wilkinson in *Westdeutsche Landesbank v Islington* (1996) from many of the rules that concern express trusts. It does appear that this form of equitable relief is as much in the form of a remedy as of an institutional trust. That means dishonest assistance is as much a form of equitable wrong (organised around a standard of good conscience) as a trust (under which identified property is held on trust for beneficiaries). The defendant is construed as, or treated as though he was, a trustee: hence the term 'constructive trustee'.

There is one underlying problem with the remedy of personal liability to account in this context. The liability attaches to the defendant either for receipt or for assistance provided that the relevant *mens rea* of knowledge or dishonesty has been satisfied. The defendant is then liable for the whole of the loss suffered by the beneficiaries, the remedy appearing to be an all-or-nothing remedy.

Tracing: understanding the nature of the claim

Introduction

This section considers the important topic of the law of tracing – literally an attempt by a claimant to establish a proprietary claim to a specific piece of property by *tracing* a pre-existing property right into it. The main principles are as follows. The law of tracing is the means by which a claimant (for present purposes, we shall assume that this is a beneficiary under a trust) seeks to trace property which was originally held on trust which was transferred away in breach of trust, or to trace substitute property for that original trust property. This 'tracing' process is merely the detective work of locating property against which a claim may then be brought. Most commonly in the cases this has related to money held in a bank account being transferred through various accounts and mixed up with other money several times so as to make the traceable proceeds difficult to identify. So-called 'common law tracing' only permits the recovery of the original trust property or substitute property which has not been mixed with other property; whereas 'equitable tracing' enables the claimant to trace into mixtures of property and offers a wide range of remedies. The remedies for equitable tracing are a choice between a constructive trust, an equitable charge, a lien, or subrogation. The principal defences are of change of position by the defendant, of estoppel by representation, or that the defendant was a bona fide purchaser of the property in question. Each of these core principles is considered in the discussion to follow.

There is therefore an important point of distinction to be made between seeking to establish title to an item of property which is precisely the property that was previously owned, and seeking to establish title to an item of property which is not the exact property which was previously owned: for example, substitute property acquired with the sale proceeds of the original property. Clearly, the former case requires the claimant to say, 'That is mine and I want it back.' In many cases this will be a case of fact and proof. However, the latter case is more complicated. How is it that a claimant can assert title in property that that claimant has never owned before? In most cases the answer will be that the claimant seeks to establish rights in property because it constitutes a substitute for the original trust property. This is an important feature of equity, that it permits property rights to be established in substitute property (on the basis of the principles considered below) and in particular that it allows such property rights to be asserted even in circumstances in which property has been mixed.

Common law tracing

In situations in which the claimant seeks to identify a specific item of property in the hands of the defendant in which the claimant has retained proprietary rights, the claimant will seek a common law following claim to require the return of that specific item of property. To return to Charlie Croker's claim for his three Mini Coopers at the beginning of this chapter, it is a common law following claim which is the claim that would return title in the three original cars to Charlie. An extension to the doctrine demonstrates that the claimant can also rely on common law tracing to establish claims to any substitute for that original property, provided that it has not been mixed with other property. So, if the cars were sold for £1 million, it would be possible to bring a common law tracing claim to recover that £1 million provided that the £1 million has been kept separate from all other money. If that money were mixed with any other money it would be necessary to bring a claim for equitable tracing, as discussed below.

This limitation on the common law tracing process makes it very brittle in that it only recovers rights in original property, or so-called 'clean substitutions'. If the property becomes unidentifiable, then the common law tracing claim will fail. The usual tactic for the money launderer is therefore to take the original money, to divide it up into randomly sized portions, pay it into accounts that already contain other money, convert the money into different currencies and move it into accounts in another jurisdiction. This type of subterfuge avoids common law tracing. Instead, the claimant would be required to rely on equitable tracing, considered below.

The Court of Appeal decision in *FC Jones and Sons v Jones* (1996), concerned an amount of £11,700 which was paid from a partnership bank account to Mrs Jones, who was the wife of one of the partners. Mrs Jones invested the money in potato futures and made a large profit. Ultimately she held a balance of £49,860: all of the money was held separately in a single bank account. Subsequently, it transpired that the partnership had committed an act of bankruptcy under the Bankruptcy Act 1914 (rendering it technically bankrupt *before* it had made the payment to Mrs Jones) and therefore all of the partnership property was deemed to have passed retrospectively to the Official Receiver. This meant that the Official Receiver was the rightful owner of the £11,700 before it had been paid to Mrs Jones. It was held that the Official Receiver could trace into both the original £11,700 and the profits making up the £49,860 at common law on the basis that all of those moneys had been held separately in a bank account and not mixed with any other property.

Equitable tracing

The more complex situation is that in which the claimant's property has passed into the hands of the defendant, but has been substituted for another item of property in which the claimant has never previously had any proprietary rights. The claimant will be required to pursue an equitable tracing claim to assert title to the substitute property as being representative of the claimant's original property. An equitable tracing claim requires that the claimant had some pre-existing equitable proprietary right in that property – although the validity of this rule has been doubted by many commentators.

It is a prerequisite for an equitable tracing claim that the claimant had some equitable interest in the original property, or that the person who transferred that property away had some fiduciary relationship to the claimant, such as being a trustee (*Re Diplock* (1948)). Similarly, the Court of Appeal in *Boscawen v Bajwa* (1995) held that there must be a fiduciary relationship which calls the equitable jurisdiction into being in a case involving the purchase of land. Particular problems with equitable tracing are considered in the sections to follow.

Tracing through electronic bank accounts

One particular difficulty arises in relation to money passed through bank accounts. English law treats each payment of money as being distinct tangible property such that, when a bank account containing such money is run overdrawn, that property is said to disappear. Consequently, there can be no tracing claim in respect of property that has ceased to exist.

One of the most vexed problems in tracing claims is that of establishing proprietary rights in amounts of money that are held in electronic bank accounts. For two reasons most of the cases in this area involve large banking and commercial institutions. First, it is only such wealthy institutions that can afford to pay for the complex and long-winded litigation that is necessary in this field. Second, the nature of electronic bank accounts raises very particular problems for English lawyers, and indeed all legal systems.

Electronic bank accounts are choses in action (debts) between depositor and bank. The bank owes, by way of debt, the amount of money in the account to the depositor (provided that the account is in credit) on the terms of their contract. Therefore, these accounts are not tangible property. Rather, they are debts with value attached to them (the amount of the deposit plus interest). It is therefore surprising that English lawyers often tend to think of money (whether held in a bank account or not) as being tangible property, as is evidenced by Lord Browne-Wilkinson's leading speech in *Westdeutsche Landesbank*. The analogy used by Lord Browne-Wilkinson on a number of occasions in explaining the nature of equitable proprietary rights was that of 'a stolen bag of coins'. This metaphor is particularly enlightening because it envisages proprietary rights in electronic bank accounts as being concerned with tangible property (the individual coins) and not intangible property (the true nature of bank accounts). When considering the way in which tracing applies to money held in accounts, conceiving of that money as being tangible, rather than being simply an amount of value, creates problems, particularly in relation to the loss of the right to trace, which will be considered next.

Loss of the right to trace

The question of loss of the right to trace is important while considering the particular problem of tracing through electronic bank accounts. In *Bishopsgate Investment Management v Homan* (1995), money was taken by newspaper mogul Robert Maxwell from pension funds under his effective control in breach of trust. The beneficiaries under those pension funds sought to recover the sums taken from their trusts on the basis of an equitable tracing claim. The money had been passed into bank accounts that had gone overdrawn between the time of the payment of the money into the account and the bringing of the claim. On the basis that the accounts had gone overdrawn (and therefore were said to have none of the original property left in them) it was held that the beneficiaries had lost their right to trace into that particular account because the property had disappeared.

The same principle appears in *Roscoe v Winder* (1915), where it was held that beneficiaries cannot claim an amount exceeding the lowest intermediate balance in the bank account after the money was paid in. The claimant will not be entitled to trace into any such property where the account has been run overdrawn at any time since the property claimed was put into it.

Similarly, it was held in *Westdeutsche Landesbank v Islington LBC* (1996) that the specific property provided by the payer was not capable of identification, given that it had been paid into bank accounts that had subsequently been run overdrawn on a number of occasions. In that eccentric way in which English lawyers think about money held in electronic bank accounts, it was said that once a bank account goes overdrawn or the money is spent, then that money disappears. This is a money launderer's paradise. Rather than say, 'if money passes out of a computer-held bank account but its value is still held in some form by the owner of that account, therefore we should treat that person as still having the money', English law actually says, 'if that electronic money has gone from that account and cannot be traced in its equivalent proprietary form, we must assume it has disappeared'. No wonder the English have such an affection for mediocre TV magicians if they are so easily convinced by disappearing tricks.

There were *dicta* of Lord Templeman in the Privy Council in *Space Investments Ltd v Canadian Imperial Bank of Commerce* (1986), to the effect that a claimant should be entitled to have a charge over all of the assets of the bank equal to the size of its claim, and therefore that there does not need to be any loss of the right to trace just because the traceable proceeds cannot be identified precisely among the bank's many accounts and assets. This idea has been rejected, *inter alia*, by the Court of Appeal in *Serious Fraud Office v Lexi Holdings plc* (2009), to the effect that a general charge would not be ordered over all of the assets of a bank on the basis that the claimant could demonstrate that the traceable proceeds of their property had passed into the bank at some point. Rather, the claimant is required to demonstrate into which fund or account that property passed for the claimant to be entitled to pursue a tracing action. Similarly, in *Re BA Peters plc, Atkinson v Moriarty* (2008), it was held by the Court of Appeal that it is impossible to trace money into an over-drawn account on the basis that the property from which the traceable substitute derives is said to have disappeared. This point was reinforced by Briggs J in *Re Lehman Brothers (Europe) (No 2)* (2009), where client money had been mixed with the bank's own money in such a way that it was impossible to identify any given money flowing from the traceable proceeds of a particular class of claimant, with the result that it was impossible for them to bring a tracing action, and further-more they could not assert a charge over the entire assets of the defendant bank.

The benefits of equitable tracing

The benefits of equitable tracing over common law tracing appear in money-laundering cases like *Agip Africa v Jackson* (1991), which upheld the core prin-ciple that there must be a fiduciary relationship that calls the equitable jurisdiction into being. In short, once that pre-existing equitable interest is demonstrated then the claimant is able to trace her property into the most complex of mixtures or through many transformations in the nature of the traceable proceeds. An example may be instructive. In *Agip*, on instructions from the plaintiff oil exploration company, the Banque du Sud in Tunis transmitted a payment to Lloyds Bank in London, to be passed on to a specified person. The plaintiff's chief accountant fraudulently altered the payment instruction to be in favour of a company called Baker Oil Ltd. Before the fraud was uncovered, Lloyds Bank paid out to Baker Oil before receiving payment from Banque du Sud via the New York payment system. The account was then closed and the money transferred via the Isle of Man to a number of recipients. The defendants were independent accountants who ran a number of shell companies through which the moneys were paid. The issue arose whether or not the value received by Baker Oil was the traceable proceed of the property transferred from Tunis.

It was impossible to trace the money at common law where the value had been transferred by 'telegraphic transfer' because it was impossible to identify the specific money that had been misapplied. On these facts, because the plaintiff's fiduciary had acted fraudulently, it was open to the plaintiff to trace the money in equity. There was also personal liability to account, imposed on those persons who had knowingly received misapplied funds or who had dishonestly assisted in the misapplication of the funds.

Equitable tracing into mixed funds

The process of tracing and identifying property over which a remedy is sought is different from the issue of asserting a remedy in respect of that property. In relation to mixtures of trust and other money held in bank accounts, a variety of approaches have been taken in the courts.

As considered in the initial hypothetical situations at the start of this chapter, one of the more problematic issues in equitable tracing claims is that of identifying title in property in funds that are made up of both trust property and other property. Where it is impossible to separate one item of property from another, it will be impossible to effect a common law following claim. Suppose that it was one of Charlie Croker's Mini Cooper cars (identifiable by their registration plates and chassis numbers) that had been taken and parked in a car park with other cars. It would be comparatively easy to identify that car and recover it under a common law following claim, as in *Jones* above. However, where the property is fungible, such as money in a bank account, such segregation cannot be easily performed. So, if that car had been sold and the money paid into a bank account and mixed with other money, then only equitable tracing will provide a claim.

Mixture of trust money with trustee's own money

The first factual situation to be considered in the context of equitable tracing into mixed funds is that where the trustee mixes money taken from the trust with property that is beneficially her own. The attitude of the courts could be best explained as selecting the approach that achieves the most desirable result for the beneficiaries.

The problem with commingling a trustee's own money with trust property is deciding whether property used, for example, to make investments was taken from the trust or taken from the trustee's own money. On the basis that the trustee is required to invest trust property to achieve the best possible return for the trust (*Cowan v Scargill* (1984)), and on the basis that the trustee is required to behave honestly in respect of the trust property, the court may choose to assume that the trustee intended to use trust property to make successful investments and her own money for any inferior investments.

This approach is most clearly exhibited in *Re Hallett's Estate* (1880). Hallett was a solicitor who was a bailee of Russian bonds for one of his clients, Cotterill. Hallett also held securities of that type on express trust for his own marriage settlement (so that he was among the beneficiaries of that marriage settlement). Hallett sold the bonds and paid all the proceeds of sale into his own bank account. Hallett subsequently died. Therefore, it was left to the trustees of the marriage settlement and Cotterill to claim proprietary rights over the remaining contents of Hallett's bank account.

It was held that it could be assumed that, where a trustee has money in a personal bank account to which trust money is added, the trustee is acting honestly when paying money out of that bank account. Therefore, it is assumed that the trustee is paying out her own money on investments that lose money and not the trust money. It was held that 'where a man does an act which may be rightfully performed . . . he is not allowed to say against the person entitled to the property or the right that he has done it wrongfully.' As such he cannot claim that 'it was your money I wasted, not mine.' Therefore, it is said that the trustee has rightfully dissipated her own moneys such that the trust money remains intact.

By contradistinction to the 'honest trustee approach', there is the 'beneficiary election' principle, which appears most clearly in *Re Oatway* (1903). It was held that where a trustee has wrongfully mixed her own money and trust money, the trustee is not entitled to say that the investment was made with her own money and that the trust money has been dissipated. Importantly, though, the beneficiaries are entitled to elect either that the property be subject to a charge as security for amounts owed to them by the trustee, or that the unauthorised investment be adopted as part of the trust fund. Hence the term 'beneficiary election approach'. It is therefore clear that the courts are prepared to protect the beneficiaries at all costs from the misfeasance of the trustee – re-emphasising the strictness of the trustee's obligations to the beneficiaries. Therefore, where the trustee confuses trust money with her own money, the court will tend to apply whichever approach is most advantageous to the beneficiaries.

In *Foskett v McKeown* (2001), a trustee had committed a breach of trust by taking trust money to pay some of the premiums on a life assurance policy that he had taken out over his own life in favour of his children. Latterly the trustee died and the policy paid out a large lump sum to the children. Because the trust money had been taken in breach of trust the beneficiaries of the trust sought to trace into the lump-sum payout so as to recover a part of that lump sum in proportion to the total value of the insurance premiums for which the trust money had paid. It was held by the House of Lords that the beneficiaries were entitled to such a proportionate share of the lump sum. Tracing was explained in that case as being part of the law of property's purpose of vindicating the property rights of the original equitable owners of the money: consequently, the beneficiaries should be entitled to trace their money from the trust into the premium payments and then into a proportionate share of the lump-sum payout after the trustee's death.

Mixture of two trust funds or with innocent volunteer's money

This section considers the situation in which trust property is misapplied such that the trust property is mixed with property belonging to an innocent third party. Therefore, rather than consider the issues that arose in the previous section concerning the obligations of the wrongdoing trustee, it is now necessary to decide how property belonging to innocent parties should be allocated between them. It was held in *Re Diplock* (1948), that the entitlement of the beneficiary to the mixed fund should rank *pari passu* (or, proportionately) with the rights of the innocent volunteer. Therefore, none of the innocent contributors to the fund is considered as taking any greater right than any other contributor to the fund. Rather, each person has an equivalent, proportionate charge over that property.

The more difficult situation, however, is that in which the fund containing the mixed property is used in chunks to acquire separate property. Suppose a current bank account from which payments are made acquires totally unrelated items of the property. The problem will be deciding which of the innocent contributors to the fund ought to take which right in which piece of property. The following facts may illustrate the problem, concerning payments in and out of a current bank account that was at zero at the opening of business on 21 May.

Date	Payments in	Payments out
21 May	£2,000 from trust A	
22 May	£4,000 from trust B	
23 May		£1,000 to buy ICI plc shares
24 May		£3,000 to buy SAFC plc shares
25 May		£2,000 to buy BP plc shares

On these facts, £6,000 was in the account at the end of 22 May, being a mixture of money from two separate trusts (A and B). By 26 May, the traceable proceeds of that property had been used to buy ICI shares, SAFC shares and BP shares. The problem is then to ascertain the title to those shares. There are two possible approaches: either particular shares are allocated between the two trust funds or both funds take proportionate interests in all of the shares. The two scenarios appear in different cases, as considered immediately below.

The long-standing rule relating to title in property paid out of current bank accounts is that in *Clayton's Case* (1816). In relation to current bank accounts, the decision in *Clayton's Case* held the appropriate principle is 'first in, first out', such that, in deciding which property has been used to acquire which items of property, it is deemed that money first deposited is used first in the first property acquired. The reason for this rule is a rigid application of accounting principles. If money is paid in on 21 May, that money must be deemed to be the first money to exit the account.

Therefore, according to the facts set out above, the deposit made from A on 21 May is deemed to be the first money to be paid out. Therefore, the ICI shares acquired on 23 May for £1,000 would be deemed to have been acquired with money derived from trust A. Therefore, the tracing claim would assign title in the ICI shares to A. By the same token, the SAFC shares would be deemed to have been acquired on 24 May with the remaining £1,000 from A and £2,000 from B. The BP shares are therefore acquired with the remaining £2,000 from trust B.

The drawback with the *Clayton's Case* approach is that it will be unfair to trust A if ICI shares were to halve in value while shares in BP were to double in value. That would mean A's £1,000 investment in ICI would be worth only £500 as a result of the halving in value, whereas B's £2,000 investment in BP would then be worth £4,000 as a result of the doubling in value.

The alternative approach would be to decide that each contributor should take proportionate shares in all of the property acquired with the proceeds of the mixed fund. This is the approach taken in most Commonwealth jurisdictions (*Re Ontario Securities Commission* (1985)). On the facts above, each party contributed to the bank account in the ratio 1:2 (in that A provided £2,000, B provided £4,000). Therefore, the ICI shares, the SAFC shares and the BP shares would be held on trust one-third for A and two-thirds for B. The result is the elimination of any differential movements in value across this property in circumstances in which it is pure chance which beneficiaries would take rights in which property.

A slightly different twist on this approach was suggested in *Barlow Clowes International v Vaughan* (1992)). In that case investors in the collapsed Barlow Clowes organisation had their losses met in part by the Department of Trade and Industry. The Secretary of State for Trade and Industry then sought to recover, in effect, the amounts that had been paid away to those former investors by tracing the compensation paid to the investors into the assets of Barlow Clowes.

At first instance, Peter Gibson J found that the rule in *Clayton's Case* (1816) should be applied. *Clayton's Case* asserts the rule that tracing claims into mixed funds in current bank accounts are to be treated as the money first paid into the bank account is to be first paid out of the account. The majority of the Court of Appeal favoured a distribution between the rights of the various investors on a *pari passu* basis. However, in the Court of Appeal, Leggatt and Woolf LJJ approved the proportionate share approach culled from the Canadian cases but did not think it was actually feasible on these facts.

It is clear from decisions in the wake of *Barlow Clowes v Vaughan* that the English courts would prefer to resile from the *Clayton's Case* principle. At the time of writing, however, *Clayton's Case* has not been formally overruled – merely criticised and distinguished. So, in *Russell-Cooke Trust Co v Prentis* (2003), Lindsay J held that the *Clayton's Case* approach was still binding but that it was also capable of being distinguished on the facts of any given case. Lindsay J relied on *dicta* of Woolf LJ in *Barlow Clowes v Vaughan* to the effect that to

> throw all the loss upon one [party], through the mere chance of his being earlier in time, is irrational and arbitrary . . . To adopt it here is to apportion a common misfortune through a test which has no relation whatever to the justice of the case.

This approach suggests that the court's purpose – when dealing with mixtures of the property of two innocent people – is to achieve justice between them if there is no obvious fault on the part of one party or the other. The same point was accepted in *Commerzbank AG v IMB Morgan plc* (2004) by Lawrence Collins J. Consequently, the current preference in the cases has been for a proportionate share approach, but only where the application of the *Clayton's Case* approach on the facts of any given case would produce a result that was irrational and arbitrary.

Claiming in tracing cases: trusts and remedies

The onus is on the claimant to claim the remedy that is most appropriate in the circumstances. Different types of remedy will be more suitable or more appropriate in different circumstances, depending on the nature of the property and whether or not there are innocent third parties involved. Usually, this issue resolves itself to a choice between a charge over the traced property, or a possessory lien over the property, or the award of proprietary rights in the form of a constructive trust over the property in favour of the claimant. Each of these remedies is considered in detail below, but their basic characteristics can be explained here. First, the charge arises only in equity and entitles the claimant to seize the property and seek a court order to sell it if the defendant does not pay the claimant, whatever the claimant is owed under the terms of the charge. Second, a lien entitles the claimant to take possession of property and to retain that property until the defendant pays the claimant, whatever the claimant is owed. Both of these types of remedy are therefore concerned with ensuring that the claimant is paid an amount of money and both require that the property can be identified separately from other property. The third 'remedy' is the constructive trust, which entitles the claimant to an equitable proprietary interest in the traced property. In theory, such a constructive trust could be constructed so that any third party with rights in the traced property would hold the equitable interest in that property in common with the claimant; more usually, a constructive trust will be claimed so that the claimant can become the absolute beneficial owner of property so that she can acquire any future increase in value in that property. A constructive trust is likely to be sought in circumstances in which the property is intrinsically valuable or when it is likely to be of use to the claimant.

The principal issue is therefore whether the appropriate remedy is to award a charge over the property or possession by way of a lien, or to award direct proprietary rights in property to the claimant. The advantage of the direct proprietary right is that the claimant acquires an equitable interest in specific property. However, a charge does grant quasi-property rights that will be enforceable in the event of an insolvency (*Re Tilley* (1967)).

A constructive trust will grant the claimant equitable proprietary rights in the property, which means that the claimant will become its owner (with the advantages of locking in any future increase in the value of the property and the burden of maintaining the property) as opposed to receiving merely a cash sum equal to its value. (Interestingly, Lord Browne-Wilkinson held in *Westdeutsche Landesbank v Islington* (1996) that a constructive trust is imposed only if the defendant has acted unconscionably, although tracing actions are not dependent on unconscionability by the defendant (e.g. *Re Diplock* (1946), where an innocent charity was required to surrender property under a tracing action). Alternatively, the court may simply order that the mixture be divided between the innocent volunteers in proportion to the size of their original contributions to that mixed fund.

Defences

While the preceding discussion has considered the contexts in which a claimant will be able to mount a tracing claim, there will be situations in which the recipient of the traceable proceeds of the claimant's property will be able to resist the claim. There are at least three defences apparently available: change of position, estoppel by representation and bona fide purchaser for value without notice.

Change of position

The defence of change of position will be available to a defendant who has received property and, on the faith of the receipt of that property, suffered some change in their personal circumstances (*Lipkin Gorman v Karpnale* (1991)). The clearest judicial statement of the manner in which the defence of change of position might operate can be extracted from the (partially dissenting) speech of Lord Goff in *Lipkin Gorman*:

> Where an innocent defendant's position is so changed that he will suffer an injustice if called upon to repay or to repay in full, the injustice of requiring him so to repay outweighs the injustice of denying the plaintiff restitution.

Suppose the following facts: B has received a valuable painting that was transferred in breach of trust. B is unaware of the breach of trust and therefore spends a large amount of money on a lease for suitable premises to show the painting to the public, on security for the painting, and on insurance. Subsequently, the beneficiaries under the trust bring a claim to trace their trust property. Lord Goff's explanation of the defence of change of position would make this circumstance a difficult one. The issue would be whether or not B's expense would be said to outweigh the value of the painting. Clearly, expenditure of a few thousand pounds would not justify B retaining a painting worth several millions and so the painting would have to be returned. B would then be required to seek a remedy from the person who transferred the property to her initially.

The defence of change of position would appear to include all sums spent by the defendant in reliance on any representation or payment made by the claimant, including the cost of financing a proposed transaction between the parties (*Sanwa Australia Finance v Finchill Property* (2001)). Furthermore, where the defendant forgoes an opportunity to take a benefit from another source in reliance on the payment received from the claimant, then the defendant is entitled to include such a reliance within his or her defence of change of position (*Palmer v Blue Circle Southern Cement* (2001)). What the defendant cannot do is seek to rely on the benefit of a contract that turned out to have been void (*South Tyneside Metropolitan BC v Svenska International plc* (1995)), or claim to have acted in good faith reliance on a payment in circumstances in which they have acquiesced in the action that rendered such payment void (*Standard Bank v Bank of Tokyo* (1995)). In any event, the defendant is required to have acted in good faith in seeking to assert a defence of change of position (*Lipkin Gorman v Karpnale* (1991)).

In *Scottish Equitable v Derby* (2000), a pensioner mistakenly received a payment from a pension fund and the fund therefore sought to recover the money from him. The pensioner argued that his change of position was contained in part in an expenditure of £9,600 on his home and also on his alleged disappointment in losing his windfall. The court would not accept that his disappointment could constitute a change of position and instead considered it to be entirely spurious, although it was held that his expenditure of £9,600 in reliance on his belief that the money was his would constitute a change of position entitling him to a defence to that extent. By contrast, in *Philip Collins Ltd v Davis* (2000), overpayments of royalties were mistakenly made to one of Phil Collins's musicians over a number of years. The musician sought to retain that money simply on the basis that he thought he was due it, even though his contract provided expressly to the contrary; the company proposed to recover the money by withholding it from future royalties which would otherwise have been paid to the musician. It was held that the musician was entitled to retain half of the overpayments on the basis that he had changed his way of life in reliance on the overpayments and could be said to have changed his position to that extent.

In *Dextra Bank and Trust Co Ltd v Bank of Jamaica* (2002), the Privy Council was prepared to hold that even incurring a future liability would constitute a change of position. So, if a person's change of position was on the basis that she had entered into a contract whereby at some point in the future she would be required to pay money to another person, that would also constitute a change of position. However, this point is not without complication. A future liability has been held not to amount to a factor sufficient to found the defence of change of position in *Pearce v Lloyds Bank* (2001). It is suggested that the approach taken in *Dextra Bank and Trust Co Ltd v Bank of Jamaica* is to be preferred because, once a liability becomes legally enforceable, the defendant can be considered to have become liable to make payment and so to have changed his position in the sense that his balance sheet will show that he owes a liability.

Estoppel by representation

Estoppel by representation is a defence that is similar, at least at first glance, to that of change of position. The significant difference between the two defences is that the estoppel is predicated on some representation being made by the claimant, as opposed to a balancing of the competing equities of the case as suggested by the defence of change of position. A good example of this defence in action arose in *National Westminster Bank plc v Somer International* (2002), in which a company received a payment of about the same amount as it expected to receive for one of its other clients at about the same time. The bank paid the money into the claimant's account. The bank told the claimant company that this amount was about to clear into the company's account. In fact the bank had made a mistake in that the money should have been paid into another customer's account. Consequently, the company shipped goods to one of its own clients, believing that that client had paid for the goods in advance. The bank that had mistakenly made the payment sought to recover the money. The Court of Appeal held that the equitable doctrine of estoppel by representation meant that the claimant should be entitled to set off the value of the goods sent to its client in reliance on receipt of the payment against the remaining value, which it would be required to return to the bank.

Bona fide purchaser for value without notice of the other's rights

A further applicable defence is that of the bona fide purchaser for value without notice (also known as 'equity's darling'). The final problem is the perennial one of deciding between the person who has lost their property to a wrongdoing fiduciary and the person who buys that property in all innocence. Let us take the example of the painting held on trust for beneficiaries, which is transferred away in breach of trust by a trustee. Suppose then that the painting is purchased by Erica, in good faith, for its full market price. Erica will necessarily take the view that she has paid an open market price for property in circumstances in which she could not have known that the property ought properly to have been held on trust. By the same token, the beneficiaries would argue that it is they who ought to be entitled to recover their property from Erica.

From a strict analytical viewpoint, the property lawyer might take a different approach and find for the beneficiaries on the following basis. At no time do the beneficiaries relinquish their property rights in the painting before Erica purchases it. Therefore, those rights ought to be considered as subsisting. Erica cannot acquire good title on the basis that the beneficial interest still properly remains in the beneficiaries. The approach of equity, though, is to protect free markets by ensuring that the bona fide purchaser for value without notice of the rights of a beneficial owner is entitled to assert good title in property in such situations. Such a person is rightly referred to as 'equity's darling'. Consequently, a good defence to a tracing claim would appear to be an assertion that you are a purchaser acting in good faith without notice of the rights of the beneficiary (*per* Lord Browne-Wilkinson in *Westdeutsche Landesbank v Islington* (1996)).

Choice between remedies

As considered above, there is a possibility of a number of remedies ranging from those associated with tracing claims, to those associated with restoration of the value of specific property, to those based on compensation (*Target Holdings Ltd v Redferns* (1996)). There is, then, a question as to the remedy which the beneficiary is required to pursue in all the circumstances. The equitable doctrine of election arises in such situations to provide that it is open to the claimant to elect between alternative remedies (*Tang v Capacious Investments Ltd* (1996)). In

Tang, the possibility of parallel remedies arose in relation to a breach of trust for the plaintiff beneficiary to claim an account of profits from the malfeasant trustee or to claim damages representing the lost profits to the trust. It was held that these two remedies existed in the alternative and therefore that the plaintiff could claim both, not being required to elect between them until judgment was awarded in its favour. Clearly, the court would not permit double recovery in respect of the same loss, thus requiring an election between those remedies ultimately.

Moving on . . .

This long chapter has raised a number of issues in outline form only – for a more detailed discussion, the reader is referred to Chapters 12 and 18 to 20 of my longer textbook, *Equity & Trusts* (Hudson, 2014). What we have achieved in the foregoing discussion is the final piece of the jigsaw relating to the treatment of the law of trusts in theory. The next two chapters consider the practicalities of trusts as used in relation to commercial transactions and also as used for charitable purposes.

Chapter 11

Quistclose trusts and commercial trusts

Trusts used as security in commercial transactions

Trusts are often used to take security in commercial transactions, not least because of the advantages which they offer in the event that a party to a contract goes into insolvency. Pension funds and unit trusts are both types of trust which are used in investment markets, and which are particularly significant in financial markets. One of the most significant forms of trusts which are used in banking transactions are *Quistclose* trusts, which can provide a lender of money with a proprietary interest in the loan moneys in the event that the borrower goes into insolvency. The analysis of those trusts forms the first half of this chapter. The second half of the chapter considers the overlap between the principles of equity and other commercial uses of trusts structures.

The principal issue, for present purposes, when taking security in commercial transactions is the form of right which the parties acquire over property so as to protect themselves. When considering how to take title in property in such circumstances, there are three principal structures to be considered. When dealing with a counterparty, the owner of property may wish to retain title in that property even though it is being used for the purposes of the contract. Often it will not be practicable to retain title if that property is being mixed with other property or if it is being used as part of a joint venture partnership. It might be possible where the property is an item of machinery that stands on its own because it will always be possible to identify that property separately from all other property.

Matters become more complicated when the property is mixed with other property, so that it is impossible to identify that property in its original form. For example, where sugar is used to manufacture chocolate: once the sugar is mixed with other ingredients to make chocolate it will not be possible to identify nor to extract the original sugar. Consequently, the former owner of the sugar would want to acquire some rights in the chocolate. That would either require some of the chocolate to be held separately for the owner of the sugar, or would have to provide that the owner of the sugar was entitled to a given proportion of the total stock of chocolate. In the former case that could be by way of trust, whereas the latter could only be by way of floating charge (*Re Goldcorp* (1995)).

Alternatively, it may be possible for the contracting party to give up title in the property, subject to an obligation on the other party to use that property only for limited, identified purposes. Such a structure would create an equitable interest in favour of that party under what is termed a *Quistclose* trust, as considered below.

What will emerge from the following discussion are examples of the allocation of property rights in commercial contracts, in partnership contracts and through the creation of ordinary companies. The fundamental objectives for a property lawyer in these contexts are the same: how can the parties demonstrate some title in assets in the event that the other party to the contract fails to perform its obligations?

Floating charges – rights over a pool of property

One example of an equitable doctrine which is used in commercial transactions is the floating charge. For all that commercial people may seek to keep equity out of their contracts on the basis that it introduces too much uncertainty into commercial life (see Goode, 1995) an increased level of commercial security has been made possible by equitable doctrines like the trust and the floating charge. The floating charge enables a claimant to establish a proprietary right without the need to demonstrate that those rights attach to specific property and to no other property, as is required for the establishment of a trust (e.g. *Re Goldcorp* (1995)).

So in *Clough Mill v Martin* (1984), a supplier of fabric was concerned to retain rights in the fabric supplied to a clothes manufacturer, lest the manufacturer go into insolvency after receipt of the fabric, but before paying for it. Therefore, the contract purported to allow the supplier to retain title in the fabric until the time of payment. The issue arose, once the manufacturer had become unable to pay, whether the supplier could assert good title in the fabric once it had been incorporated with other material and added to the manufacturer's stock of garments. Goff LJ held that the contract would create a mere charge on the facts because of the difficulty that would arise if more than one seller sought to assert a like right – that is, that there would be too many claimants and not enough stock to satisfy the claims. The decision is one reached, necessarily, on its facts after consideration of the precise terms of the contract.

A floating charge does not retain equitable rights for the chargee; rather, it establishes rights of an identifiable value (in the form of a charge), which attach from time to time to a changing fund of property. As such, in insolvency, the floating charge offers a weaker form of security than either the '*Romalpa*' clause (which establishes that no rights transfer to the insolvent party) or the *Quistclose* trust (which similarly establishes that only limited equitable rights transfer to the insolvent party: *Barclays Bank Ltd v Quistclose Investments Ltd* (1970)).

Quistclose trusts

Quistclose *trusts in outline*

A *Quistclose* trust enables the lender in a loan contract to retain an equitable proprietary interest in the loan money, which provides protection, *inter alia*, in the event that the borrower were to go into insolvency. The equitable interest is created by inserting a term into the loan contract to the effect that the borrower may only use the loan money for specified purposes. In short, where a lender transfers loan moneys subject to a contractual provision that the borrower is only entitled to use that money for specified purposes, then the borrower will hold those moneys on trust for the lender if they are used for some purpose other than that set out in the loan contract. Significantly, in the event that the borrower purports to transfer the loan money to a third party in breach of that contractual provision then it has been held by Lord Millett in *Twinsectra v Yardley* (2002) that the transferor will be deemed to have retained its rights under a resulting trust that will preclude the transferee from acquiring rights in that property. The traditional explanation of the *Quistclose* trust in trusts law scholarship is that if the borrower were to go into insolvency, then the loan moneys would be held on resulting trust for the lender, who consequently was protected by means of that trust against the borrower's insolvency. This structure is not without difficulties (as considered below), although it is no more difficult than the previous decision of the House of Lords in *Barclays Bank v Quistclose* (1970): these competing analyses are the focus of this section.

At present, the *Quistclose* arrangement has been applied only to loan moneys but there is no reason in principle why it should apply only to money and not to other forms of property and contractual relationships. The following discussion will examine the *Quistclose* decision and the various alternative explanations for the nature of the trust created.

The decision in Barclays Bank v Quistclose

In *Barclays Bank v Quistclose* (1970), a loan contract was formed by which Quistclose lent money to Rolls Razor Ltd solely for the purpose of paying dividends to its shareholders. That money was held in a share dividend bank account separate from all other moneys. At the time of making the loan, Rolls Razor was in financial difficulties and teetering on the edge of insolvency. Harman J described the company as being 'in Queer Street'. In the light of these difficulties, the lender Quistclose was determined that if it lent money to the company, it should be able to control how that money was used. Therefore, a purpose for the use of money was specified in the loan contract: it provided that the company was permitted to use the money only to pay a dividend to its shareholders and for no other purpose. In the event Rolls Razor went into insolvency before the dividend was paid. Quistclose contended that the money in the share dividend account was held on trust for

Quistclose itself. The House of Lords held that the loan money held separately in a share dividend bank account should be treated as having been held on trust for Quistclose. The real question is the proper analysis of that trust arrangement.

Lord Wilberforce upheld the resulting trust in favour of Quistclose on the basis that it was an implied term of the loan contract that the money be returned to the bank in the event that it was not used for the purpose for which it was lent. Lord Wilberforce held that there were two trusts: a primary trust (which empowered Rolls Razor to use the money to pay the dividend) and a secondary trust (which required Rolls Razor to return the money to the bank if it was not used to pay the dividend). As his Lordship held:

> In the present case the intention to create a secondary trust for the benefit of the lender, to arise if the primary trust, to pay the dividend, could not be carried out, is clear and I can find no reason why the law should not give effect to it.

This bicameral trust structure is unique to the case law in this area – although it would be possible to create a complex express trust that mimicked it. The House of Lords was asked to approve a resulting trust on the appeal to it, and therefore the trust at issue has generally been taken to be a resulting trust.

However, if you read the short judgment of Lord Wilberforce, the term 'resulting trust' is not used explicitly. Instead, Lord Wilberforce's judgment is concerned with the interaction of concepts of common law and concepts of equity. This makes more intuitive sense to a banking lawyer than to a trusts lawyer. In a loan contract, the parties' interaction is governed entirely by common law: the lender transfers the loan money outright, the borrower becomes the absolute owner of the loan money with a right to spend it, and then the borrower faces a contractual obligation to pay interest on the loan and then to repay the capital amount of the loan at the end of the transaction.

So, in an ordinary loan contract there is no trust involved at all. Lord Wilberforce held that in a *Quistclose* arrangement the doctrines and 'remedies of equity' would supplement the contract law position if the borrower purported to use the money for a purpose which was not permitted by the terms of the contract. Therefore, his Lordship's judgment was concerned with the interaction of common law and equity in general terms until he came to the passage quoted above, which made specific reference to the primary and secondary trust concept. The primary trust can be understood to be a power for the borrower to use the loan money for its contractually specified purpose; the secondary trust then appears to be a resulting trust which carries the equitable interest back to the lender. There are, however, other explanations which are considered in the following sections.

A sui generis structure

The most tempting suggestion is simply to accept that the *Quistclose* trust is in a category all of its own (a *sui generis* category) which has been developed for the particular circumstances of loan contracts. The *Quistclose* trust has been described in *Carreras Rothmans Ltd v Freeman Mathews Treasure Ltd* (1985) on the basis that:

> equity fastens on the conscience of the person who receives from another property transferred for a specific purpose only and not therefore for the recipient's own purposes, so that such person will not be permitted to treat the property as his own or to use it for other than the stated purpose.

This statement could be taken to be authority for one of three competing understandings of the *Quistclose* arrangement as an express, resulting or constructive trust.

At first glance, the reference to the 'conscience' of the recipient equates most obviously to a constructive trust, although those *dicta* are capable of multiple analyses. As considered in *Westdeutsche Landesbank*, to define the *Quistclose* trust as operating solely on the conscience of the recipient of the money is merely to place the situation within the general understanding of the trust as part of equity, rather than to allocate it necessarily to any particular trust categorisation. This issue is considered in detail in Chapter 22 of Hudson (2014).

The Australian case of *Re Australian Elizabethan Theatre Trust* (1991) has held that there is no need for a separate analysis of the *Quistclose* trust and that, instead, ordinary principles of express trust law are sufficient to explain the appropriate property law principles. Thus, it is said, there is an express trust with two limbs: one granting a power to the borrower to use the loan moneys for the contractually specified purpose, and the second which provides that any misuse of the loan moneys causes the entire equitable interest to be held for the lender (*General Communications Ltd v Development Finance Corporation of New Zealand Ltd* (1990)).

The Twinsectra model

In the House of Lords in *Twinsectra v Yardley* (2002), Lord Millett suggested that the equitable interest in the loan moneys remains in the lender throughout the transaction on resulting trust. Therefore, the borrower takes the money with a right to use it only for the purposes specified in the loan contract, but always subject to the lender's equitable interest in that money. Lord Millett held that the *Quistclose* trust should be considered to be akin to a retention of title by the lender whereby the lender effectively retains an equitable interest in the property throughout the transaction. In that case a solicitor permitted loan moneys to be used by his client in breach of the express terms of a loan contract. On this analysis, a *Quistclose* trust enables a party to a commercial contract to retain their equitable interest in property provided as part of a commercial agreement. Lord Millett held specifically (at para 81) that 'The money remains the property of the lender unless and until it is applied in accordance with his directions, and in so far as it is not so applied it must be returned to him.' However, confusingly, his Lordship went on to hold (at para 100) both that the money was held on resulting trust and that the money must be returned to the lender. It is difficult to see both how the lender should *retain* the equitable interest in the loan money and how the loan money should be *returned* to the lender. After all, how can property be returned to someone if that person had retained that property all along? If you ask to borrow my umbrella but I refuse to lend it to you, and so I retain it, how could I ask you to return my umbrella the next day?

An attempt to resolve these issues

The most satisfying analysis is that the property is held on express trust as considered above in relation to the *Australian Elizabethan Theatre* case, or that the resulting trust operates eccentrically so as to retain the ownership of the loan money in the hands of the lender. However, if the lender retains the equitable interest in the money then it complicates the way in which the borrower can be understood as spending the loan moneys. The answer, suggested above, is that the borrower must be deemed to have a power to spend the loan moneys in accordance with the contractually specified purpose.

It would be possible to change this analysis in any given case *if* the loan contract itself provided for something else. For example, in a loan contract the bank making the loan would be better advised to make it plain exactly what equitable interests are retained by the bank, what powers the borrower acquires, and so forth. Given the complexities in the case law it would be bizarre for a bank to leave these issues unspecified in the contract. A better structure yet would be for the bank to open a new account in the name of the borrower, to pay the loan money alone into the bank account, and then for the bank to pay the money directly for the specified purpose when it is prompted to do so by the borrower. In this way, the money would not pass to the borrower; instead the contract would specify that the loan money remains absolutely the property of the lender until payment is made. In this analysis, the *Quistclose* trust is just another means by which commercial people retain title in property and the precise form of the parties' rights will require careful consideration from case to case.

Commercial trusts are not contracts

There is a growing trend in a number of jurisdictions towards the explanation of commercial trusts as being, in truth, a species of contract. It has been suggested that the foundation of trusts in modern practice is the creation of a contract between settlor and trustee which sets out the terms of the trustee's obligations and also sets out the circumstances in which the trustee's liabilities will be excluded (Langbein, 1995). In consequence it has been suggested that contracts are in truth only to be thought of as contracts because the terms of their enforcement are limited by contract.

In parallel with this notion has been the development of trusts practice in those jurisdictions, known as 'tax havens', which offer financial services to clients who want to reduce their liability to tax in the jurisdiction in which they are resident by having them invest in the tax haven, in which no tax will be payable. In an attempt to ensure that the clients who invest in such trusts are not treated as being liable to tax in their home jurisdictions on any profits made by the trust, the sellers of these trusts have attempted to construct trusts in which the investors have no vested beneficial interests; instead their interests are represented by a 'protector', who is empowered to act against the trustees where necessary. It is said that the client's rights are purely rights in contract with the provider of the trust scheme, rather than the rights of beneficiaries under a trust in English law as considered in Chapter 4. The relevant trusts statutes in many of the tax havens have been altered so as to admit these schemes. The danger that these jurisdictions run is that an English court, in relation to their English resident clients, will refuse to recognise the validity of such a trust and so deem the client to remain the owner of that property and so impose a liability to tax on such clients.

The proper response to these developments is simple, I would suggest. First, it is important to remind ourselves of the position in English law: for there to be a valid trust, there must be some person for whose benefit the court can decree performance of the trust. This is the so-called 'beneficiary principle', considered in Chapter 4. Therefore, any person who enters into a trust scheme in a tax haven is either disposing of his property outright, subject only to a contractual right to receive some share in the profits in the future, or else he is a beneficiary with proprietary rights in the trust property, and so liable to tax in the ordinary way as the owner of that property (*Baker v Archer-Shee* (1927)). In English law there is no intermediate category of person who has a right to identified property held on trust, but who can be treated for tax purposes as having no proprietary rights in the trust fund. An English court ought not to change its centuries-old analysis in the English law of trusts as to the nature of a beneficiary's rights under a trust simply so that a group of rich investors can avoid their liabilities to pay tax by investment in offshore trusts.

As to the broader point whether or not trusts are capable of being considered to be merely contracts, this is not correct. It is the case that recent English decisions have held that trustees are entitled to limit their liabilities by contract (*Armitage v Nurse* (1998)). Nevertheless, trustees bear fiduciary obligations of the kind considered throughout this book that are not created by ordinary contracts (although contracts of agency and partnership do create fiduciary obligations). Consequently, there is a clear distinction between contracts on the one hand and trusts on the other. Furthermore, it is not true that there are always contracts between settlors and trustees. Constructive and resulting trusts are not predicated on any contract between settlor and trustee, but rather on the control of the trustees' conscience as considered in Chapters 7 and 6, respectively, in this book. Similarly, express trusts of the kind found in *Paul v Constance* (1977), in which the courts infer the existence of the trust from the circumstances, do not necessarily require any contract to be in place between the parties; rather the trust arises on the basis of conscience and the parties' intentions as to the treatment of the property at issue.

For commercial people it is reassuring to think of trusts as being an extension of the contractual principles that are familiar to them. There are forms of trusts, such as unit trusts, which seem to combine contractual and trusts law principles in investment contexts, and therefore there is a tendency to want to collapse those principles into one another. However, it is very important that the trust is recognised as being something distinct from contract, precisely because the law of trusts deals with a number of significant parts of our non-commercial life in which the principles of the law of contract have no place, including the allocation of rights in the home and the administration of will trusts. To dispose of such non-commercial situations by reference to commercial law principles would mean that inappropriate rules would be used to resolve disputes, for example in familial situations. Furthermore, it is difficult to see why commercial people should have their own transactions, subject to entirely different laws from those that apply to ordinary people. Why should those who have the resources to hire expensive legal representation be subject to less onerous legal codes than the rest of the population, and why should professional trustees be entitled to limit their own liabilities when non-professional trustees would not know to create such contracts and so limit their liabilities? This is one of the key challenges facing the modern law of trusts.

Conclusion – how commercial lawyers think about property rights

What is remarkable is the difference between the manner in which property lawyers consider questions of title in property and the manner in which commercial lawyers consider those same questions. To put the point crudely, commercial lawyers are concerned to give effect to contracts wherever possible without concerning themselves as to the niceties of title, whereas property lawyers typically agonise more over which precise rights attach to which precise property (see, for example, *Re Goldcorp* (1995)). Property lawyers and trusts lawyers can be expected to take a more careful approach to rights in property. The one exception to this difference arises in relation to insolvency, when commercial lawyers become greater advocates of certainty as to the identity of property.

The clearest example of the difference between a property lawyer and a commercial lawyer arises in relation to the discussion of certainty of subject matter in Chapter 3. The property lawyers' strict approach is personified by the decision in *Re Goldcorp* that there must be segregation of property before that property can be held on trust. Other concepts, like the floating charge in which property rights of a certain value can attach loosely to a fluctuating pool of property, have grown out of equity and been seized upon by commercial lawyers as providing a different form of security for commercial parties. The commercial lawyer will not want a contract to be invalidated simply because some formality as to the segregation of property has not been complied with. So it is that the Sale of Goods (Amendment) Act 1995 was enacted to provide that, even where property has not been segregated, if the claimants have rights to part of a mixed fund of property those claimants can assert rights as tenants in common of the entire fund.

So, it is said that the one context in which commercial lawyers follow as strict a line as the property lawyers is in relation to insolvency. It is a central principle of insolvency law that no unsecured creditor be entitled to take an advantage over any other unsecured creditor under the *pari passu* principle, and that no property may be taken from an insolvent person's estate under the anti-deprivation principle (*Belmont Park Investments v BNY Corporate Trustee* (2011)). That explains the decision in *Goldcorp*. In that case there were more claims than there was property to go round. Consequently, all of the creditors who could not identify any property which was held separately on trust for them were required to wait with the other unsecured creditors in the forlorn hope that there would be some assets left when the insolvency process was worked through.

What emerges from this short discussion is an impression that commercial law is concerned to develop principles that are likely to support the efficacy of commercial contracts. There is a great suspicion among the commercial community of equitable principles because they are wrongly considered to be unpredictable by virtue of their being generally discretionary. This is in spite of the fact that most of the significant commercial structures were developed by equity: among them the ordinary company, floating charges and express trusts. See generally Hudson, *Equity and Trusts* (2014) Chapter 21.

Chapter 12

Charities

The outline of the law on charities

Introduction

Charities constitute a distinct category from the rest of the law of trusts because charities are public trusts that do not have beneficiaries. Rather, the trustees of charities are obliged to use the charity's property for a charitable purpose, which in turn, must be for the 'public benefit'. The bulk of this chapter asks whether or not a variety of purposes will constitute charitable purposes so that they will constitute valid charities. In Chapter 4 we considered how an abstract purpose trust would be void. What emerges from this chapter is that a trust can be created validly to pursue an abstract purpose provided that that purpose is a charitable purpose. Another advantage of charitable trusts is that they are exempt from most forms of taxation – something that arises in many of the cases in which taxpayers have sought to avoid tax by using charities, with the result that much of charities law has been bent out of shape to prevent inappropriate tax avoidance.

The definitions of the various forms of 'charitable purpose' were set out in case law before the passage of the Charities Act 2006, which introduced further categories of charitable purpose. That Act was consolidated into the Charities Act 2011. The old case law divided between: trusts for the relief of poverty; trusts for the advancement of education; trusts for the advancement of religion; and trusts for other purposes beneficial to the community. However, the enactment of the Charities Act 2011 has had the effect of expanding the categories of 'charitable purpose' beyond those categories set out by case law. The first three categories – the relief of poverty, the advancement of religion and the advancement of education – remain after the passage of the Act, but in large part, the fourth category has been replaced by a new statutory list of purposes, as set out below, although the old fourth category cases continue to be effective as charitable purposes. This chapter will consider each of these charitable purposes in turn and will consider the interpretation of some of the new statutory purposes in the light of the decided cases.

The requirements of the Charities Act 2011

A 'charity' is defined in the Charities Act 2011 as being 'an institution which is established for charitable purposes only' and which 'falls to be subject to the control of the High Court in the exercise of its jurisdiction with respect to charities' (Charities Act 2011, s 1(1)). A charitable purpose is one that fulfils two requirements. First, it must fall within the list of purposes set out in s 3(1) of the 2011 Act, as considered in the remainder of this section; second, it must satisfy the public benefit test, as considered below.

The definition of 'charitable purposes' in the Charities Act 2011 is found in s 3(1). There are 13 categories, of which the first three refer back to pre-existing case law on the definition of a charitable purpose:

(a) the prevention or relief of poverty;
(b) the advancement of education;
(c) the advancement of religion.

These first three categories are therefore very similar to the initial three case law categories of charitable purpose; whereas the following categories are new:

(d) the advancement of health or the saving of lives;
(e) the advancement of citizenship or community development;
(f) the advancement of the arts, culture, heritage, or science;
(g) the advancement of amateur sport;
(h) the advancement of human rights, conflict resolution or reconciliation, or the promotion of religious or racial harmony, or equality and diversity;
(i) the advancement of environmental protection, or improvement;
(j) the relief of those in need by reason of youth, age, ill-health, disability, financial hardship, or other disadvantage;
(k) the advancement of animal welfare;
(l) the promotion of the efficiency of the armed forces of the Crown, or of the efficiency of the police, fire and rescue or ambulance services;
(m) any other purposes within subsection (4) (that is, categories of charitable purpose which are already accepted under case law on charities).

What is particularly important is that categories of charity which have been accepted in old case law continue to be valid under the 2011 Act. Thus, it is provided in s 3(4) of the 2011 Act that any purposes that are 'recognised as charitable purposes under existing charity law', for example under old case law, will continue to be recognised as charitable purposes, regardless of whether they appear in the list of charitable purposes in s 3 of the 2011 Act. Consequently, it is still important to consider those categories of charitable purpose which have been upheld by pre-2006 case law because the 2011 Act maintains their validity. Therefore, we shall first consider the three substantive heads of charity under pre-2006 case law before turning to new statutory heads of charitable purpose.

The requirement for a public benefit

The requirement for a public benefit is generally conceptualised in the cases by considering what will *not* constitute a public benefit. So, in the House of Lords in *Oppenheim v Tobacco Securities Trust* (1951), Lord Simonds held that there could not be a public benefit if there was a nexus between the people who established the charity and the people who were intended to benefit, if the people who stood to benefit could not be said to constitute a section of the public. (A 'nexus' is a form of connection.) In that case, where a company sought to establish a trust to pay for the school fees of the children of its employees, it was held that there was no *public* benefit because there was a nexus between the children who were to benefit and the company that was establishing the trust. The children of employees did not constitute a section of 'the public' and therefore there was no 'public' benefit. In relation to charities that are created for general purposes, it was suggested by Russell LJ in *ICLR v Attorney General* (1972) that where a trust purpose removes the need for statutory or governmental action by providing a service voluntarily, the organisation providing that service should be deemed to be acting for the public benefit and so to be acting charitably.

There have been recent cases, particularly relating to the advancement of religion, which have suggested that if a purpose could possibly be interpreted so as to be for the public benefit then that purpose can be considered to be for the public benefit (*Re Hetherington* (1990)). Similarly, it has been held that even if the trust could not be subjected to such a purposive interpretation, it could nevertheless be held to be a valid charitable purpose if the trustees would operate the trust so that there would be a public benefit in practice. These principles are considered in greater detail in the various discussions of 'public benefit' in relation to each of the heads of charity discussed in this chapter.

The three established heads of charity

The prevention or relief of poverty

The first category of charitable purpose is that of the prevention or relief of poverty. This is the clearest category of charitable purposes in many ways. The birth of the law on charities is best understood as being in the activities of the church when dealing with impoverished people in individual parishes. It was the Charities Act 2006 that introduced for the first time the notion of a charitable purpose encompassing the *prevention* of poverty, which persists in the 2011 Act.

The test for the relief of poverty

The leading decision is that of the House of Lords in *Dingle v Turner* (1972), which forms the centrepiece of this section – characteristic of the approach of the courts in this area is the 'purposive' decision of Lord Cross. The trust in *Dingle v Turner* concerned a bequest of £10,000 to be applied 'to pay pensions to poor employees of E. Dingle & Company'. Those arguing that the bequest be held invalid sought to rely on *Oppenheim v Tobacco Securities Trust* (1951), a case relating to educational purpose trusts, which held that there must be some public benefit beyond a private class of persons. Lord Cross did not agree with that argument. He explained that the rule in *Oppenheim* was one of universal application in the rest of the law of charities, but not in relation to trusts for the relief of poverty.

The point of distinction from the *Oppenheim* line of cases was said to be the fact that those cases involved trusts whose purpose was to acquire 'an undeserved fiscal immunity' (i.e. a tax break), whereas trusts that were genuinely for the relief of poverty would not fail because they would not have such an ulterior motive if they were genuinely for the relief of poverty. In short, the court would be prepared to support a genuine motive to relieve the poverty of even only one or two individuals as being charitable; although in the absence of such a motive the court would refuse to find the trust charitable. It is suggested that charitable motives are more obviously demonstrated in relation to the relief of poverty (provided those receiving the benefits can be shown to be genuinely impoverished) unlike cases in which companies are seeking to acquire tax benefits for their directors and other employees by setting up educational trusts that benefit only the children of their own employees. Lord Cross described this as the 'practical justification . . . if not the historical explanation' for the distinction between trusts for the relief of poverty and other charitable trusts.

What is 'poverty'?

The difficulty for the courts is then to establish a test for deciding in any particular situation whether or not a particular trust is sufficiently directed at the relief of poverty. The cases have taken the view that poverty does not necessitate proof of outright destitution; rather, it can encompass simply 'going short' (*Re Coulthurst* (1951)). There are a number of examples of situations in which the courts have held cases of general financial hardship, rather than absolute grinding poverty, to be within the technical definition of 'poverty'. For example, a trust for 'ladies of limited means' has been held to be charitable (*Re Gardom* (1914)) together with the (gloriously expressed) trust for the benefit of 'decayed actors' (*Spiller v Maude* (1881)).

Whether or not there needs to be a public benefit

It is unclear whether or not charities relating to poverty must be for the public benefit. Old case law did not require that there was a public benefit; as considered above it was sufficient that the settlor had a genuine charitable intention. The Charities Act 2011 defines a 'charitable purpose' as requiring that there be a public benefit in s 2(1)(b). However, ss 3(4) and 4(3) of the 2011 Act provide that old case law continues in effect. Consequently, it is not clear whether the old case law rule not requiring a public benefit for poverty charities will continue in effect or whether the requirement in the Charities Act that there must be a public benefit will now expunge the old case law approach to poverty.

A significant question in relation to the breadth of public benefit, necessary to create a valid trust for the relief of poverty, is the question of the closeness of the links between the settlor and the people who are to be benefited. For charitable purposes other than the relief of poverty, it is important that the class of purposes to be benefited must not be defined by reference to their proximity to the settlor, that is, by all being relatives of the settlor or something of that sort. In terms of trusts for charitable purposes, it stands to reason that a settlor could not create a settlement 'for the benefit of my two children who have little money' and then claim that it is a charitable trust for the relief of poverty. However, it has been held that to define a charitable purpose for the relief of poverty of the settlor's poor relations would not affect its validity as a charitable bequest (*Re Scarisbrick* (1951)), provided that that would genuinely relieve the poverty of those people. It is from this line of decisions that trusts for the benefit of poor relations have been upheld as being valid charitable trusts, no matter that that does seem a little anomalous at first blush because that seems to be a private express trust of the sort discussed in Chapters 2 through 5.

Educational purpose trusts

What is 'education'?

The first issue is to decide what exactly is meant by the term 'education' in the context of the law of charities. Clearly, trusts purposes involving schools and universities would fall within the analogous cases to the preamble of the Statute of Charitable Uses 1601. The contexts in which there is greater confusion surround trusts set up for the study of more esoteric subjects, or even simply to advance an ideological position, which are not annexed to any accepted educational institution.

Research, teaching and ideology

In the leading case of *McGovern v Attorney General* (1982), Slade J set out the principles on which a court would typically find that research work would be held to be charitable, namely: if the subject is a useful subject of research and if it is intended to publish the results of that research, whether or not carried on in an institution of education. Therefore, the term 'education' will encompass research carried out outside schools or universities, provided that there is an intention to publish that research or make its benefits available to the public.

Sport and education

In the leading case of *IRC v McMullen* (1981), the House of Lords approved the charitable status of a trust created to promote the playing of association football and the playing and coaching of other sports, provided that it was done within schools or other educational establishments. The contention was made that the playing of sport ought properly to be considered to be a part of education, in the same way that sitting in a classroom is generally supposed to be educational. The leading speech was delivered by Lord Hailsham, who held that this purpose was indeed educational because sport was essential to the development of young persons at schools and colleges.

Sporting purposes outside schools or colleges will not, in themselves, be charitable under the case law. So, a trust to provide a cup for a yachting competition was not held to be charitable (*Re Nottage* (1895)), although trusts in relation to the conduct of sports and cultural activities, which were carried on at university, were held to be charitable purposes (*London Hospital Medical College v IRC* (1976)); the difference being that the former were not at an educational establishment whereas the latter was. In this writer's opinion, all this supposes that drinking while wearing a rugby shirt counts as either a sport or culture.

The public benefit requirement

It has become important in the context of educational trusts to look beyond the apparent purpose of the trust to require some evidence that the trust is intended to be run as a de facto charity. Therefore, the requirement of sufficient public benefit has emerged. It might be possible to set up a trust that has only one purpose: 'to provide educational opportunities for young people in the UK', giving the trustees unfettered discretion to receive applications for grants and to apply the money as they see fit. However, if that trust were being operated by a company with the real intention of educating only the children of its directors, that would not be a trust for the public benefit, even though, on its face, the trust's purpose as drafted looks straightforwardly charitable. The question would be the extent to which money was paid solely to the children of directors as a private class. If the money was paid out to children who had no family connection with the company then the trust would be a charitable trust. Whereas, if it was a sham which purported to be for the public benefit while in fact it only paid for the school fees of the children of directors, then it would not be a charitable purpose for the public benefit.

The difficulty would come if money was given out for the benefit of children of the 200,000 ordinary employees (otherwise than on the basis of their poverty). One argument might be that such children formed a sufficiently large section of the public to enable the trust to be considered to be a charitable one. Alternatively, it could be said that the trust remains a private trust de facto because money is only applied to those with a nexus to the settlor. The trustees may, for form's sake, pay 10 per cent of the available money to children entirely outside any nexus to the company. In such a situation, the argument would still appear to be that the trust is predominantly a private trust. The question would then be: what if the trustees paid 50 per cent to those outside any nexus with the company, and 50 per cent to those who were the children of employees? The possible answers to this conundrum which are presented in case law are considered next.

The 'personal nexus' test

The leading case is that of *Oppenheim v Tobacco Securities Trust* (1951), in which the House of Lords considered a trust that held money from which the income was to be applied for the education of the children of employees of British-American Tobacco Co Ltd. That company was a very large multinational, employing a large number of people. The trust would have been void as a private trust on the basis that it lacked a perpetuities provision. It was argued, however, that the purpose was charitable and therefore that no perpetuities provision was necessary. Lord Simonds followed *Re Compton* (1945), in holding that there was a requirement of public benefit to qualify as an educational charity and that the management of this trust did not satisfy that requirement because the money was only for the benefit of a private class (i.e. the children of employees of that company).

The phrase that was used by the court to encapsulate the test was whether or not those who stood to benefit from the trust constituted a sufficient 'section of the community'. Lord Simonds held that:

> A group of persons may be numerous, but, if the nexus between them is their personal relationship to a single *propositus* or to several *propositi*, they are neither the community nor a section of the community for charitable purposes.

Therefore, it was held that the trust at issue could not be a charitable trust because of the nexus between those who stood to benefit from the trust and the *propositus* (the company), which was settlor of that trust.

Fee-paying 'public schools'

One of the greatest problems facing charities law in this area has been the charitable status which has been accorded to fee-charging, so-called 'public schools'. Those schools only accept pupils whose parents can afford their very high fees. Therefore, those schools are not open to the public, nor are their facilities available to the public; but nevertheless those schools have been entitled to be registered as charities and consequently to receive the tax advantages which come from that status (which in effect means that the public purse is subsidising those schools instead of raising tax revenue from their profits so as to fund state schools). This issue arose in *Independent Schools Council v Charity Commission* (2012), where it was held that schools which did not permit any pupils who paid no fees to attend could not be charities, whereas schools with programmes to admit students who did not pay fees could be charitable. The issue would revolve around the extent of their public benefit in each case. It was held that, by definition, charging fees which many people could not afford would mean that such a school could not be acting prima facie in the public benefit. Therefore, fee-charging schools would be required to demonstrate that they provided education for all regardless of ability to pay, or else that they performed other substantial and sufficient acts of public benefit.

Trusts for religious purposes

The definition of 'religion' in the case law

In *Re South Place Ethical Society* (1980), Dillon J gave a taste of the meaning of the concept of a 'religious purpose' in the law of charity: 'religion, as I see it, is concerned with man's relations with God'. Therefore, on the facts of *South Place*, the study and dissemination of ethical principles does not constitute religion because, in the words of Dillon J, 'ethics are concerned with man's relations with man' and not with God. The focus is therefore on a system of belief in a god. Other forms of spiritual observance are not included. Therefore, New Age religions concerned with belief in the power of crystals, for example, would not constitute a religion under the case law definition.

The leading case of *Gilmour v Coats* (1949) in the House of Lords took the view that mere religious observance was insufficient to constitute a charitable purpose unless there was also some demonstrable public benefit. So, simply arguing that the prayers of a cloistered order of nuns would be for the benefit of mankind was not considered to be a valid charitable purpose for the advancement of religion. Religious observance is generally not a public matter: usually people would pray in private. Yet it is necessary for a trust to be a valid charitable trust for the advancement of religion that the trust has some public benefit. However, the courts have begun to adopt increasingly relaxed approaches to the interpretation of such public benefit. In *Neville Estates v Madden* (1962), the issue arose whether a trust to benefit members of the Catford Synagogue could be a charitable purpose. The central issue was whether the members of that synagogue could be considered to be a sufficient section of the population to constitute a 'public benefit'. It was held that, because the religious observance practised in the synagogue was (in theory) open to the public, the requirement of public benefit would be satisfied.

Similarly, in *Re Hetherington*, the issue concerned a trust to provide income for the saying of masses in private. On the facts it was found that it was not susceptible of proof in these circumstances that there would be benefit to the public. However, Browne-Wilkinson J was prepared to construe the gift as being a gift to say masses in public on the basis that such an interpretation would render the trust valid; thus demonstrating a very purposive approach because it was found that there was a genuine charitable intention.

This purposive approach indicates the attitude of the courts to validate chari-table trusts wherever possible, in contradistinction to the stricter interpretation accorded generally to express private trusts. It also illustrates a generational approach by judges like Lords Wilberforce, Goff and Browne-Wilkinson (when in the High Court) to uphold the validity of trusts wherever possible, in contrast to the approaches of judges like Viscount Simonds and Harman J to invalidate trusts in circumstances in which there was some apparent incongruity in their drafting.

Religion where there is no god

A more complex idea is contained in s 2(3)(a) of the Charities Act 2011, where that paragraph provides that the term 'religion' includes 'a religion which does not involve belief in a god' or one that involves belief in a number of gods. Previously, charities law had separated religions off from other forms of belief by reference to a requirement that there be a belief in a god or gods. In cases such as *Re South Place Ethical Society*, Dillon J made reference to belief in 'God' in the singular, which is characteristic of a Judeo-Christian attitude to the nature of god. Thus, it is suggested that the principal effect of this provision in the 2011 Act was to confirm that major world religions such as Hinduism and Buddhism would be a religion for charitable purposes, without needing to show belief in a single god. The Charity Commissioners had always accepted such major world religions as falling within the charities law definition of 'religion' in any event.

Now that there is no need for the presence of a god, further to the 2011 Act, how will a religion be distinguished from, for example, a merely ethical system of belief, or a belief in the existence of hobbits, or a belief in Spider-Man as the ulti-mate power for good in the universe? It is unclear what will constitute a 'religion' for these purposes in the future. It may be limited to the *Oxford English Dictionary* definition of religion that there must be a 'belief in or sensing of some super-human controlling power or powers, entitled to obedience, reverence, and worship, or in a system defining a code of living'. This still leaves the question whether or not Spider-Man is a 'superhuman' in this sense, because he is understood to be a comic book character as opposed to being understood to be a god. But what if there were people who genuinely believed that Spider-Man was real and genu-inely believed that he was a god? Thor was considered in Nordic cultures to be a god (the god of thunder to be precise); so the question might arise whether or not his modern cultural representation as the comic superhero and film character 'Thor' could also be treated as a god in relation to anyone who considers his superhuman personality to be godlike. After all, it is difficult to prove the exist-ence of a god; that is, after all, a matter of *belief* rather than *proof*.

Even more interesting perhaps in this context is the belief of Rastafarians that a person who lived at the same time as them, the late Emperor Haile Selassie I (Emperor of Ethiopia from 1930 until 1974) was to be venerated as a god in spite of living as a human being. (If you listen to the opening track on Bob Marley's magnificent live album *Babylon by Bus*, it is clear that it is religious music.) After all, the Christian belief in Jesus is a belief in a person who also lived as a human being. The Rastafarian belief was a genuine religious belief which was created in the 20th century; but in what circumstances could a new movement establish that such a belief was similarly genuine, and that it was deserving of legal recognition? At what stage does a genuine belief in a human being's godlike status constitute a religious belief? These questions remain at large. What is clear is that the Emperor Haile Selassie I existed in the flesh. Therefore, this is a question of *belief* in a person's godliness and not a question of *proof* of their existence.

Furthermore, a 'code of living' could mean the sort of life led by a monk or it could mean (if taken literally) the activities of an athlete who lives by a strict diet, who begins training very early in the morning and who eschews all of the other pleasures of life outside athletics. What is missing from the athlete's activities, it is suggested, is any connection to belief in a supernatural entity or power. Therefore, a code of living in a religious sense should probably include belief in such a power. The precise meaning of this provision, however, is clearly open to interpretation.

In the Supreme Court decision in *R (on the application of Hodkin) v Registrar General of Births, Marriages and Deaths* (2013), not relating directly to charities law, it has been held that Scientology does constitute a religion for the purposes of licensing its premises to be used as places of marriage under the Places of Worship Registration Act 1855. Lord Toulson was careful not to decide any questions about charities law when he defined a religion in the following terms:

> I would describe religion in summary as a spiritual or non-secular belief system, held by a group of adherents, which claims to explain mankind's place in the universe and relationship with the infinite, and to teach its adherents how they are to live their lives in conformity with the spiritual understanding associated with the belief system.

This definition involves a number of difficulties, as any definition of this concept would. For example, why must a religion explain mankind's place in the universe? That would seem to encompass astrophysics (which provides an explanation of our place in the universe) but not necessarily pagan beliefs which worship individual animal spirits (such as Herne the hunter in the form of stags). Yoga training teaches adherents how to live in accordance with a belief system. Is that a religion?

Specific charitable purposes under statute

What follows is a selection of the new purposes introduced originally by the Charities Act 2006. For a more detailed discussion of these and other charitable purposes under statute see Hudson, *Equity and Trusts* (2014), Chapter 25. It is worth noticing that many of the heads of charity considered here were already considered by cases before 2006 under the old case law head of 'other purposes beneficial to the community', and therefore it may be important to consider whether the 2011 Act has had the effect of overturning that case law in some circumstances.

The advancement of health or the saving of lives

Section 3(2)(b), referring to the advancement of health, includes the 'prevention or relief of sickness, disease or human suffering'. Research into medical procedures would ordinarily have fallen under educational purposes under the research category in any event. The *advancement* of health' could even encompass activities that promote healthy eating, as well as healthcare directly or public information campaigns promoting good health. The 'saving of lives' could encompass anything from medical care to lifeboat services that save lives at sea (and which were accepted as charitable under the old case law).

The advancement of citizenship or community development

Section 2(2)(e) deals with 'the advancement of citizenship or community development'. The Act contains a gloss to the effect that it includes 'rural or urban regeneration' and 'the promotion of civic responsibility, volunteering, the voluntary sector or the effectiveness or efficiency of charities'. What is not clear is what is meant by 'citizenship'. It could be linked to whatever is taught in schools as part of the national curriculum under 'citizenship'. There are references elsewhere in s 2(2) to religious or racial harmony and equality, although the reference to 'community development' could include the organisation of youth groups, and other activities that are directed at social harmony.

The advancement of the arts, culture, heritage or science

Each of these four elements should be considered separately. None of these terms is defined in the Act. First, 'the arts' – it is suggested that the reference to 'the arts' in the plural is not a reference simply to 'art'. Thus, it is a reference to activities that ordinarily constitute a part of 'art' in the singular and so refers to painting, to sculpture and so forth, but it could also be said to refer to theatre performances, opera, classical music and so forth, which all generally fall under the rubric of 'the arts'. The advancement of art, in the singular, could include not only the display of artworks (*Abbott v Fraser* (1874)), and the maintenance of museums (*Trustees of the British Museum v White* (1826)), but its advancement might also refer to the funding of future artworks, provided the Charity Commission can accept that it is genuinely of sufficient artistic merit. The general reference to 'heritage' suggests the maintenance of historic land, gardens and buildings, and also monuments and so forth, beyond artworks. Heritage need not be purely physical: there are, for example, a large number of folk music societies whose work is concerned with the preservation and conservation of cultural heritage items like songs, poems and so forth. This should be said to merge into 'culture'.

The advancement of amateur sport

This category refers to 'the advancement of amateur sport'. Under old case law the mere advancement of sport did not in itself constitute a charitable purpose: thus, paying for a cup for a yachting competition and to promote yachting was not held to be a charitable purpose (*Re Nottage* (1895)), nor was the promotion of cricket (*Re Patten* (1929)). Recreational charities have been held valid under old case law as charitable purposes only if they improved the conditions of life of the people using them, and either if they are available to all members of the population without discrimination or if they are made available by reason of their users' 'youth, age, infirmity, disability, poverty or social and economic circumstances'. This has changed under s 5 of the Charities Act 2011. The Charity Commission has decided that it will accord charitable status to 'the promotion of community participation in healthy recreation by providing facilities for playing particular sports'. The terms of the Charities Act 2011 have confirmed this approach. The remaining questions relating to recreational charities, discussed next, may similarly be disposed of by this regulatory development.

Recreational charities

Recreational charities have long been contentious in the law of charities. Under old case law, charitable status was not given to social clubs or sports clubs that did not alleviate any material lack in the lives of a section of the public (*IRC v McMullen* (1981)). 'Recreation' and 'leisure-time occupations' are valid charitable purposes further to s 5(1) of the Charities Act 2011.

Political purposes

The leading case of *National Anti-Vivisection Society v IRC* (1947) in the House of Lords considered the question whether or not an organisation's work promoting the care of animals could be held to be a charitable purpose by treating the society's political campaigning as being merely ancillary to a charitable activity. The type of political campaigning undertaken was to procure a change in the law so that vivisection would be banned outright. Lord Simonds considered the society's aims to be too political to qualify as a charity on the basis that an aim to change legislation is necessarily political. Therefore, advancing a change in the law as a core aim of the trust will disqualify that trust from being a charity.

The rationale for the rule is that there is a problem for the court in having to decide whether a political purpose is beneficial because that would require the court to decide whether one side of a political argument (e.g. vivisection) outweighs another. Suppose, for example, a trust with a purpose to advance the medical utility of experiments on animals by conducting such experiments to search for a cure for cancer. By admitting the medical trust to charitable status the law is impliedly accepting that side of the political argument.

As with all trusts law issues, the question is to use the correct structure for the statement of aims. The RSPCA is registered as a charity, even though it works to stop vivisection in some contexts. The reason why it is upheld as being charitable despite its attempts to stop vivisection is that the anti-vivisection attitudes it holds are only one part of its total activities. Similarly, in *Bowman v Secular Society* (1917), Lord Normand held that a society whose *predominant* aim was not to change the law could be charitable, even though its campaign for a change to legislation was a subsidiary activity. It is a question of degree whether a society seeks to change the law *per se*, or whether it espouses ends that *require* a change in the law. It is unclear where the law of charities draws that particular line.

Issues with the law of charities

Conceptualising the approach of the cases

There has been a general distillation in the courts' attitudes to purportedly charitable trusts over the years into one of two conflicting approaches towards the validity of charitable purposes. First, a requirement that the applicant merely show a general charitable purpose, as in *Dingle v Turner*. Second, a requirement that the applicant demonstrate that there is no personal nexus between the settlor and the class of people to be benefited, but rather that there be sufficient *public* benefit, as in *Re Compton*. The former approach considers the intrinsic merits of the trust purpose that is proposed. The latter looks instead to see how the trustees are actually running the trust and whether or not the practical approach achieves suitably public, charitable effects. This latter approach is more concerned with demonstrating that the intention behind the trust is to affect the public rather than to attract the tax benefits of charitable status to something which is a trust really intended for a private class of beneficiaries. This is particularly true in relation to some of the educational charities, in which companies sought to acquire tax benefits for paying for the school fees of their employees' children (see *Oppenheim*). In those cases, the issue resolves itself to a question of whether or not the company can prove that a sufficiently large proportion of the public will benefit from the trust.

Issues with the notion of 'public benefit' in case law

On the one hand we have the *Re Compton* line of cases, which require that there must be no personal nexus between the people who will benefit from the charitable trust and the settlor of that trust. Thus, the benefit must be available to a sufficiently large section of the public outside any direct connection to the settlor. This, it is suggested, does not tell us much about the nature of the trust – it only tells us that the settlor must be acting selflessly in the provision of some communal benefit. The core point, as suggested by Lord Cross, is that there must be some genuine charitable intention on the part of the settlor. Thus, trusts for the relief of poverty may be valid, even if there are only a few people who will take a benefit from the trust, provided that there is a genuine intention to relieve poverty. Lord Cross's approach requires that there is something intrinsically charitable in the creation of a trust, compared with the *Compton* approach, which is concerned with a merely evidential question of demonstrating that there is a predominantly public rather than a private benefit in the purposes of that particular trust. The former approach considers the intrinsic merits of the trust purpose that is proposed, whereas the latter looks instead to see how the trustees are actually running the trust and whether or not the practical approach achieves suitably public, charitable effects.

There are two other doctrines that have an effect on the free operation of the *Compton* test as applied to all charities other than charities for the relief of poverty. First, the intention disclosed in *Re Hetherington* to validate genuine charitable intentions wherever possible, even if that means effectively altering the purpose of the trust or requiring the trustees to undertake to manage the trust in accordance with the court's directions, so as to make it compliant with charities law. Thus, a trust need not necessarily be drafted so as to disclose a pure public benefit because the court may well order that the trust be performed in a compliant manner. Second, the *cy-près* doctrine enables the court to give effect to otherwise invalid or impossible purposes and thus, again, validates a trust that is performed in accordance with charities law. What these two doctrines illustrate is that, for all the apparent rigidity of the *Compton* test, the law of charities operates on a flexible basis. The basis for this flexibility is the general understanding that charities are a good thing, and that in consequence a genuinely charitable intention should be implemented wherever possible.

The cy-près doctrine

The *cy-près* doctrine gives the courts a power to reconstitute the settlor's charitable intentions so as to benefit charity if the original purposes cannot be achieved, for whatever reason. The charities legislation provides for broader powers to apply property *cy-près* than was available under case law (see the excellent Mulheron, 2007). Before the enactment of the Charities Act 1960, case law provided that the *cy-près* doctrine could be invoked only if it was either impossible or impracticable to perform the purposes of the trust. The aim of the 1960 Act was to widen the powers of the court to reconstitute a charitable trust if its terms were merely inconvenient or unsuitable, as opposed to being genuinely impossible. The settlor must have intended to settle property for a genuinely charitable purpose. If that purpose cannot practicably be carried out, then the court will permit the property to be used for different purposes, which achieve broadly the same charitable goals.

Moving on . . .

That concludes our contextual discussion of equity and trusts. In the following chapter we return to some of the fundamental principles of equity as a general concept which is concerned to achieve conscionable outcomes in individual cases with a discussion of the law on injunctions.

Chapter 13

Injunctions and other equitable remedies

The place of the equitable remedies within equity's canon

This chapter considers the principal remedies (as opposed to trusts) that equity uses. Equitable remedies tell us as much about the principles of equity as the law of trusts and proprietary estoppel. We shall focus primarily on injunctions, which are in many ways the purest form of equity in that they operate on the basis of general equitable principles so as to achieve the best result in the circumstances of any given case.

The nature of equitable remedies

Remedies in this context, not trusts

The equitable remedies considered here are injunctions, specific performance, account, rescission and rectification. As considered in earlier chapters, the trusts imposed by equity are institutional and not remedial. That means that trusts arise automatically without the exercise of the court's discretion. The matters considered in this chapter are remedial, and therefore do grant the court some discretion as to the nature and extent of the remedy, in line with established principles.

The use of only weak discretion by courts of equity

There are two possible kinds of discretion: strong and weak discretion. Strong discretion would mean that a judge could decide to do anything that she considered to be appropriate in the circumstances, whereas weak discretion means that even though a judge could conceivably do anything she wished, she will nevertheless follow case law precedents and limit the exercise of her discretion in accordance with those principles. The type of discretion used by the courts of equity is the weak variety. An example of this is the decision of the Court of Appeal in *Jaggard v Sawyer* (1995) in relation to the award of an interim injunction. The Supreme Court Act 1981 empowered the court to make any such order as it saw fit; something that could have been taken by the Court of Appeal to have granted it a strong discretion. However, the Court instead considered itself to be limited to the exercise of this statutory power only in accordance with five clear principles that had been set out in previous decisions. Thus, the English courts tend to consider themselves as having only a weak discretion in the award of equitable remedies, even though we might otherwise have considered the potential breadth of equity as discussed by Aristotle as granting them a stronger discretion.

able principles on which injunctions are awarded

An injunction is an equitable remedy. It is at the discretion of the court to make an order to either party to litigation, or by way of a final judgment, to take some action or to refrain from some action. The broadest discretion of the court is required at this point. Injunctions can be used in a broad range of factual situations from family law disputes to commercial litigation. Sometimes the injunction forms a part of the relief sought by one or other of the parties in parallel to claims for damages and other remedies, whereas at other times the injunction is the sole remedy required by the claimant.

The courts have an extremely broad power to grant injunctions in general terms, over and above any specific statutory power to grant an injunction in any particular context. Lord Nicholls described the breadth of the power of the courts to grant injunctions in *Mercedes Benz AG v Leiduck* (1996) to the effect that:

> the jurisdiction to grant an injunction, unfettered by statute, should not be rigidly confined to exclusive categories by judicial decision. The court may grant an injunction against a party properly before it where this is required to avoid injustice . . . The court habitually grants injunctions in respect of certain types of conduct. But that does not mean that the situations in which injunctions may be granted are now set in stone for all time. . . The exercise of the jurisdiction must be principled, but the criterion is injustice. Injustice is to be viewed and decided in the light of today's conditions and standards, not those of yesteryear.

Two things emerge from this passage. First, the power to grant injunctions is unfettered (unless there is a specific statutory rule to the contrary in a particular context). Therefore, judges can grant injunctions whenever they consider it to be appropriate. In practice, judges will follow the principles set out in previous cases as to the award of injunctions in that type of case. Second, the purpose of injunctions is to prevent injustice being suffered on the facts of any individual case. In this sense, the principles governing injunctions constitute one of the purest forms of equity (in the sense we discussed it in Chapter 1) in that it empowers the judge to ensure justice in any situation. Nevertheless, the courts have developed principles governing the situations in which this discretion to award injunctions will be used in particular types of case. The principles governing injunctions – as discussed in this chapter – divide between permanent injunctions, temporary (interim) injunctions and the recent furore over super-injunctions.

Given that the injunction is an equitable remedy, a number of typically equitable requirements apply. As set out in *Shelfer v City of London Electric Lighting Co* (1895), common law damages must not be a sufficient remedy. In keeping with the role of equity in supplementing the deficiencies of the common law, if the common law has a suitable remedy to cover the situation in the form of damages, then there will not be any call for the imposition of an injunction. If damages would not completely remedy the harm suffered by the applicant, however, then an injunction may be appropriate. In deciding whether or not to grant an injunction, the court will consider its effect on the respondent and therefore will not award the injunction if it would be oppressive to the defendant.

The decision of the Court of Appeal in *Jaggard v Sawyer* (1995), contains an important restatement of the application to the award of injunctions of the core equitable principles that were considered in Chapter 1. Thus, the applicant must not have delayed in seeking the injunction so that the events that gave rise to the application have long passed. This principle is similar to the other equitable principle that the award of the injunction must not be in vain; for example, on the basis that the harm suffered by the applicant is not capable of being resolved by the imposition of an injunction. To borrow from the old metaphor: the court will not award an injunction to prevent the respondent from opening a stable door if the horse that was kept in those stables has already bolted and escaped. In such a situation, the award of an injunction could not prevent the horse's escape and therefore would be in vain. Importantly, another core equitable principle applies here in that the applicant must have come to equity with clean hands. Therefore, someone who has herself committed a wrong cannot claim an injunction in support of her wrongful act: for example, a thief could not claim an injunction to prevent the rightful owner of property from recovering her stolen property.

It is also important that some right of the applicant must have been affected. So, in *Paton v British Pregnancy Advisory Service Trustees* (1979), it was held by Sir George Baker P that 'the first and basic principle is that there must be a legal right enforceable in law or in equity before the applicant can obtain an injunction from the court to restrain an infringement of that right'. The award of an injunction will therefore be made to support some right of the applicant.

Types of injunction

Injunctions divide between those that require some action from the respondent (mandatory injunctions) those that require the respondent to refrain from some action (prohibitory injunctions) and those that seek to prevent some action that it is feared may be performed in the future (injunctions *quia timet*). Another division between types of injunction is between interim injunctions, which are made during litigation to preserve the parties' respective positions until the litigation is resolved, and final or permanent injunctions, which are made at the end of litigation as part of the court's resolution of the dispute between the parties. The following discussion considers interim injunctions in particular.

Interim injunctions

Interim injunctions in general

Interim injunctions (formerly known as interlocutory injunctions) are awarded on an interim basis during litigation. Their award is based on a balance of convenience between the potential harm suffered by the applicant if no injunction were awarded, and the potential inconvenience caused to the respondent if the injunction were to be awarded. The universal application of this approach has been doubted in some more recent cases. The applicant must therefore demonstrate a strong prima facie case.

The test for the availability of an interim injunction was contained in *American Cyanamid v Ethicon Ltd* (1975). In the words of Lord Diplock, 'The court must weigh one need against another and determine where "the balance of convenience" lies.' The court is thus required to consider, in all the circumstances, whether it would be more convenient on balance to award or deny the award of an interim injunction. There are four elements to the test: (i) that the balance of convenience indicates the grant of an award; (ii) seemingly, that the applicant can demonstrate a good prima facie case; (iii) that there is a serious question to be resolved at trial; and (iv) that there is an undertaking for damages in the event that the applicant does not succeed at trial.

Significantly, the applicant must also demonstrate that, even though the application for the injunction is made before litigation has begun in earnest or before the litigation has been completed, he has the makings of a good case once the matter does come on for trial. Clearly, the court would not wish to award an injunction to someone who had no reasonable prospect of success at trial or else the respondent could suffer harm or injury as a result of the injunction, which might not be capable of compensation in the future.

Freezing injunctions

Another form of interim injunction is the freezing injunction (colloquially known as '*Mareva* injunctions'). A freezing injunction will be awarded to prevent the respondent from removing assets from the English jurisdiction before the completion of litigation to avoid settlement of a final judgment.

The applicant is required to demonstrate three things: a good arguable case; that there are assets within the jurisdiction; and that there is a real risk of the dissipation of those assets which would otherwise make final judgment nugatory. Another formulation has provided that freezing injunctions will be awarded when the court is convinced that the applicant will recover judgment against the defendant, that there is good reason to believe that the defendant has assets within the jurisdiction to meet that liability, and that the respondent may well take steps to put those assets beyond the applicant's reach (*Z Ltd v A-Z* (1982)). The courts will not impose such an injunction if the burden placed on the defendant would be more than is just and convenient (*Fourie v Le Roux* (2007)).

The English courts have decided that, in some circumstances, they have the jurisdiction to grant freezing injunctions over assets held outside England and Wales: the so-called worldwide freezing injunction. In one of the cases arising out of the BCCI bank collapse, Rattee J awarded a worldwide freezing injunction on the basis that, in the context of 'the complex international nature of the financial dealings' concerned in a case in which neither respondent was resident in England or Wales, it was necessary to make the injunction similarly international (*Re Bank of Credit and Commerce International SA (No 9)* (1994)). In a comparative relaxation of the principle, the Court of Appeal in *Credit Suisse Fides Trust v Cuoghi* (1997) has held that the worldwide freezing injunction can be granted in circumstances in which 'it would be expedient', rather than being limited to a situation in which exceptional circumstances justify the order. Nevertheless, the applicant must still demonstrate a likelihood of assets being put beyond its reach in circumstances in which the respondent is both able and likely to act in that way.

Search orders

A search order (colloquially known as an '*Anton Piller* order') permits the applicant to seize property belonging to the defendant to protect evidence for any future trial. Typically, the order will be obtained *ex parte* (without the defendant being aware of the hearing) to enable the applicant to exercise it before the defendant realises the risk of having property seized (*Universal Thermosensors Ltd v Hibben* (1992)). In many cases, a freezing injunction and a search order are obtained at once in respect of the same defendant and over the same property: a case of 'freeze' and 'seize', if you will.

Recent decisions have emphasised that such an order ought to be a remedy of last resort, given that the impact on the respondent is potentially enormous. In *Anton Piller KG v Manufacturing Processes Ltd* (1976), Lord Denning MR held that such an order should be made 'only in an extreme case where there is grave danger of property being smuggled away or of vital evidence being destroyed'. In that case it was established that for the award of such an order the applicant must have an extremely strong prima facie case; further that the potential damage for the applicant must be very serious; and finally that there must be clear evidence that the defendants have in their possession incriminating documents or things that they may well destroy.

Super-injunctions and privacy

Confidential information in equity and in tort

Since at least the 16th century, equity has sought to protect confidences – such as commercial secrets, intellectual property, secrets contained in private correspondence, and even the notes of lectures which would defeat the lecturer's copyright in the lecture itself – generally by awarding injunctions to prevent the dissemination of confidential information. One of the leading cases in this area, *Prince Albert v Strange* (1849), involved Queen Victoria's husband suing Mr Strange when Strange had gained access to some etchings of paintings which Queen Victoria and her family had made of their private life, their pets and so on. Strange had intended to exhibit those etchings to a paying public and to publish a catalogue of the contents of that exhibition. It was held by the House of Lords that the contents of this catalogue (let alone the etchings themselves) were private information and that the publication of this private information would be prevented by a permanent injunction. The principle which was set down by Lord Cottenham was that the court will enjoin the publication of confidential information where that would constitute a 'breach of trust, confidence, or contract'. Some of the most significant cases have involved the publication of information passed between husband and wife, which is necessarily considered to be private. So, in *Duke of Argyll v Duchess of Argyll* (1967), the Duke of Argyll was enjoined from publishing information about his wife's attitudes to sexual morals and the sanctity of marriage in a story in *The People* newspaper. (The noun 'injunction' goes with the verb 'enjoin'.)

In *Coco v AN Clark (Engineering) Ltd* (1969), Megarry J held that there are three prerequisites in this area: the information must be confidential or have arisen in a confidential context; the information must have been passed in a context which suggested it was confidential; and the use of the information must be unauthorised and to the detriment of its owner.

These principles were upheld in the Court of Appeal in *Imerman v Tchenguiz* (2011), when Lord Neuberger emphasised the difference between common law and equitable principles in this area. Here a husband was entitled to have his personal data, which had been stored on a server which he used in common with his brother-in-law, kept in confidence and not used in divorce proceedings. The same approach to the protection of confidential information, such as wedding photographs at a private ceremony, was taken in *Douglas v Hello! Ltd* (2001).

The movement towards tort law in this context

Latterly, Lord Nicholls explained in *Campbell v MGN* (2004), how the traditional equitable doctrine was now giving way in the context of privacy specifically to a 'tort of the misuse of private information' (colloquially known as the tort of privacy) which would provide a remedy in damages but which would continue to provide a right to injunctions to prevent publication. Otherwise, the equitable doctrine continues in existence as before, as evidenced by *Imerman v Tchenguiz* (2011). It is in relation to this tort and injunctions sought in relation to it that the issues relating to super-injunctions have arisen. The law on super-injunctions and injunctions to protect privacy are considered next.

The law on super-injunctions

The public debate about super-injunctions

There was a media storm through 2010 and 2011 about the freedom of the Press to report whatever it chose to report: in particular there was great concern about the use of so-called 'super-injunctions' by the courts so as to prevent the Press from reporting not only the detail of legal proceedings but also from reporting the fact that an injunction had been awarded. Furthermore, the so-called 'super-injunction' made the parties anonymous so that it was impossible to report the identities of the parties in any event. At the outset these cases were principally concerned with footballers, pop stars, television presenters and senior bankers trying to keep their extra-marital, sexual affairs secret. It became bound up, in the public debate at least, with a different scandal concerning the habit of journalists at News International, and the private detectives whom they hired, 'hacking' into the voicemail accounts of celebrities and non-celebrities alike; something which was a criminal offence. The Press argued that they had a right to freedom of expression; whereas the celebrities argued that they had a right to privacy, that the tabloid press was out of control and that super-injunctions were consequently necessary to protect their privacy. The allegation that the voicemail of a teenage murder victim had been hacked into by journalists, and her messages deleted (with the tragic result that her parents thought she was still alive) led to a step-change in the seriousness with which the general public began to take these issues. Suddenly it was clear that such issues affected ordinary people and not just those who made their fortunes from their exposure in the same Press which they now demonised.

On the one hand, there were grave concerns about the way in which the Press operated (including examples of widespread illegal activity); on the other hand, there were concerns about the ability of the Press to report court proceedings freely (part of the long-established principle of 'open justice' in Britain) in the shadow of the courts creating super-injunctions. In turn, this led to the establish-ment of the 'Leveson Inquiry into the Culture, Practice and Ethics of the Press' in 2011 and, significantly for present purposes, the publication of a report by a committee empanelled by the Master of the Rolls titled the *Report of the Committee on Super-Injunctions* (2011). As emerged from the latter report, all of the 18 cases involving applications for super-injunctions decided at that time had had reasoned judgments published by the relevant judges and all of those injunctions (where they had been granted) had been only temporary in nature. Therefore, the public debate about super-injunctions had appeared to be slightly overblown when it was alleged that the judges were silencing the Press.

The nature of super-injunctions

The term 'super-injunction' has been bandied around in the Press so as to cover a number of different legal devices. From a lawyer's perspective, it is important to distinguish between a 'super-injunction' and an 'anonymised injunction' and other forms of injunction. All super-injunctions are at root just interim injunctions (as discussed above) with the following added features. The *Report of the Committee on Super-Injunctions* (2011) established by the Master of the Rolls defined a super-injunction as being:

> an interim injunction which restrains a person from:
>
> (i)   publishing information which concerns the applicant and is said to be confidential or private; and
> (ii) publicising or informing others of the existence of the order and the proceedings (the 'super' element of the order).

It is important that these are merely temporary injunctions pending a trial of the underlying issues. However, it is often argued by journalists that even a temporary delay in publication can, in effect, destroy a story by making it old news. Although, if the story does quickly become old news, it is unclear to what extent it was an important story in the first place.

An 'anonymised injunction', where the parties' identities are kept secret, was defined as being:

> an interim injunction which restrains a person from publishing information which concerns the applicant and is said to be confidential or private where the names of either or both of the parties to the proceedings are not stated.

It is common to have anonymised proceedings in criminal and in family law matters. Similarly, the principles governing interim injunctions generally apply to super-injunctions with the addition of certain principles considered below. However, it is in relation to the area of privacy in particular that super-injunctions have acquired their own peculiar lustre; after all, the media is never more excited than when talking about the media, as will emerge in the following section.

The balancing act in relation to awards of injunctions for privacy

The law on super-injunctions and the law on other injunctions seeking to protect the applicant's privacy therefore run together. The principles of equity in relation to confidences have given way to the law of tort and, significantly, the principles of human rights law which were incorporated into UK law by the Human Rights Act 1998. As Lord Steyn made clear in the House of Lords in *In re S (A Child) (Identification: Restrictions on Publication)* (2005), neither the right to privacy nor the right to freedom of expression necessarily has supremacy over the other; instead the court must apply the concept of proportionality when deciding in any given context which of the two is to take priority. Applying those principles, in *Murray v Express Newspapers plc* (2009), Sir Anthony Clarke MR held that, in deciding whether or not to award an injunction to protect private information, the courts must balance the claimant's human right to respect for her private and family life under Art 8 of the European Convention on Human Rights with the competing right to free expression of newspapers and others under Art 10 of the Convention.

Therefore, the court must first consider whether or not the information is such that there will be a right under Art 8 at all on the facts of the case. If Art 8 does not apply, then no injunction nor any other remedy will be granted. In general terms, sexual activity (e.g. *Donald v Ntuli* (2010)) and information relating to the existence of children outside a marriage would be the sorts of matters which would ordinarily fall within Art 8. The decided cases have tended to involve this sort of circumstance. However, where the applicant in *Hutcheson v News Group Newspapers Ltd* (2011) sought to keep his second family secret, it was held that the fact that their existence was already publicly known would prevent Art 8 from apr'ying. In the leading case of *Campbell v MGN* it was held that the fact that a supermodel was receiving treatment for drug addiction was something which would engage Art 8. The court is likely to seek to protect children in general terms: as in *CTB v News Group Newspapers Ltd* (2011), where a famous footballer sought to keep an adulterous relationship a secret in part to protect his children, or more importantly in *re S* where the identity of a young boy was kept confidential when his mother was on trial for the murder of that young boy's brother. This was also the approach where the Press took unauthorised photographs of a famous novelist's children (*Murray v Express Newspapers* (2009)).

Only if there is a situation which calls the Art 8 right into existence will the court consider whether or not that should be outweighed on the facts by the Art 10 right to freedom of expression. What is clear is that the courts are prepared to allow a very broad range of material to be published as being in the public interest which might otherwise be thought of as mere tittle-tattle; for example, the 'news' that a supermodel had lied in interviews about having taken drugs when she was in fact receiving treatment for drug addiction in *Campbell v MGN*, and the 'news' that the chief executive of a bank had had an extra-marital sexual relationship with a fellow employee of that bank in *Goodwin v NGN Ltd* (2011).

What is particularly important, of course, is that significant matters which impact on our political system (such as the MPs' expenses scandal disclosed first in the *Daily Telegraph*) or on public safety (such as the allegations of dumping of toxic waste in the *Trafigura* case) are able to be made public. As part of the concern about super-injunctions, Paul Farrelly MP raised a question in Parliament about the dumping of toxic waste which, unbeknown to him or the Parliamentary authorities, had been made subject to a confidentiality order and an anonymised injunction. This raised the concern about politicians using Parliamentary privilege to make public things which the courts had ordered should remain confidential. There is a clear principle that Parliament can and should debate anything which it considers to be appropriate. Nevertheless, to do so when a court has issued a temporary injunction requiring confidentiality is to interfere with the independence and freedom of the judiciary. These constitutional issues are considered in detail in the *Report of the Committee on Super-Injunctions*.

Specific performance

The nature of specific performance

The remedy of specific performance is concerned to hold the parties to a contract to the proper performance of their obligations. Specific performance achieves this goal by imposing a personal obligation on the defendant to perform specific contractual obligations. It is not necessary that there has been a pre-existing breach of contract for the award of an order for specific performance. As with all equitable remedies, its award depends on common law remedies, such as an award of damages, being insufficient remedies in the circumstances (*Wilson v Northampton and Banbury Junction Railway Co* (1874)), thus emphasising equity's role in supplementing shortcomings in the common law. Specific performance has been explained by Lord Hoffmann in *Co-operative Assurance v Argyll* (1997) as being part of the discretionary jurisdiction of the Court of Chancery to do justice in cases in which the remedies available at common law were inadequate. There are, however, types of contract in relation to which specific performance will not be available, as will emerge from the following sections.

Those types of contract to which specific performance will apply

Specific performance will be available in relation to contracts where the particular subject matter of the contract has some significance; therefore, a contract for the sale of a particular parcel of land will be specifically enforceable because that particular land will be of significance to the contracting parties (*Adderley v Dixon* (1824)). Such an order will only be made in relation to chattels where a particularly significant chattel is concerned, that is one which is not reasonably capable of being substituted with another chattel (*Adderley v Dixon*). If the claim concerns a payment of money, then the court will usually not award specific performance on the basis that an award of damages would ordinarily be sufficient remedy (*Cannon v Hartley* (1949)).

Specific performance will typically not be available in circumstances where the contract is illegal or immoral, or where there is no consideration, because these are matters that the law of contract would neither usually enforce nor recognise as being valid contracts in any event. There are also types of contract in relation to which the court will not make an award of specific performance because it would not be possible for the court to judge at what point there had been sufficient or suitable performance. Examples of this are contracts that involve the exercise of some particular skill by the defendant or where the contract requires supervision. The example commonly used in this context, as by Megarry J in *CH Giles and Co Ltd v Morris* (1972), is that in which an opera singer is under contract to sing at a theatre six nights per week for three months. The court would not award specific performance because it would not be possible to know whether or not the singer was singing sufficiently well to constitute performance of the contract (given that the court will not assume that it has the expertise to judge such matters) and in any event this would require the court to supervise the performance of this contract (*Ryan v Mutual Tontine Westminster Chambers Association* (1893)), something that the court would not be prepared to incur the time and expense to do. Specific performance will also not be awarded in circumstances in which the contract is for an insubstantial interest or where the contract is not mutually binding.

Defences to specific performance include: the lack of an enforceable contract; the absence of some necessary formality in the creation of the contract; and some misrepresentation, undue influence or unconscionable bargain bound up in the formation of the contract. Alternatively, specific performance will not be awarded where there has been some mistake or lapse of time.

Account

The doctrine of account was considered in Chapter 10 in relation to the obligation of trustees and of strangers to account to beneficiaries in the event of a breach of trust. More generally, the remedy of account has been developed by equity to compel one person to render an account to another person of amounts owed to that other as the result of the breach of some equitable obligation. Its roots are therefore in a procedural obligation to value either the amount of the loss that has been caused to the claimant and for which he or she will require compensation, or to calculate the amount of the profit that has been earned by the defendant at the claimant's expense and which must be given up to the claimant by way of the obligations of a constructive trustee (as in *Boardman v Phipps* (1967)) or otherwise. There is no particular intellectual basis to the remedy of account which can be identified here; rather, the remedy of account is generally confined to a process of adding the amounts that are owed between the parties at the end of litigation once substantive liabilities, such as those discussed in the breach of trust and constructive trust chapters in this book, have been established.

Rescission

The nature of rescission

Another form of equitable remedy concerned with contracts is rescission, the purpose of which is to unpack a contract so as to achieve a *restitutio in integrum*: that is, to restore the parties to the position that they had occupied originally. The grounds on which an order for rescission might be made are many. Rescission is available only in relation to contracts that are voidable; if a contract is found to have been void *ab initio* then rescission will not be available because such a contract is deemed never to have existed (*Westdeutsche Landesbank v Islington* (1994), per Leggatt LJ).

Rescission in relation to misrepresentation

A fraudulent misrepresentation will render a contract merely voidable where that misrepresentation was made with an intention that it should be acted upon by the person to whom it was made (*Peek v Gurney* (1873)). The type of fraud required for a fraudulent misrepresentation is a misrepresentation made knowingly, or without belief in its truth, or with recklessness as to whether or not it was true (*Redgrave v Hurd* (1881)). The rationale for permitting rescission of contracts made on the basis of a fraudulent misrepresentation is that it would be inequitable to permit a person with such a fraudulent motive to profit from their common law rights. As such, it is a principle that is easy to reconcile with the underlying tenets of equity. Even where a person makes an innocent misrepresentation it will be sufficient to give the other party to the contract a good defence to an action for specific performance of that contract (*Walker v Boyle* (1982)). The court has power to order that a contract continues in existence in cases of innocent misrepresentation where it would be equitable to do so (Misrepresentation Act 1967, s 2(2)).

Rescission in relation to undue influence

Rescission will be generally available in cases of unconscionable bargains or in cases of some undue influence that induces one party to enter into the contract (*Barclays Bank v O'Brien* (1993)). In common with general equitable principles, it would be unconscionable to allow someone to benefit from some undue influence exerted over the other contracting party. Equity has always conceived of undue influence as a form of constructive fraud. Another way in which this can be thought about is as the victim of the undue influence having failed to give free consent to the formation of the contract (*Royal Bank of Scotland v Etridge (No 2)* (2002), per Lord Scott). This latter explanation is more typical of a commercial lawyer's approach than the traditional equitable explanation.

Mistake

A material mistake made by both parties to a contract will enable that contract to be rescinded (*Cooper v Phibbs* (1867)). Unilateral mistake may lead to rescission only where there has been some unconscionability in the formation of the contract. Mistakes of law and of fact may both give good grounds for rescission (*Kleinwort Benson v Lincoln CC* (1998)).

Loss of the right to rescind

The right to rescind will be lost where it is impossible to return the parties to the positions they occupied previously (*Erlanger v New Sombrero Phosphate Co* (1873)) where the contract has been affirmed (*Peyman v Lanjani* (1985)) or (in common with the general equitable principles considered in Chapter 1) where there has been delay (*Life Association of Scotland v Siddal* (1861)).

Rectification

The remedy of rectification is available to amend the terms of a contract so as to reflect the true intentions of the contracting parties (*M'Cormack v M'Cormack* (1877)). It is restricted to situations in which there is a written document which fails to reflect the true intention of the parties (*Racal Group Services v Ashmore* (1995)). The effect of the order is to effect an alteration in the written document itself (*Craddock Bros Ltd v Hunt* (1923)). However, what rectification does not do is alter the parties' contractual intention, on the basis that equity will not intervene in the contractual freedom of the parties to a contract. Instead, rectification merely effects an alteration better to reflect its true contractual intention (*Mackenzie v Coulson* (1869)). Rectification will not be ordered where there is some sufficient, alternative remedy available, such as common law damages (*Walker Property Investments (Brighton) Ltd v Walker* (1947)) or where the issue forming the subject matter of the application could be dealt with by a simple correction of, for example, a clerical error (*Wilson v Wilson* (1854)).

As considered above in relation to rescission, there is a need to distinguish between cases of common mistake and cases of unilateral mistake. Rectification will be available in circumstances of common mistake (*Murray v Parker* (1854)) whereas rectification will only be available in relation to a unilateral mistake in cases of fraud or similar unconscionable behaviour (*Hoblyn v Hoblyn* (1889)) or, alternatively, if the defendant knew that the claimant considered the mistaken element to be a term of the contract (*A Roberts and Co Ltd v Leicestershire CC* (1961)). Buckley LJ considered this principle to turn on the issue of whether or not the conscience of the defendant was affected by failing to draw the mistake to the claimant's attention in circumstances where the defendant knew that it would benefit from the claimant entering into the contract under the influence of that mistake (see *Thomas Bates and Sons Ltd v Wyndham's (Lingerie) Ltd* (1981)).

Alternatively, where one party to the transaction knows of the mistake and allows the other party to enter into the transactions nevertheless, a form of equitable estoppel will prevent that person from resisting a claim for rectification (*Whitley v Delaney* (1914)). It is sufficient for the operation of this form of estoppel that the defendant recklessly shut her eyes to the fact that a mistake has been made – it is not necessary that actual knowledge of the mistake be demonstrated (*Commission for New Towns v Cooper* (1995)). This latter principle accords with equity's general purpose to avoid unconscionable behaviour.

Rectification will be available in circumstances of common mistake. Rectification will only be available in relation to a unilateral mistake in cases of fraud or similar unconscionable behaviour. Rectification may also be available in respect of voluntary settlements to reflect the settlor's evident intention. Alternatively, the court may order the delivery and cancellation of documents.

Moving on . . .

In the final chapter, we consider some of the key themes that have run through this book and the future for equity.

Chapter 14

Themes in equity

The foundations of equity

Reconnecting modern equity with its philosophical roots

I have tried quite deliberately not to allow my own enthusiasm for this subject to interfere with a clear discussion of the principles up to now. My assumption has been that you would be most interested in an account of equity and of the law of trusts, which would make the complexities somewhat clearer, which would be easy to read from cover to cover, and which would cover all of the key principles.

However, it seems to me that you might nevertheless enjoy a short, concluding chapter that shines a light on some of the interesting possibilities presented by equity, many of which are bound up with the philosophy underpinning the idea that a strict legal rule should be vacated if justice so demands it. I warn you that to many flinty-hearted trusts lawyers and to those who practise Chancery law in Lincoln's Inn, some of what I am about to say appears to be dangerously progressive. By contrast, I prefer to think of it as reconnecting the practice of the courts of equity with ancient ideas about equity and justice.

The development of the courts of conscience

In Chapter 1 we considered the birth of the Courts of Chancery out of the jurisdiction of the Lords Chancellors as holders of the Great Seal of England and thus as conduits for the powers of the monarch as the monarch's principal minister. The early Lord Chancellors were ecclesiastics – that is, they were bishops – and therefore the equitable principles that were developed under their leadership by the courts of equity were informed by religious notions of conscience as well as by secular ideas. The Lord Chancellor was known as the Lord Keeper of the Great Seal – a reflection of his political office – and also as Keeper of the King's Conscience – a reflection both of his religious office and also of the mission of the court to examine the conscience of a case. Indeed this double meaning of 'conscience' is significant. The conscience referred to was originally a reference to the monarch's conscience, which was preserved by the Lord Chancellor. This suggests that the conscience of the monarch was both *outside* the monarch (in that it could be controlled by the Lord Chancellor) and that there was something sublime and religious about it. By contrast, the more modern sense of conscience has focused on the conscience of the defendant as opposed to the conscience of the monarch at whose behest the Courts of Chancery operated originally. In time, the Lord Chancellors were no longer ecclesiastics and therefore their function was primarily a secular function, more akin to the modern Prime Minister, but also acting as a judge.

It was Lord Nottingham (real name Heneage Finch, who was appointed Lord Chancellor in 1673) who was generally attributed with having conducted the work of developing those forms of action that have formed the basis for modern Chancery practice. Lord Eldon was significant in ordering many of the strict rules of trusts law in the early 19th century; this was significant in introducing rigidity to some aspects of equity. It would be true to say, however, that doctrines such as constructive trust and proprietary estoppel developed markedly in the second half of the 20th century. The principles of equity have hardened in recent cases into more formalistic rules – such as those evidenced by *Lloyds Bank v Rosset* (1990), *Tinsley v Milligan* (1994), and *Twinsectra v Yardley* (2002) – and so appeared to move away from very broad philosophical principles. That said, leading cases such as *Westdeutsche Landesbank v Islington* (1996) and *Paragon Finance v Thakerar* (1999) have nevertheless sought to re-establish the basis of equitable doctrines such as the trust on the control of the conscience of the defendant. What these cases have left unclear, however, is the precise meaning of the term 'conscience'. It is to the possible meanings of that word and the intrinsic nature of equity that we now turn.

Equity is like improvised jazz

The question then is how do we understand this equity which is both full of detailed rules (especially in relation to express trusts) and yet which is at times flexible and inventive? Well, to quote Woody Allen, 'it's like anything else': sometimes a person is calm, collected and organised, and at other times they are confused, responding instinctively to a situation, and just trying to do their incompetent best (Allen, 2003). Sometimes the weather is calm and warm; at other times it is tempestuous and cold. It is like anything else. There is nothing unusual in that; in truth, there is nothing more natural. Our best-laid plans often go wrong, just as our best-drafted laws often generate injustice. This is the natural way of things. As Samuel Beckett put it, all one can do is try again, and fail again, but fail better (Beckett, 1983). That is the human condition: to flounder through life, perhaps mastering one small corner of it (trusts law, car maintenance, the saxophone) but simply doing the best one can in every other context while trying to learn from your mistakes as you go.

My suggestion is that equity is like freestyle jazz music in that it is based on carefully thought-through ideas and concepts but it reacts to the situation in front of it in the way that best fits the situation. Therefore, it is a combination of rigid rules (just as any jazz music has a solid core to it) and what appears to be random improvisation but which is actually a principled response to circumstances. A review of the jazz group The Dave Brubeck Five in *Time* magazine in 1954 sums up my feelings about equity in the following terms:

> It is tremendously complex, but free. It flows along, improvising constantly but yet it is held together by a firm pattern. . . . The essence is the tension between improvisation and order; between freedom and discipline.

The firm pattern is set down by the high-level equitable principles, by centuries of precedent illustrating those principles, and by the more detailed rules in areas like trusts law. And yet in relation to areas such as injunctions, equitable estoppel and constructive trusts what the courts do is to take those established principles and then adapt them to fix the situation. So, in *Porntip Stallion v Albert Stallion Holdings Ltd* (2009), it was held that Albert Stallion's widow and former wife could be ordered in effect to live together so as to protect the claimant's entitlement to occupy a property for life; but that esoteric outcome was predicated on the requirements of representation, reliance and detriment, and the ability to fix the remedy to the context. The same test was used in *Baker v Baker* (1993) to identify the existence of the estoppel before ordering that, while the claimant could have been awarded rights in the family home, he should be entitled to receive an amount of money sufficient to pay for his sheltered accommodation for the rest of his life because that suited his circumstances better. The law on interim injunctions is even more clearly organised so as to permit general principles to be used in the circumstances of any given case so as to achieve a conscionable result: a firm pattern nevertheless allows improvisation.

Equity exhibits a tension between order and flexibility. To its denigrators, equity is disorganised, chaotic and unprincipled; to its adherents it exhibits clear patterns in compliance with subtle but meaningful principles. At its centre is the idea of conscience, a concept to which we turn next.

The meaning of the term 'conscience'

In 1705, Lord Chancellor Cowper had the following to say in the case of *Lord Dudley v Lady Dudley*:

> Now equity is no part of the law, but a moral virtue, which qualifies, moderates, and reforms the rigour, hardness, and edge of the law, and is a universal truth; it does also assist the law where it is defective and weak in the constitution (which is the life of the law) and defends the law from crafty evasions, delusions, and new subtleties, invested and contrived to evade and delude the common law, whereby such as have undoubted right are made remediless: and this is the office of equity, to support and protect the common law from

shifts and crafty contrivances against the justice of the law. Equity therefore does not destroy the law, nor create it, but assists it.

Lord Cowper was clear that moderating the rigour of the common law in individual circumstances so as to achieve a fair outcome is in itself a moral virtue. The courts have accepted that equity is based on an idea of good conscience. Lord Cowper's model of equity as a moral virtue is similar to that advanced by Aristotle in his *Ethics*, in which he considered it to be 'right' for equity to rectify ordinary law in circumstances in which it would be just to do so.

Thus we can see the moral content in the operation of equity. So much for the functional purpose of equity. By contrast there are two ways in which equity extends this function of rectifying legal wrongs into the interaction of individual citizens with the state. First, by preventing the unjust application of legal rules, the courts of equity prevent individuals from suffering injustice, regardless of any larger principle that justice must be applied to all evenly. That is, in itself, a moral imperative to recognise the value of each individual human being, which also supports human rights law. Second, equity looks at the conscience of individual defendants to ensure that they will not be able to take any unconscionable advantage of a strict legal rule by means of fraud, breach of trust or some similar behaviour. As Lord Ellesmere said in the *Earl of Oxford's Case* (1615), it is in this sense that equity uses the notion of conscience to inquire into the ethics of the defendant's actions or omissions by asking whether or not that defendant has acted properly or improperly.

That consciences are formulated objectively

At this juncture we might begin to think that this is an odd type of conscience. It is common to think of a conscience as being something peculiar to each individual person. Consequently, it would be impossible for a court to *impose* a conscience on someone from outside; rather, that person might be thought to have a conscience *within* herself and therefore it might be thought that a legal jurisdiction acting on the basis of conscience would be limited to asking whether or not that individual believed her action to have been wrong. This is the basis of the *dicta* of Lord Hutton in the House of Lords in *Twinsectra v Yardley* (2002), in which his Lordship twisted the test of dishonesty in dishonest assistance (considered in Chapter 10), such that a person would only be held to have been dishonest if she had both failed to act as an honest person would have acted and also if she had known that such behaviour would have been considered to be dishonest by an honest person. I would suggest that the addition of the second half of that test by Lord Hutton is due primarily to a squeamishness about the notion of judging someone for their unethical behaviour without being able to demonstrate that that person knew that their actions were unethical.

I would suggest that a different approach would be better both pragmatically and philosophically. First the pragmatic reason: in *Walker v Stones* (2001), the

Court of Appeal rejected the notion that a person should only be considered to have been dishonest if they knew themselves that their actions were dishonest. That is, they rejected the notion that the test should be entirely subjective. Their objection was that a person might perfectly reasonably believe, for example, that she was justified in stealing from a rich person because she was comparatively poor herself. Such a person is considered to be dishonest in the equitable sense because to do otherwise would be to allow people to excuse socially unacceptable and otherwise unlawful behaviour on the basis of their own peculiar ethics. More pragmatically still, it would be a very difficult job to prove the contents of someone's conscience. On that basis why could not every thief in the land stand in the dock and say, 'I see nothing wrong at all in stealing' and so insist on being set free? The courts would need to be full of psychoanalysts inquiring into the souls of each litigant. No, instead the courts must use objective notions of what sort of behaviour is acceptable and what behaviour is unacceptable. But is this approach philosophically acceptable?

So we come to the second justification for a different approach. I will suggest that consciences are in truth objectively formulated. This will seem, at first, a surprising suggestion because we tend to consider our consciences to be as much our own as our dreams and our senses. Nevertheless, I suggest that consciences arise objectively. The social theorist Norbert Elias, in his book *The Society of Individuals* (2001), reminds us that from the moment we are born we are dependent on other people. Principally, we are dependent upon our mothers at first, not only for nourishment and warmth, but also for all of our emotional learning. Through our interaction with our parents and other family members we come to learn language, how to behave among other people, how to walk and so on. In this early stage, psychoanalysis tells us that we acquire knowledge of ourselves and of our capacities in dealing with other people. Jacques Lacan's famous mirror stage talks of the infant first becoming aware of itself in a mirror when next to its mother: the infant recognises the mother's reflection in the mirror first and subsequently realises that the shape next to the mother is actually itself. In this way we are said to take the first floundering steps towards self-awareness. And so, throughout our lives, it is our interaction with other people that creates us. We acquire knowledge of our own history and of society's views of right and wrong through our schooling, our parents and the world around us. Mass media carry messages to us of things that are meant to delight us, to disgust us and to stimulate us. We grow and change in response to these messages from outside.

So it is, I suggest, that our consciences are formed. In Sigmund Freud's analysis, conscience is that voice inside us which makes us feel shame primarily. It is conscience that whispers quietly, 'That's wrong, you should not do that.' From our earliest moments our understanding of right and wrong, acceptable and unacceptable, comes from other people – whether our parents, our teachers or other people around us. These messages are then internalised and grow into our consciences. But, you might say, couldn't my conscience then be something that develops inside me in a way that is unique to me – after all, don't different people have slightly different consciences? I would reply that it is still only when someone or something in the outside world challenges you or makes you question your own conscience that you are aware of whether or not you personally are affected. For example, before you first learn from a friend, or from reading a book or from watching the television that there are doctors who will terminate a pregnancy so that the mother runs no risk of dying, I would suggest that you would not know whether or not you would consider that action to be unconscionable. Similarly, until you are actually abandoned on a deserted railway station forecourt at midnight for the first time with no ticket and no inspector in sight, just as the last train to your destination is pulling onto the platform, you cannot know for sure whether you would simply dash onto the train or whether you would heed the call of conscience and try to buy a ticket from the recalcitrant ticket machine. Until something or someone external to you poses the question, you cannot know how your conscience will actually respond. Your conscience is not a set menu; rather, it develops in response to the world. It is true that as we grow older we are able to predict with greater certainty how our consciences would respond, but only because we have met sufficient challenges to our consciences in our lives to be confident of how we will feel.

So I would suggest that conscience grows due to external stimulus. Therefore, I would suggest further that it is perfectly acceptable for the law to judge conscience objectively: that is, if conscience comes from outside it is perfectly proper for the outside world to construct ways of measuring whether or not the individual is responding appropriately to the messages that society is generating. As Freud suggested in *Civilisation and Its Discontents* (1930), the very fact that we have societies means that we humans have to repress our animal urges to eat the first food we see, to take another's property or to indulge other base desires. Instead, we wait (most of us) patiently in queues, we do not leave shops without paying and, so far as possible, we refrain from murdering one another. A court of conscience can perfectly properly call an individual to question because her actions transgress the common morality. Therefore, a court can judge such a person's conscience objectively.

Natural law humanising positivism

There are two contradictory currents in modern jurisprudence. On the one hand, there is positivism, which suggests that law becomes law once it has been properly enacted through the appropriate procedures, and that law is obeyed because law has the power to issue commands to us all. On the other hand, there is natural law, which suggests that law is imposed and obeyed because we accept that it springs from some essential morality: in short, that law is a good thing and we ought to obey it. In England, positivism holds sway with most jurists, particularly as identified with HLA Hart's *The Concept of Law* (1961). The difficulty with hard-line positivism is that it requires laws to be enforced without regard to other considerations, provided that the law has been properly created. As a result, it is tempting to develop models on which laws should operate so that there is certainty in the manner in which the law does operate. This is particularly true of areas of the common law such as the law of contract and commercial law. However, there are other areas, such as family law, in which it is considered more appropriate to leave it to the judge in any given case to decide what is best for a divorcing couple and their children without being bound by rigid precedent. It is suggested that equity functions so as to humanise the positivist tendencies of most common law and of most lawyers. Rather than repose complete, unquestioning confidence in the correctness of the law in all circumstances, equity permits us to question the application of those laws in particular cases. If we remember that to err is human, then man-made laws must also be capable of being wrong in some circumstances.

Lawyers like order. They have tidy minds and want the world to conform to their patterns. Occasionally, however, the world will not work in the way we want it to and we have to acknowledge that a particular result may be unfair. It is common to hear academic lawyers attempting to create 'taxonomies' of certain areas of law in the same way that biologists seek to categorise different types of butterfly. This important work is only useful up to a point. The greatest strength of common law systems, as opposed to systems based on a civil code, is that common law systems have an inbuilt flexibility to develop their concepts and to adapt their principles to accommodate changing social mores or to prevent unfair exploitation of a strict legal principle. One clear example considered in Chapter 1 was the equitable principle that a statute should not be used as an engine of fraud. The entire purpose of equity is bound up in that one lyrical expression. Equity exists precisely to prevent abuses of the law.

The use of taxonomies also raises an interesting issue. When biologists create a taxonomy of the different types of plant, they are doing so by observing what actually exists in nature; but when lawyers create a taxonomy, they are merely doing so as part of an ideology. Lawyers do not create taxonomies as a result of observing something that exists in nature. As the philosopher Nietzsche put it, the greatest artists in abstraction are the people who create the categories into which ideas are placed. Lawyers who create taxonomies (and thus a series of categories) are therefore simply making categories up; albeit that they often do so by pretending that there is something innate or ineffable about them.

Equity and its recognition of the fragility of the individual

It is a feature of the modern world that individuals think of themselves as being individuals and not simply as archetypes within society more generally. If one were to ask people to give an account of themselves they are unlikely to limit themselves to generic categories such as labourer, husband or housewife. Instead, one is likely to receive more esoteric descriptions such as fly-fisherman, sado-masochist, raver, Manchester United fan, software technician, personnel manager, short-order cook or alcoholic. In the modern world we expect to be valued entirely for ourselves and not simply considered to be a part of the general mass of the population. So the more esoteric descriptions of individuals reflect their sense of themselves, of the things that are most important to them and their determination to be valued as an individual.

Sociology has begun to emphasise the fragility of the individual at the same time as we have started to focus on individuals as individuals. Anthony Giddens (1991) has identified a crisis caused by the increasing burden that individuals are required to bear both in making their own choices about their lives and looking after their own welfare without the protection of the state. The crisis is then found in the insecurity that people feel about the extraordinary breadth of the choices open to them and the risks of failure. An example might be that sense that undergraduate law students begin to feel in their second year when they have to begin to make detailed career choices and to face the agony of application, selection and rejection. As individuals come to expect that they will be treated as individuals at the same time as they come to feel ever more alienated and alone, then it is important that there is a branch of the legal system in the form of equity which takes into account the individual's own, personal circumstances (see Hudson, 2004b).

The changes in our understanding of property

The focus in this book on the trust is on an important part of the law of property. In our discussion of cases such as *Re Goldcorp* (1995), we saw that the law of trusts requires that the specific property to be held on trust be segregated from all other property. By contrast, in *Attorney General for Hong Kong v Reid* (1994), a constructive trust was imposed over property bought with bribes paid to a public official in favour of people who had never previously had any rights in that property. The purpose of the trust in this instance was to punish that official for the breach of his duties, but it was not so concerned with the identity of the property at issue. Latterly, there have been instances in which even assets that are not capable of being transferred have nevertheless been defined as being property. For example, in *Don King v Warren* (1998), the benefit that might be drawn in the future from a promotions contract was found to have been capable of forming the subject matter of a trust, even though the contract itself was clearly expressed as being non-transferable.

What this last case illustrates is that the things that constitute property have changed significantly (see Hudson, 2004a). More generally, however, our treatment of property has changed enormously. As people have generally come to own more property than their forebears would have done – for example, people now own televisions, tablet computers and washing machines, which their great-grandparents did not own – they have come to value their property less. The French thinker Jean Baudrillard (1970) has expressed this phenomenon as being part of the 'compulsory obsolescence' that is built into most property. Electrical goods are not expected to last in perpetuity but rather are expected to break down at some point when they pass out of warranty. They will become obsolete also in the sense that technology will develop other items that will replace the utility of the original object.

Furthermore, the desires of the individual to be fashionable or to have possession of at least the base level of modern consumer goods will render the original goods obsolete. The demands of the fashion industry insist that we change and reject our clothes on a regular basis; the demands of the music industry require that we treat our CD collections in much the same fashion. There again, few people (except the most cutting-edge DJs) now have record players; many older people have cassette players somewhere in their home but they buy few cassettes to play in them now because they tend to have compact disc players instead. As a student reader of this book, you may never have owned a cassette player. It is likely that a lot of your music is held on a computer, on an mp3 player or somewhere else. All of these technologies will be displaced in time by other technologies which can hold many thousands of songs, pictures and videos. Now even the concept of a hard drive is being displaced by storage in 'the cloud'. All property becomes obsolete: that has become the point.

So, just as trusts law has come to accept as property things that would not previously have constituted property (such as non-transferable contracts) so our attitude to property is changing generally. Zygmunt Bauman refers in his book *Liquid Modernity* (2002) to our social relations as being liquid in that we no longer have rigid ties to our property, to our careers, nor to one another. So industrialists consider their business assets as being things that can be disposed of because their owner will not have forged any strong emotional bonds with them; people tend to change jobs regularly during their lifetimes (it is estimated that the average Briton will change job 11 times during her adult life); and an example of our weakening social relations is the rising incidence of divorce and the ubiquity of broken families. Consequently, equity has a different task in hand to divide between the value that people might attach to their property and to their commitments to one another, whereas traditional property law has always worked on the premise that the trust fund is comprised of property that has an intrinsic value to the beneficiaries and that should be protected as such. Ensuring a just result in the modern context may create a greater focus on compensation for the loss of the value of property rather than on tracing and recovering the very property itself, whether that is in relation to the family home or other property.

Modern equity

From the ancient to the modern

Equity is both something ancient and something very modern. Academics such as Maitland in the late 19th century tried to present equity as being something quintessentially English. While it is true that equity has grown out of its own history and not directly from Roman law (unlike the European civil codes) it is not true to suggest that these ideas have been completely insulated from other cultures. There are suggestions that the earliest forms of the trust were brought back to England by the crusaders after they had come into contact with the Islamic *waqf*, which is an ancient form of charitable institution often used privately within extended families (Lim, 2001). Similarly, the core notion of equity is found in Aristotle and in the German philosopher Hegel: there is nothing necessarily English about those ideas, just as there is nothing necessarily English about human rights law.

Therefore, we might argue that, on the one hand, equity is an ancient institution. On the other hand, we must recognise that the law of trusts, while growing out of that equitable jurisdiction, has become a more rigid institution than ever before, providing for both big corporations and ordinary citizens to achieve their commercial and welfare needs. So, is the trust equitable or is it a form of institution similar to the contract?

In truth, it is both. The ethics of the 20th century saw a more educated population around the world come to realise that they were entitled to their own aspirations and goals. Commerce and profit were increasingly viewed as good things by the end of that century, with even leftist politicians voicing a desire for prosperity and markets as well as for social justice and equality. It is not surprising, therefore, that in the extraordinary technological and social advances of the 20th century (both good and bad) the trust device would be put to use in a number of ways that were convenient in that new, global economy. As early as the 1890s, English company law was formed by the decision in *Saloman v Saloman* (1897), which held that the commercial trusts used for investment purposes should be treated as companies with their own distinct personality; similarly unit trusts developed as a means for mutual investment, and cooperatives used similar combinations of partnership and trust for social investment (Hudson, 2000). This added an extra dimension to the use of formal marriage settlements and will trusts to hold private family property over the generations. These developments have all served to develop the trust beyond its roots in family settlements into something infinitely more supple and ubiquitous.

The continued role of equity

So is there any use for equity now? In my opinion there is. The form of equity that has been discussed hitherto has been limited specifically to the sense in which it is understood in English law. There are, however, other uses of the concept of equity in the social sciences. To an economist or a political scientist, the term 'equity' relates to the concept of the provision of social justice through public policy. Equity in this context correlates to the provision of a form of equality between citizens. Its converse in modern economics is typically 'efficiency'. That means that economists subscribing to social democracy typically argue for fairness between different classes of citizen, whereas right-wing monetarists generally advocate the merits of efficiency in economics over equality, assuming that efficiency will create the environment in which social justice in the form of freedom will take hold. It is these broader contexts and debates about the meaning of equity which lawyers will be required to seize on in the future.

The philosophical reasons for the maintenance of equity reach back into the broader question as to how well does the English legal system currently serve the population. Aristotle maintains that within a system of formal justice there is still an important place for a system of equity which will achieve fairness on a case-by-case basis and thus protect the freedom of individuals from the indifferent determination of the law machine. The legal system works well for companies and individuals with large amounts of money and good legal advice, but in a world in which legal aid is not broadly available it is very difficult for ordinary citizens to access the legal system. In consequence, equity and trusts have become ever more focused on commercial cases because it is only the large commercial organisations that can afford to get to court.

In conclusion

As you hold this book in your hands you will be conscious that the end is near; you can feel that there are only a few remaining pages. What remains to be done, having considered at lightning speed some of the key components of equity and principally of the law of trusts, is to think why it is that a broadened and deepened equity is so important as part of ensuring justice in any legal system, whether in England and Wales or anywhere else. We shall consider the significant part that equity plays in the conversation about justice which we have in any system of law.

One of the lessons of the 20th century was the possibility of man's inhumanity to man. In the two world wars in that century untold millions of people were killed, tortured and put through extraordinary levels of misery, and that is not to mention many hundreds of other conflicts which took place around the world. And yet in that century we also developed remarkably humane ideas about the need to recognise each individual as having inalienable human rights. We also saw reductions in the levels of disease, and improvements in the living standards of most people in the rich, capitalist countries of the West. It was a time of contradictions: the century of the concentration camp and of clean, piped water. Through that century we tried fascism and communism, capitalism and socialism, and a range of religions beyond them. We created new forms of ecological and social risks through phenomena as disparate as global warming, mass unemployment and nuclear weapons.

In that context it strikes me as remarkable that anyone could think it possible to create rigid rules of law which could hope to meet all circumstances without the need for some flexible long-stop jurisdiction such as equity. If we learned nothing else from the contrasting sights of skeletal people emerging from the gulags and of financial traders betting trillions of dollars every day, we must have learned that our world will always throw up new challenges, new technologies and new threats. The biggest risk we run is that, in the face of this chaotically developing world, we forget to look after individuals and to cherish and nurture ordinary people. In such a situation it is vital that we retain the possibility of equity – or something akin to equity – so that we never overlook the right of individuals to be heard and to be treated on their own merits aside from the rigid rules that legal systems create.

I admit there is a tension in my argument. By arguing for the strength and flexibility of equity I am also arguing for judges to be given extraordinary power to decide individual cases outside the parameters of established statutory and common law rules. For some people this is to rob the democratic process of the power to create the context within which social justice is possible. They would argue that unelected judges drawn from the privileged class of people who make up the judiciary are the wrong people to be given that sort of power. All I can do is acknowledge that there is that tension in my argument. It is not my goal to pass political power to judges. Rather, for me, writing about equity and discussing the future development of equity is a political act in which we ensure, in Bevan's phrase, that not even the apparently enlightened principle of ensuring the greatest good for the greatest number can excuse indifference to individual suffering (Bevan, 1978). In other words, equity enables us to recognise situations of individual injustice within our desire to promote the greatest good for the greatest number in our statutory legal models.

Human rights law has a similar project: to protect individuals from the evil that humans can do to one another. However, human rights are built on principles that emerged after the 1939–1945 war as part of a determination to ensure that such suffering is prevented in the future. Critics of those principles suggest that the only product of expanding human rights is to export capitalism around the world. Creating democracy and respect for human rights, it is said, acts as a blind for opening new markets for the western capitalists. Whatever the rights and wrongs of that situation, equity belongs to a more ancient tradition which holds that it is wrong to treat individuals unfairly in promulgating larger objectives. For the future, the development of equity will need to consider the development of ideals of good and bad conscience in the context of a world in which individuals expect that their human rights will be respected. It may be that these two codes begin to blend around the edges given their common goal of protecting the individual from the might of the many.

In our complex world we must not seek simply to shroud ourselves in a process of rule-making which attempts to control that which cannot be controlled. Rather, we must accept the richness of our world and we must cherish our diversity. Within a broader programme of ensuring the greatest good for the greatest number, we can also work to ensure justice for individuals.

To be effective, that project requires equality of access to the justice system for all of our citizens. To lose our way in a system that applies formal rules on a literal basis – whether in the form of the restitution of unjust enrichment or related to strict pre-requirements of financial detriment – would be to overlook the importance of these rights to ordinary citizens. Too often it is to treat *people* as being worthy of our attention only if they are *consumers* with money to spend. Equity supplies a conscience to our legal system in many senses: it gives private law itself a conscience by preventing strict rules from generating unfair outcomes; it ensures that litigants act in good conscience; and it allows claimants to have their stories heard by the courts so that they can be treated as individuals who matter. It is only by allowing all of our citizens to participate in the conversation about the nature of our legal and equitable rights that we will be able to build the strong communities and successful societies that befit the 21st century.

Bibliography

Allen, W, *Anything Else*, 2003, Metro Goldwyn Meyer, written and directed by Woody Allen.

Baudrillard, J, *The Consumer Society (La Société de Consommation)*, 1970, Paris: Gallimard.

Bauman, Z, *Liquid Modernity*, 2002, Cambridge: Polity.

Beckett, S, *Worstward Ho!*, 1983, London: Calder Publications.

Bevan, A, *In Place of Fear*, 1978, London: Quartet.

Birks, P, *Introduction to the Law of Restitution*, 1989, Oxford: Clarendon Press.

Birks, P, 'Trusts raised to avoid unjust enrichment: the *Westdeutsche* case' [1996] RLR 3.

Cooke, E, *The Modern Law of Estoppel*, 1995, Oxford: Clarendon Press.

Cotterrell, R, *Sociology of Law*, 1993a, London: Butterworths.

Cotterrell, R, 'Trusting in law: legal and moral concepts of trust' (1993b), 46(2) *Current Legal Problems* 75.

Dworkin, R, *Law's Empire*, 1986, Cambridge, Mass: Harvard University Press.

Elias, N, *The Society of Individuals*, 2001, New York: Continuum.

Freud, S, *Civilisation and Its Discontents*, 1930, Harmondsworth: Penguin.

Giddens, A, *Modernity and Self-Identity*, 1991, Cambridge: Polity.

Goff, R and Jones, G, *The Law of Restitution*, 1966, London: Sweet & Maxwell.

Goode, R, *Commercial Law*, 1995, Harmondsworth: Penguin.

Goode, R, 'Proprietary Liability for Secret Profits – A Reply' (2011) 127 LQR 493.

Hart, HLA, *The Concept of Law*, 1961, Oxford: Clarendon Press.

Hayton, D, 'The extent of equitable remedies: Privy Council versus Court of Appeal' (2012) 33 *Company Lawyer* 161.

Hegel, GWF, *Philosophy of Right*, Knox (trans), [1821] 1952, Oxford: Clarendon Press.

Hudson, AS, 'Money as property in financial transactions' (1999a), 14(6) JIBL 170.

Hudson, AS, 'Seller liability in credit derivatives', in Hudson, AS (ed), *Credit Derivatives*, 1999b, London: Sweet & Maxwell.

Hudson, AS, *Swaps, Restitution and Trusts*, 1999c, London: Sweet & Maxwell.

Hudson, AS, 'Termination and restitution of credit derivatives', in Hudson, AS (ed), *Credit Derivatives*, 1999d, London: Sweet & Maxwell.

Hudson, AS, *Towards a Just Society: Law, Labour and Legal Aid*, 1999e, London: Pinter.

Hudson, AS, *The Law on Investment Entities*, 2000, London: Sweet & Maxwell.

Hudson, AS (ed), *New Perspectives on Property Law, Obligations and Restitution*, 2004a, London: Cavendish Publishing.

Hudson, AS (ed), *New Perspectives on Property Law, Human Rights and the Home*, 2004b, London: Cavendish Publishing.

Hudson, AS, *Understanding Company Law*, 2010, Abingdon: Routledge.

Hudson, AS, *The Law on Financial Derivatives*, 5th edn, 2012b, London: Sweet & Maxwell.

Hudson, AS, *The Law of Finance*, 2nd edn, 2013a, London: Sweet & Maxwell.

Hudson, AS, *Securities Law*, 2nd edn, 2013b, London: Sweet & Maxwell.

Hudson, AS, *Great Debates in Equity and Trusts*, 2014, Basingstoke: Palgrave Macmillan.

Hudson, AS, *Equity and Trusts*, 8th edn, 2014, Abingdon: Routledge.

Hunt, M, 'The "horizontal effect" of the Human Rights Act' [1998] *Public Law* 423.

Langbein, J, 'The contractarian basis of the law of trusts' (1995) 105 *Yale LJ* 625.

Lim, H, 'The *waqf* in trust', in Scott-Hunt, S and Lim, H (eds), *Feminist Perspectives on Equity and Trusts*, 2001, London: Cavendish Publishing.

Lupoi, M, *Trusts: A Comparative Study*, 2000, Cambridge: Cambridge University Press.

Maitland, FW, *Equity*, 1909, Cambridge: Cambridge University Press.

Marley, B, *Babylon by Bus*, 1978, Island Records (opening track: 'Positive Vibration', by B Marley).

Master of the Rolls, *Report of the Committee on Super-injunctions*, 2011: http://www. judiciary.gov.uk/Resources/JCO/Documents/Reports/super-injunction-report-20052011.pdf.

Matthews, P, 'The efficacy of trustee exemption clauses in English law' [1989] *Conv* 42.

McGhee, J, *Snell's Equity*, 32nd edn, 2011, London: Sweet & Maxwell.

Millett, P, 'Bribes and secret commissions again' (2012) 71 *CLJ* 583.

Moffat, G, *Trusts Law*, 2nd edn, 1999, London: Butterworths.

Morse, G (ed), *Palmer's Company Law*, 1992, London: Sweet & Maxwell.

Mulheron, R, *The Modern* Cy-près *Doctrine*, 2007, London: UCL Press.

Oakley, A, *Constructive Trusts*, 3rd edn, 1997, London: Sweet & Maxwell.

Rickett, C and Grantham, R, 'Resulting trusts – a rather limited doctrine', in Birks, P and Rose, F (eds), *Resulting Trusts and Equitable Compensation*, 2000, London: LLP.

Sin, K, *The Legal Nature of the Unit Trust*, 1997, Oxford: Clarendon Press.

Spry, I, *Equitable Remedies*, 6th edn, 2001, Sydney: The Law Book Co.

Swadling, W, 'A new role for resulting trusts?' (1996) 16 LS 110.

Thomas, GW, *Powers*, 1998, London: Sweet & Maxwell.

Thomas, GW and Hudson, AS, *The Law of Trusts*, 2nd edn, 2010, Oxford: Oxford University Press.

Time, 'The Man on Cloud No. 7', *Time*, 8 November 1954.

Index